Strong Female Lead

Strong Female Lead

Lessons from Women in Power

ARWA MAHDAWI

HODDER*studio*

First published in Great Britain in 2021 by Hodder Studio
An Hachette UK company

1

Copyright © Arwa Mahdawi 2021

The right of Arwa Mahdawi to be identified as the Author of the Work has been
asserted by her in accordance with the Copyright, Designs and Patents Act 1988.

A CIP catalogue record for this title is available from the British Library

Hardback ISBN 9781529360639
Trade Paperback ISBN 9781529360646
eBook ISBN 9781529360653

Typeset in Bembo MT by Hewer Text UK Ltd, Edinburgh
Printed and bound in Great Britain by Clays Ltd, Elcograf S.p.A.

Hodder & Stoughton policy is to use papers that are natural, renewable
and recyclable products and made from wood grown in sustainable forests.
The logging and manufacturing processes are expected to conform
to the environmental regulations of the country of origin.

Hodder & Stoughton Ltd
Carmelite House
50 Victoria Embankment
London EC4Y 0DZ

www.hodder-studio.com

Contents

To E&O, my strong female leads

Prologue

Do you know how expensive sperm is? My bank balance does. Perhaps this is Too Much Information, but in early 2020 I went on a sperm-buying spree. My female partner and I started trying for a baby and sperm is something of a key ingredient in the process. Trying to choose a donor is a weird experience. You leaf through reams of intimate information about each anonymous dude: you go through their childhood photos, their medical history, and an essay where they answer questions about their favourite food, their interests and role models.

Want to guess who the overwhelming majority of guys picked as their role model? Elon Musk.

Want to guess how many guys named a woman as their role model? Almost none. And when they did it was usually their mum or grandma.

The plural of anecdote is not data; a hundred or so sperm donors is obviously not a representative sample of men in general. Nevertheless, my very unscientific observations are hardly unique: when you ask men who their role models or heroes are, women are rarely mentioned.[1] When they are mentioned, they tend to be women they are related or married to. While there are certainly exceptions to this rule, men aren't routinely encouraged to look up to or emulate women. When

Jodie Whittaker was cast as the first female Doctor Who, for example, there were men who lamented the 'loss of a role model for boys'.[2] Powerful women are often framed as being role models for girls and other women rather than being viewed as an inspiration for everyone. You can see this in some of the reactions to US Supreme Court Justice Ruth Bader Ginsburg's death in September 2020. 'Justice Ginsburg was an inspiration to countless young women and girls across our nation and around the globe,' the (male) Governor of New Jersey tweeted at the time.[3] Obviously, it was unthinkable to him that young men and boys might have also been inspired by a woman.

Why do so many men see Elon Musk as a role model? It's because we associate heroism and leadership with a very specific set of stereotypically male qualities. Musk has these qualities in spades: confidence verging on arrogance, competitiveness, aggressiveness, risk-taking, charisma. There's nothing wrong with these things *per se* – what's problematic is the extent to which they define our idea of leadership. For decades women have been told that if we want to get ahead in politics or business we need to develop those sorts of qualities. We're sent to management training courses where we're told we need to raise our voices, be more assertive, and never say 'sorry'. We're told that stereotypically 'feminine' qualities like collaboration and empathy are weaknesses and 'masculine' traits are strengths. We're told that, in order to succeed, we need to act more like men.

For a long time there was nothing subtle about this messaging. Margaret King, who was Margaret Thatcher's stylist, for example, said that the prime minister primarily wore suits because 'she was in a man's world, and she had to look the part'.[4] It was accepted that women had to look and act like men to succeed. Then, in the early 2010s, Corporate Feminism™ took off and the messaging around female leadership became a little more insidious. 'I want every little girl who was told she is bossy to be told that she has leadership skills,' Sheryl Sandberg wrote in her 2013 bestseller *Lean In*.[5] The conversation around leadership became focused on how women shouldn't need to apologize for being assertive; how we should reclaim words like 'bossy' and 'bitch'. There was no substantive redefinition of leadership, just a rebranding. Women should continue to act like men, the message was, just more unapologetically and with 'The Future is Female' stickers on their laptop. A generation of #Girlbosses used feminism as a marketing tool while leaning into the same old leadership styles.

And it's not just women who have been leaning in; men have been trying to emulate a fixed idea of what a 'leader' is, too. Leadership has a conformity problem: while the people at the top love to tell everyone that we live in a meritocracy where only the 'best' get ahead, there's a very rigid idea of what 'best' looks like. The 'best' all seem to have gone to the same schools and come from the same backgrounds. The 'best' all have the same interests and characteristics. The 'best' even look the same. The archetype of a Silicon Valley tycoon, for example, is a nerdy white guy in a hoodie or turtleneck. In the advertising industry, creative directors and head strategists generally walk around in the 'creative genius' uniform of black T-shirts, stubble, and unkempt hair. (But only if they are a man, of course.) In politics, a leader looks like an old white guy in a suit.

Actually, 'old white guy in a suit' underplays just how eerily similar many politicians look. In 2015, Argentinian

3

photographer Alejandro Almaraz[6] layered photos of world leaders on top of each other in a series called Portraits of Power. The finished product? A composite that shows how leaders around the world all look the same. Each country adopts its own aesthetic of power, of course, and it changes over time. Twentieth-century United States presidents, for example, have all been clean-shaven. Mexican presidents traditionally sit back from the camera in official portraits and like to pose in front of bookshelves. Leaders only started to smile more in recent years; in the twentieth century, official portraits showed them looking stern.

Homogeneity in leadership would be one thing if it resulted in effective leadership and the people at the top really were the best. But, very often, they're not. The bar is set very low for privileged white guys; everyone else is held to far higher standards. Not only do women have to work harder to get to the top, they have to work harder to stay there: a 2016 study,[7] for example, found that women receive far harsher punishments than men for ethical violations at work. And a study[8] commissioned by the Rockefeller Foundation found 80% of news reports about female CEOs involved in a crisis cited the CEO as the source of the problem. When a man was CEO, however, only 31% of stories blamed him for the company's issues.

When you make leadership less homogenous, you raise the bar, you don't lower it. Look at Sweden, for example. In 1993, Sweden's Social Democratic party introduced a strict gender quota for its candidates. Immediately a subset of men started complaining that this was unfair and would end up lowering the bar. A study looking at Swedish politics published in 2017 by researchers at LSE found quite opposite. 'Gender quotas increase the competence of the political class in general, and among men in particular,' the researchers concluded.[9] On average, a higher female representation by 10 percentage points raised the proportion of competent men by 3 percentage points (the researchers developed a model which looked at a number of social variables to measure competence[10]). Rather than reducing meritocracy, quotas force out mediocre men – which is why Sweden's quota system was informally dubbed 'the crisis of the mediocre man'.

Because the pathway to power is often more about who you know than what you know, style often seems to trump substance in leadership. Which is all very well when things are going well, but doesn't cut it when shit hits the fan. You know what happens in both business and government during periods of crisis? Mediocre men hastily turn the reins over to women; it's a well-studied phenomenon called 'the glass cliff'. One reason for the phenomenon is pure self-interest; men don't want to be put in charge of a situation with a high likelihood of failure, so a senior woman is finally given a go at the top job. Another reason, however, is that women are simply better at leading during times of crisis. While this has long been noted by academics, it started getting mainstream attention during the pandemic. The coronavirus crisis put an unflattering spotlight on the deficiencies of strongmen; meanwhile people started noticing that many of the countries that responded the best to the crisis were those led by strong women. And that's not just anecdotal: a 2020 study[11] by economists from the University of Liverpool and the University of Reading 'matched' female-led countries with their closest 'neighbour' based on socio-demographic and economic characteristics considered important in the transmission of coronavirus and found female-led countries did better. Similarly, a separate study that looked only at the US found that states with female governors had lower fatality rates.

It wasn't just female politicians who excelled during the pandemic; business leaders did, too. A 2019 study that examined the performance assessments of over 60,000 leaders (22,603 women and 40,187 men) found that women rate higher than men on 17 out of 19 leadership competencies that differentiate excellent leaders from average or poor ones. In light of the pandemic,[12] Zenger Folkman, the (male-led) consultancy behind that study, looked at similar data gathered during the first phase of the Covid-19 crisis to see if these ratings had changed. It turns out women were rated even higher than men. The study found that, during the pandemic, people put greater importance on interpersonal skills, such as 'inspires and motivates', 'communicates powerfully', 'collaboration/teamwork', and 'relationship building', all of which women rated higher on.

I hope to god that by the time this book is published the pandemic is over. However, even if lockdowns are a distant memory, make no mistake that we are still very much in a crisis. Let's just review the last few years, shall we? An infestation of 'murder hornets'. A global pandemic. Unprecedented wildfires in America. Unprecedented wildfires in Australia. Unprecedented wildfires in the Arctic. Brexit. Huge chunks of Greenland's ice cap toppling into the sea. The worst economic downturn since the great recession. The worst swarms of locusts in many decades. A massive mouse plague in Australia. Record flooding in Sudan. Devastating floods in Indonesia. Civil unrest in America. A devastating explosion in Beirut, that was a direct result of government corruption. Did I mention 'murder hornets'?

The past few years have been rough but, without drastic change, the next will be even worse. Climate change is accelerating and many climate scientists[13] believe that we're going to look back on the decade after the financial crash and marvel at how good we had it. (Horrifying, I know.) The word 'unprecedented' will lose all meaning. There will be more unprecedented fires, more unprecedented floods, more unprecedented heatwaves; a 2020 study postulated[14] that the earth could see a greater temperature increase in the next fifty years than it did in the last 6,000 years. By 2100, temperatures could rise so much in certain areas that going outside for a few hours will result in certain death. Heat could kill as many people as infectious diseases. It's not just temperatures that are rising, inequality is too. The pandemic triggered the most unequal recession in modern history. Billionaires saw their wealth balloon; meanwhile, millions of people around the world were pushed into extreme poverty.

Thanks to the changing climate, millions of people are also going to be pushed out of their homes. The World Bank estimates that three regions (Latin America, sub-Saharan Africa and Southeast Asia) will generate 143 million more climate migrants by 2050.[15] But where will those migrants go? Nationalism and nativism are on the rise, often wrapped up in populism. Between 1990 and 2018 the number of populist leaders around the world increased from four to twenty: many of those were elected into power on the basis of anti-immigrant messaging. Populism has moved from the fringes to the mainstream: research from 2018 found that one in four Europeans vote for populist candidates and more than 170 million Europeans[16] are governed by a cabinet that has a populist member. And while Donald Trump may have lost the 2020 election, he still got nearly half of US voters to vote for him.

From climate change to massive inequality to the decline of trust, the world is facing a number of interconnected crises. Above all else, however, it's facing a crisis of leadership. One of the reasons the world is in this mess is that we have confused confidence with competence and elevated charlatans into the highest positions of power. We have developed a rigid and very masculine model of leadership that is ill-suited to handle the problems the world faces.

It's time to change the narrative around leadership. It's time we stopped pathologizing femininity and recognized that the traits we associate with women – things like empathy and collaboration – are strengths, not weaknesses. It's time we stopped telling women to act like men and started telling men to lead like women. Not for politically correct reasons, but for existential ones. While this book may have 'women' and 'female' in the title, it is absolutely not a 'woman's book'. Rather, it is a reassessment of the sort of leadership qualities that we should value; the sort of qualities that we desperately need in a world grappling with populism, pandemics and the climate crisis. Our current authoritarian model of leadership has got us into this mess; we need a different, more empathetic, more feminine style of leadership to get us out of it. Because one thing is clear: bluster and bravado will not help us navigate the challenges ahead. Now more than ever (to invoke the cliché of our times), we need to elevate different role models and embrace a different, more feminine, style of leadership.

Am I trying to say that the world would be a better place if it were run by women? Barack Obama suggested as much during a 2019 conference on leadership.[17] 'Now women, I just want you to know; you are not perfect, but what I can say pretty indisputably is that you're better than [men],' he declared. 'I'm absolutely confident that for two years if every nation on earth was run by women, you would see a significant improvement across the board on just about everything.'

Thanks, Obama, but I disagree. I want to make very clear that the point of this book is not to argue that we should put women in charge of everything – although since only nineteen countries in the world are run by women and there are the same number of men called Peter running FTSE 100 companies[18] as there are female CEOs, it's high time we put women in charge of more things. The idea that women are hardwired to be more cooperative and compassionate than men is sexist and unscientific; there are only negligible differences between men and women's brains. There is a big difference, however, in how we are socialized. Women are taught to be people pleasers; we're taught to listen and cooperate. We're socialized to have many of the qualities that have been found to result in effective leadership. It's no good putting women in charge of everything if those women simply replicate toxic leadership styles; what we need are more leaders (of every gender) that lean into these traditionally female qualities.

The women profiled in this book aren't necessarily the most powerful or famous women in the world, although a few of them are certainly up there. Nor are they necessarily a *Who's Who of Women Arwa Thinks are Cool*; I almost certainly don't entirely agree with everything they've ever said or done. (Not to mention, Sod's Law practically dictates that one of them is going to do something embarrassing as soon as this book is published.) Again, this isn't a book about individuals so much as it's a book about the characteristics that define effective leaders. The women profiled demonstrate (to varying the degrees) the qualities inherent in a new model of leadership. While I have looked at leaders from around the world, this book is skewed Anglo–American because those are the areas I'm most qualified to write about. The book combines research with interviews and original data. And don't worry, the data is not all collected from sperm banks!

There are, it should be said, men who embody 'feminine' qualities. In every chapter of this book I could probably have found an example from a male leader. I focused purely on women, however, for two reasons. First, there is already plenty of writing praising male leadership. In Harvard Business School's 2019 MBA program, for example, just 16%[19] of case studies featured a female protagonist. Second, the qualities this book argues are needed in a new model of leadership are very much coded female.

Unlike some books on leadership, I'm not going to make any promises about how the lessons here will empower you. Reading this book will not make you rich and successful, I'm afraid. But I hope it changes the way you think about leadership. Every single crisis the world faces right now – from the climate to inequality – is also a crisis of leadership. Meaningful change is impossible if we don't change the sort of people who are in charge.

I

Lean Out

Nero fiddled while Rome burned; Elizabeth Holmes bought a dog.

It was September 2017 and Theranos, the blood-testing company Holmes had founded in 2003 when she was just nineteen, was in crisis. Holmes had launched Theranos with a tantalizing promise: it was going to revolutionize the medical industry through a cheap finger-prick test that would let you screen for multiple diseases with a single drop of blood. People bought into that vision in droves: at one point the company was valued at $9 billion and Holmes was a media darling. But things started to go downhill in 2015, after a series of damning exposés were published by the *Wall Street Journal*'s John Carreyrou. An important deal with Safeway folded. One of the company's labs had been found to be a threat to patient health, leading to Theranos agreeing to stay out of the blood-testing business for two years; which was kind of a big deal since that *was* their business. The company was under investigation by pretty much every government agency you could name, from the SEC to the FDA to the FBI. Holmes had once topped *Forbes*'s list of America's richest self-made women with an estimated net worth of $4.5 billion; in 2016 the magazine lowered that estimate to zero.

In short: things were bad. But Holmes took it all in her unblinking stride. She was an entrepreneur, a hustler, a disruptor. She'd been on the covers of *Forbes* and *Fortune*; she'd made *Time*'s '100 Most Influential People' list; she'd doled out inspirational advice to the masses from prestigious stages around the world. 'You'll get knocked down over and over and over again, and you get back up,' Holmes told the Forbes Under 30 Summit[1] in 2015, inadvertently echoing Chumbawamba. So Theranos had suffered a setback? It was no biggie, she knew exactly how she was going to get back up again. Holmes hopped in a plane (first class, of course) to see a man about a dog. She picked up a Siberian husky puppy, who she named Balto, and flew him (first class, of course) back to her company's Palo Alto headquarters to execute her cunning comeback plan.

Balto wasn't just a dog. He was a symbol; a beacon of hope. Balto's namesake, Holmes explained in a speech to her exhausted employees, was a heroic husky who galloped into history after transporting life-saving medicine to Nome, a city in Alaska. A popular version of the story goes like this: it was 1925, and a number of children in Nome were sick with diphtheria; the nearest medicine was in Anchorage, 800 brutal miles away. Balto fearlessly led a team of sled dogs to their destination; thanks to the dog's courage and gritty determination, the kids survived. The husky inspired a Disney movie and a statue in Central Park.

So what was this latter-day Balto going to do, you ask? Was he going to drag a sled to the FBI's headquarters and bark at them until they stopped investigating? No, as it turns out, he was just going to wander the halls of Theranos, defecating in conference rooms, and reminding employees to be resilient.

He was a walking, pooping, barking, motivational poster. He was also, Holmes later decided, actually part wolf. 'He's a wolf,' Holmes reportedly told anyone who would listen. 'He's a wolf.'[2]

Wolf or not, Balto couldn't save Theranos. Things continued to unravel and, in June 2018, Holmes stepped down as CEO and was charged with wire fraud by the Department of Justice. In September, Theranos shut down.[3] It turned out that the Edison, the printer-sized blood analysis machine that was the heart of the company, had never worked; Theranos had been running its tests through third-party machines. Holmes went from being a fêted figure to a figure of fun; Theranos became the subject of incredulous podcasts and documentaries. Hollywood signed on to adapt *Bad Blood*, John Carreyrou's book about the company, into a movie; Jennifer Lawrence would play Holmes. People couldn't get enough of the story. How on earth had Holmes pulled this off? Why had she done it? Had things simply gotten out of hand? Was she a sociopath? 'I'll leave it to the psychologists to decide whether Holmes fits the clinical profile,' Carreyrou wrote. 'But there's no question that her moral compass was badly askew.'[4]

But it's not just Holmes's moral compass that was badly askew: her rise to fame shows how warped society's preconceptions about leadership are. The real question we should be asking when it comes to Holmes isn't *what's wrong with her?*, but rather *what's wrong with the way we think about leadership?* How did a nineteen-year-old build a company valued at $9 billion with nothing more than an enticing vision and a lot of chutzpah? How did Holmes get powerful men like Henry Kissinger to sit on the board of a company built on lies? How did she create a mirage so effective that the likes of Joe Biden, then vice president of the United States, waxed lyrical about how 'inspirational' Holmes was after a tour of the company? How did she get inducted into Harvard Medical School's Board of Fellows? Scientists had been trying to develop affordable, accurate finger-prick blood tests for decades: how did Holmes, a college drop-out, convince so many powerful people that she'd achieved what people far more qualified than her had found impossible?

The reason I'm starting a book about women and leadership with the story of a woman who was a fraud is because I think answering those questions tells us a lot what's wrong with the current model of leadership. While Holmes is often described as a con artist, it might be more accurate to call her a performance artist. She was able to hoodwink the media for so long because she turned herself into a reflection of what they wanted to see. From her clothes to her cadence, Holmes fashioned every inch of herself to fit the mold of what we think a certain sort of leader is like. Which encompasses the following five pillars:

1. Individual brilliance

Our current model of leadership is highly individualistic; it fetishizes the extraordinary individual and diminishes collective action. Even Balto is an example of that: no offence to the poor dog: like Holmes, he wasn't so much a brilliant leader as he was a carefully constructed brand. It seems that Balto didn't actually do most of the work he was lauded for; it was very much a team effort. If any dog deserved more of the glory it was probably Togo, who, it has now been established, ran more than the other dogs. Balto just swooped in at the end and got all the glory.

Truly great leaders are not demi-gods. Rather, they're fallible people who know their limits. They know how to collaborate; don't let their ego get in the way; and recognize they don't have all the answers. Alas, we seem to want to see our leaders as heroes. And so we reward people who act like they're special. Holmes, recognizing this, very clearly modelled her image on Steve Jobs. She dressed the same way every day, adopting a uniform of black turtlenecks and black slacks; she had a very strict diet and subsisted mainly on green juice. The message she was sending with all this was that she was a perfectionist completely dedicated to her work. She wasn't distracted by the mundanities and frivolities the rest of us are; she was special.

2. Authoritarian control

When you think of leaders as extraordinary individuals, then a hierarchical style of leadership naturally follows. If they know it all, then it stands to reason they should control it all. And Holmes, who reportedly demanded absolute loyalty from her employees, was incredibly controlling. A former employee, for example, told ABC[5] Holmes would fire anyone who disagreed with her. Her staff would also reportedly 'friend' Theranos employees on Facebook and report back on what they were posting. This kind of control was a necessary part of ensuring that nobody realized Theranos wasn't exactly what it seemed, but it also played into the image of a visionary leader.

3. Unwavering self-belief

One of the biggest problems with our current model of leadership is that it confuses confidence with competence. Forget actually being good at your job: bluster, lofty promises and unwavering self-belief will get you anywhere! Self-help culture has contributed to our fetishization of confidence. It's entrenched the idea that if you just believe deeply enough and hustle hard enough, you can do anything. Even something you're completely unqualified for. Holmes had perfectly internalized this sort of empowerment culture; when she spoke, she often sounded like a kind of inspirational quote generator. 'I think the minute you have a backup plan, you've admitted you're not going to succeed,' Holmes told the Stanford Business School in 2015, for example. 'Our approach is to take the most swings at the bat. We'll get the most home runs, we'll also get the most strikeouts, and we're just not going to make the same mistake twice.'[6] Completely meaningless, right? And yet so perfectly in tune with today's leadership advice that Stanford Business School, which costs $118,000 a year to attend, happily printed it an 'Insights' article[7] about Holmes's leadership.

4. The right background and credentials

Not everyone could have pulled off Holmes's con. Crucially, she was starting from the right foundation: she was white, conventionally attractive and well-connected. She didn't drop out of community college, she dropped out of Stanford. After which, her dad used his connections to introduce Holmes to a prominent venture capitalist. Her great-great-grandfather had married the heir to the Fleischmann's Yeast empire; a fact she brought up frequently to bolster the idea that business was in her blood. She had the right background for the job. While the right background isn't always essential, it helps immensely.

5. Masculinity

Our model of leadership is still very much coded male. Indeed, studies show that leadership is so gendered that tools like Google Translate assume leaders are male. In one study,[8] Google Translate changed '*Die Präsidentin*' (German for female president) to '*il presidente*' in Italian, although the correct translation is '*la presidente*'. Meanwhile '*Der Krankenpfleger*' (the male nurse in German) became '*l'infirmière*' (the female nurse) in French. While Holmes used the fact that she was a woman in a heavily male industry as a marketing tool, she also shed herself of anything that might seem feminine. She told the New Yorker she didn't date, even though she was dating Sunny Balwani, the company's COO. She cultivated an air of authority by staring intensely at people when she spoke; an intimidating, wide-eyed, unblinking gaze. And then there was her voice: Holmes spoke in what many people believe to be a fabricated baritone, designed to make her sound more powerful. Sometimes she slipped and her real, more high-pitched, more feminine, voice would come out, but she'd revert to character quickly.

The ironic thing about our current model of leadership is that while we have this image of leaders as extraordinary individuals who stand out from the crowd, we have a very rigid idea of what a leader looks like. That image varies according to industry and geography, as discussed in the introduction, but the pillars above are pretty much consistent. Because our current model of leadership prizes conformity, the quickest route to success is often just shaping yourself to fit that model. A lot of us do this every single day, to some degree, without even realizing it. While Holmes's fake voice has attracted a lot of ridicule, for example, she's far from the only woman who has changed her voice to conform to expectations about leadership. Studies[9] show that, in Western cultures, people with lower voices are generally seen as stronger and more electable; women, in response, have been lowering their voices in order to sound more authoritative. Sometimes this is conscious and deliberate: the former British prime minister Margaret Thatcher, for example, used a professional speech coach and reportedly dropped the pitch of her voice by 60 Hz. (To put this in context: adult women tend to speak in a range from 165 to 255 Hz, while a man's range is 85 to 155 Hz.) Most people don't have voice coaches; instead, we alter our voices subconsciously depending on our environment. A study[10] conducted by researchers out of the University of South Australia in the 1990s found that as more women have entered the workplace, female voices appear to have lowered. The researchers compared the voices of two groups of Australian women aged eighteen to twenty-five: the first group of voices were recordings taken in 1945, the second group were recordings taken in the early 1990s. The researchers found that the 'fundamental frequency' of the voices had dropped by 23 Hz over the five-decade period – from an average of 229 Hz to 206 Hz. If you're musical, that's the equivalent of an A# below middle C changing to a G#. I'm not musical (as a kid I was asked to lip sync the recorder during a school concert because I was so out of tune), so I have no idea what that means. But I have it on good authority that it's an audible difference. So while Holmes's voice was exaggerated, what she was doing wasn't unusual. She was doing what many of us have been told to do in order to be successful, she was *leaning in*.

A large part of the conversation around women and leadership in recent years has been dominated by Sheryl Sandberg's 2013 bestseller, *Lean In: Women, Work and the Will to Lead*. While Sandberg's book addressed some of the structural issues holding women back, the key message many people took from it was that if you play the guys' game, if you act like a man, then you can have it all. Sandberg's book has been thoroughly bashed in recent years, and there's no need for me to provide yet another takedown. But it's worth reiterating that telling women to lean into male-centred power structures simply isn't productive. As Michelle Obama noted during a 2018 book tour: 'It's not always enough to lean in, because that shit doesn't work all the time.'[11] Lowering your voice may make you sound more authoritative, but guess what? It also makes you more unlikeable: research[12] shows that women with lower voices are considered less agreeable than women with higher voices. This sort of catch-22 is everywhere when you're a woman. You have to speak up and prove you're assertive, but you can't be too assertive because otherwise you'll be a Nasty Woman, a bitch. Studies[13] show that wearing a 'professional' amount of make-up in the office makes you seem more competent, capable, reliable and amiable than your colleague without make-up – but if you accidentally slap on a little too much warpaint then both men and women are likely to rate you less human, less warm and less moral. It's a tricky tightrope to walk and, as Holmes demonstrated, eventually you're bound to fall off.

I didn't pick the phrase 'lean out' as the lesson for this chapter as a dig at Sandberg's book. I picked it because it's crucial that we – both men and women – start challenging these archetypes about leadership. We need to take a step back and really interrogate the sort of qualities we associate with leaders. And rather than trying to lean into an out-of-date model of leadership we need, to start redefining what a leader looks like.

I want to introduce you to someone I think is doing an exemplary job of very consciously leaning out of the traditional leadership model: Nadia Whittome. If you're British, or pay attention to British politics, you'll already be very familiar with Whittome. She became the UK's youngest sitting Member of Parliament (MP) when she was elected MP for Nottingham East in the 2019 election, aged twenty-three. Whittome wasn't groomed for Westminster through the usual channels; rather, she entered politics through left-wing activism. She certainly hadn't expected to become a MP so quickly. Whittome won an internal vote to be selected as Labour's parliamentary candidate for the inner-city safe seat of Nottingham East in October 2019. Less than twenty-four hours after that, a snap general election was announced for December: the UK's third general election in less than five years. Whittome found herself thrust into the limelight at lightning speed. She was living with her mum at the time; she'd never lived away from home before. All of a sudden, she was being interviewed on the news and was heading to London to represent her constituency. She wasn't sure what to expect but she was very clear about what she wanted to achieve and what kind of leader she wanted to be. 'I will be a new kind of MP, inspired by radical women of colour across the world,' Whittome tweeted after winning her seat.[14]

Because the election had been such a whirlwind, Whittome hadn't had any time to prepare for her new life. In the US there are a few months in between being elected as a new congressmember (roughly the equivalent of an MP) and starting the job and you attend a week of orientation where you meet your colleagues and learn the ropes. In the UK you start your new job almost immediately with very little preparation; you get given an envelope congratulating you on becoming an MP with a few cursory instructions on where to show up for your first day and how to get your laptop. That's about it.

Even extensive training courses, however, couldn't have prepared Whittome for the culture shock of Westminster, she tells me when I call her up for an interview in late 2020. It's the middle of the pandemic and Whittome is working from home; she's rattling around in her kitchen getting a cup of coffee, she explains apologetically, which is why she's not on video. (This is great news for me and my quarantine hair and I immediately turn my own video off.) Being a young, working-class, mixed-race, female politician felt alienating, Whittome says. The place wasn't designed for people like her and there were constant reminders of that. She quotes one of her colleagues, the Labour politician Kate Green, who'd once counted the number of women in the paintings on Parliament walls – 'there aren't many,' Green had said, 'we're easily outnumbered by paintings of horses.'[15]

Young women of colour are particularly outnumbered. There were quite a few women of colour in the 2019 intake of Labour MPs and they were constantly getting mistaken for each other or for the staff. On one occasion a Tory MP gave her colleague Abena Oppong-Asare (Labour MP for Erith and Thamesmead) his bag to hold, thinking she was the help.

Getting the keys to her office was also an ordeal. She was sharing with her friend and colleague Olivia Blake, the MP for Sheffield Hallam, (who's 'pretty awesome', Whittome says) and people kept calling it 'Olivia's office' and asking why she wanted the key.

There were moments where Whittome would have conversations with some of her colleagues and it would feel like they were just from different planets. She was sitting in one of the Parliament bars, for example, when a Conservative MP plopped himself down next to her and started a conversation.

'Nadia,' he said gravely, 'do you own your own home?'

'No,' she replied.

'Well, you will one day,' he said confidently. 'And, you know, Nadia, new homeowners are some of the most marginalized people in this country.' The MP then proceeded to speak in great detail about the conveyancing process. Which, as it happened, Whittome already knew a thing or two about; she'd studied law at Nottingham University for two years before dropping out for financial reasons. She'd been taught conveyancing law, she'd just never realized new homeowners were so oppressed. You live and learn!

Whittome was twenty-three at the time of the conversation, which is half the age of the average MP: most are between fifty and fifty-nine; it's been that way since 1979.[16] She was also a decade younger than the average first-time buyer in the UK. The idea that she'd be able to buy a house was laughable – although obviously not as laughable as the idea that new homeowners are some of the most marginalized people in the UK.

The Patron Saint of New Homeowners isn't a bad person, Whittome stresses. He just had a completely different life experience and, subsequently, a completely different world-view. To a large extent, that's generational. The average MP grew up in a Britain where university tuition was free and low-income students got a grant to study. When Whittome went to university, tuition fees were £9,000 a year and low-income kids had to take out large student loans to study. The average MP left university with no debt; the average student graduating from an English university now leaves with £40,000 in debt. When the average MP was in their twenties, buying a house in Britain cost around four times the average wage; now it's eight times average earnings. 'We're the first generation since the 1800s that are set to be worse off than our parents,' Whittome says. 'We're a generation defined by insecurity: insecure housing, insecure work, an insecure planet.' That insecurity, Whittome thinks, has made her generation of young millennials look at leadership very differently. The system simply hasn't worked for people her age. They've lived through two big global recessions and a pandemic that widened economic inequality further. Now that they're slowly starting to take the reins of power, there's a desire to do things differently. 'We're pushing back against the old, broken way of doing things,' Whittome says.[17]

What does that mean? To begin with, it means *acting* differently rather than just *looking* different. The 2019 election resulted in Britain's most diverse Parliament ever. For the first time, both the Liberal Democrats and Labour had more women MPs than men; one in ten of the 650 MPs elected were non-white compared to just one in forty MPs a decade before. While to some degree that represents progress, Whittome has very little interest in skin-deep diversity. What does it matter if there are more young brown women in politics if they just act like the old white guys they're replacing?

'The goal isn't more diverse, oppressive structures. It's changing those oppressive structures and achieving liberation, not diversity,' Whittome stresses. She gives Priti Patel, Britain's Home Secretary, as an example. A ten-year-old boy had recently written to Patel and begged her to stop his dad, a direct Windrush descendant, being deported to Jamaica. 'I don't think it mattered at all to that little boy that the person who ultimately was responsible for deporting his dad was a woman of colour,' she says dryly.

Like Whittome, Patel doesn't come from the private school–Oxbridge background many MPs do; she was educated at state schools and her parents were immigrants. That's about where the comparison between Patel, who is highly social conservative, and Whittome, who is very left-wing, ends, though. Patel idolized Margaret Thatcher growing up and adopted Thatcher's autocratic leadership style. 'Collaborative' and 'kind' are not words that tend to be associated with Patel; rather, she has been accused of bullying and having a bulldozer-like style. Patel has done very well for herself, becoming the first woman of colour to ever be Home Secretary. But she has leaned into the establishment rather than done anything to change it. Whittome doesn't want to do that. It's important, she says, 'that you don't just occupy space but that you transform it'. But that's often easier said than done; there's a lot of pressure to conform to the norms of Westminster. 'You are expected to fit neatly into a box and be compliant.'

Instead of fitting in, Whittome began her job with a gesture that immediately differentiated her: she promised to take home only £35,000 of her £79,468 salary and donate the rest. She didn't tell other MPs they should all do the same. She didn't criticize others for taking their full salaries. She simply did what she thought was right for the community and activist movement she came from.

'It's not like an act of charity and it's not saying that MPs don't deserve a high salary,' she explains.

> It's just that everyone deserves a high salary. I'm not going to take mine until the people who I was elected to represent, like firefighters, nurses, cleaners, teaching assistants, care workers – like my former colleagues – until they get theirs. It's just a practical way of showing solidarity with the people I represent and being able to practically contribute to the material fight-back against austerity in my community.

She rattles off a few of the places she donated her salary to, speaking about the work these charities are doing with genuine admiration and enthusiasm. While my interview with her is supposed to be about the work she's doing, she takes every available opportunity to name-check people she admires and amplify their achievements and voices. At one point in our interview she rummages around to find a quote by the Egyptian–American journalist Mona Eltahaway about challenging 'patriarchy in the streets, in our homes and in our minds'.[18] I'm in full agreement with the quote, but what strikes me the most is the very fact of Whittome going to the words of another woman, crediting her and giving her ideas space. I'm not sure any man I've interviewed has ever said 'this guy says it better'.

Talking to Whittome doesn't feel like having a conversation with a politician; it reminds me of being back at university and having passionate conversations at the pub about how we were all going to put the world to rights. And then, of course, you get a mortgage and you get jaded and you grow out of that idealism. Whittome hasn't done that yet. She sounds young and earnest. I don't mean that to sound condescending. On the contrary, it's refreshing. Our current model of leadership is incredibly cynical; if you want to succeed, you've got to play by the rules. But a new cohort of leaders is making it clear they don't want to play by those rules, they want to change them.

Perhaps the most high-profile example of this new style of leadership is the diverse group of progressive congresswomen known as the 'Squad' in the United States. The four original members of the ever-growing Squad (Alexandria Ocasio-Cortez, Ayanna Pressley, Rashida Tlaib, Ilhan Omar) all made history in various ways when they were elected to Congress. Pressley became Massachusetts's first Black female congressperson in the state's 7th district; Omar, who came to the US as a refugee, was the first ever Somali–American in Congress and, along with Tlaib, one of the first Muslim women in congress; Tlaib was the first Palestinian–American woman; Ocasio-Cortez became the youngest woman ever elected to Congress. Much has been made of this 'diversity' but, again, it's not how they look that's important, it's how they behave. The Squad have refused to be tokens. They haven't toned themselves down or tried to conform. They have been very clear that they want to change what leadership looks, acts and sounds like.

Pressley's hair is one example of this. In January 2020, Pressley revealed that she had been diagnosed with alopecia, an autoimmune disease that can cause hair loss, and announced that she was going to stop wearing wigs to disguise her hair loss and show the world her bald head. 'I do believe going public will help,' she said in a video published by The Root.[19] 'I'm ready now, because I want to be freed from the secret and the shame that secret carries with it. Because I'm not here just to occupy space – I'm here to create it.'

There might be some readers who think 'that sounds dramatic, it's just hair'. Believe me, it's not. When I was fourteen I was anorexic and started losing my hair. I'd be washing my hair in the shower and would find myself suddenly holding a clump of hair in my hand. It was traumatic. You don't really understand the significance of your hair until you start to lose it. Back in 2001, Hillary Clinton told the Yale College graduating class: 'Your hair will send significant messages to those around you: what hopes and dreams you have for the world, but more, what hopes and dreams you have for your hair. Pay attention to your hair, because everyone else will.'[20] Clinton was being sarcastic, of course, but there was a lot of truth to it. People pay attention to women's hair. People judge you for it. Which is why a lot of women spend so much time and money on our hair. You don't see a whole lot of bald female politicians.

Pressley rocking a bald new look, however, was about far more than her being unafraid to look different. Black hair is highly politicized. Pressley explained that one reason she'd chosen to speak up about her alopecia is because she'd become well known for her Senegalese twists. She'd walk into rooms and see little girls wearing T-shirts saying 'My Congresswoman Wears Braids', she got letters from Black women saying how her hair give them pride in their own. 'The reality is that I'm Black, and I'm a Black woman, and I'm a Black woman in politics, and everything I do is political,' the forty-five-year-old congresswoman said at the time. Pressley refused to let her hair simply be looked at as a woman making a fashion statement. She used it as an opportunity to talk about how her personal informs her political. 'We don't need any more Black faces that don't want to be a Black voice,'[21] Pressley said on a previous occasion. What does that mean? It means that 'diversity at the table doesn't matter if there's not real diversity in policy'.

Pressley has been very clear about how her life experience has shaped her world-view and the policy she wants to enact. Pressley's husband, for example, spent ten years in prison. Her father also spent time in prison. Pressley has been vocal about that and talked about how her personal experience with the criminal-justice system has influenced her work trying to change that system. She hasn't pretended to be completely 'objective', she's explained how her personal and political fit together. Some people dismiss this as 'identity politics' but here's the thing: all politics is identity politics. Being a privileged white man is an identity too!

The Squad are often described as 'outspoken'. Which, as we all know, is code for 'irritating woman with an opinion'. While the Squad have a lot of fans, they've also ruffled a lot of feathers. Republicans can't stand the new America they represent, and nor, to some degree, can some members of their own party. House Speaker Nancy Pelosi, for example, has been less than complimentary about the congresswomen and has openly criticized the way they've occasionally spoken out about the Democratic party. In 2019, for example, the Squad were the only four Democrats to vote against the House's border funding legislation because they thought it wasn't progressive enough. Pelosi wasn't impressed that they voiced their concerns with it. 'All these people have their public whatever and their Twitter world,' Pelosi said in a *New York Times* interview. 'But they didn't have any following. They're four people, and that's how many votes they got.'[22]

The Squad isn't just 'like, four people', though. While it's still too early to properly assess their legislative achievements, you can see their impact in the amount of media coverage they get and the influence of their endorsements; you can measure their popularity in the number of grassroots donations they get. They are the new face of politics and, as Whittome makes clear, they are recruiting an international army.

While Whittome and the Squad are still in the early days of their career, they are representative of a new generation of politicians who aren't afraid to go against the establishment and stand up for their convictions. They refuse to quietly fit in and are unapologetically themselves. And not in an obnoxious way; being 'unapologetically yourself', after all, is often code for being entitled, but in a way that shows how they don't want to just take up space, they want to change it. They've all gone into politics because the current style of leadership hasn't worked for them, their communities, or the world. Why would they replicate a model of leadership that has resulted in massive inequality and a breakdown of institutional trust? They've made it very clear that they are not interested in repeating the mistakes of the past but in forging a more inclusive and effective style of leadership.

2

Build Trust (by banishing bullshit)

Sometimes it starts with a fever. Sometimes it starts with a cough, a headache and a growing sense of confusion. Sometimes there are no symptoms at all to begin with, but that doesn't mean you're safe; the Nipah virus works quietly and efficiently, attacking your brain. Violent seizures are possible and death is highly probable: the bat-borne virus has an estimated case fatality rate of a massive 40 to 75%. While it was first identified in 1999, you may not have heard of Nipah before; there have only been a few known outbreaks in Asia. Although you've almost certainly heard of the 2011 Steven Soderbergh film *Contagion* which is partially inspired by the virus. (Matt Hancock, Britain's Health Secretary, told the media that watching *Contagion* helped inspire his coronavirus vaccine strategy, which did not exactly inspire trust in the government!) There are no cures for Nipah, no established protocols for treating it. If you get it, there's very little that can be done for you. If you survive, then you might suffer long-term effects such as shaking and personality changes. Nipah, in short, is terrifying. Even more terrifying? Some scientists are worried that it could be the next big pandemic.

K. K. Shailaja, the Minister of Health and Social Welfare in the Indian state of Kerala, first heard about Nipah on 9 May

2018. Mohammed Salih, a twenty-eight-year-old architect, had died the night before in a hospital in Kozhikode, a sprawling city on the Malabar coast once known as the City of Spices. His symptoms were unlike anything the doctors at his hospital had seen before; a virologist called Govindakarnavar Arunkumar was summoned to help. After identifying the pathogen, Arunkumar called Shailaja with the grim news that they were dealing with the first Nipah outbreak in India. It seemed Salih wasn't the first victim; his twenty-six-year-old brother, Muhammad Sabith, had died of similar symptoms[1] a couple of weeks earlier. Now it looked like other members of the family who shared the same house were sick. If Nipah continued to spread, Arunkumar told Shailaja, there was no knowing how many people could die.

The first thing Shailaja Teacher, as the former physics teacher is affectionately known, did after getting that phone call was get on the internet and Google 'Nipah'. She is, after all, only human. The second thing she did was calmly snap into action. A task force was assembled, quarantine facilities were proactively built, testing centres were established, personal protection equipment was ordered. Everyone who had been in contact with the brothers was traced and put under quarantine. Shailaja didn't do all this from behind a desk; as soon as she got the call, she set off to Soopikada, the small village where the brothers were from.

Soopikada would be a lovely place to visit under other circumstances. It's nestled alongside the lush Janaki forest; brightly coloured butterflies flit through the trees and there is a hum of birdsong. As dusk falls, the bats come out. Lots and lots of bats: the village is thick with them, hundreds of fruitbats hanging upside down from the mahogany trees, rustling and squeaking in protective groups. The bats were the most energetic presence in an eerily quiet Soopikada when Shailaja, along with a team of health experts, arrived. News of the virus had spread fast and people were panicked. Rumours and misinformation were circulating on WhatsApp; some villagers had already fled. Others were locked in their houses, afraid to come out. Nobody knew how the brothers had been infected, but there were plenty of theories. Could it have come from a pet duck that lived with the family? Did the brothers get sick after cleaning out an abandoned well on their property? Had they eaten a mango infected by bat saliva? Could the virus spread in the air or did it spread through touch? There were lots of questions and Shailaja, who spent the next couple of weeks camped out in the village, set about trying to provide people with answers. Some of her colleagues weren't thrilled she was doing this in person; they had cautioned her against visiting the village. 'My team said if the minister catches the virus, everything will collapse,' Shailaja later said in an interview. 'But I said no, people will not listen if you don't go there.'[2] Her trip to the village wasn't a show of bravado; it was very different from Boris Johnson boasting about shaking hands with coronavirus patients in the early days of the pandemic, weeks before he tested positive for Covid-19. Shailaja wasn't trying to look tough, she was trying to quell fear by communicating the facts clearly and in person. And, of course, she listened to scientific advice and took precautions. Her trip to the village was brave but it wasn't reckless.

Over the next few days, things on the ground steadily got worse. The brothers' aunt died. So did their dad. A thirty-one-year-old nurse called Lini Penthussery, who'd treated the family, started recognizing symptoms in herself and, on 22 May, went to the hospital asking to be quarantined. 'Take care of our children,' she wrote in a final note[3] to her husband from the hospital's isolation unit shortly before she became the fifth person to die. Deep down, Shailaja was terrified but, she later said, she knew she could 'couldn't afford to show fear'.[4] Along with her team of scientists and health officials, she continued to meet with residents and calmly explain what the government knew so far and what they were doing. She explained that the virus didn't spread through the air but through droplets and so people should wear masks and physically distance. Shailaja also liaised with religious leaders – the village is both Hindu and Muslim – and ensured that the victims were buried in a way that was both sanitary and allowed people to mourn.

There's something calming about Shailaja Teacher – Google Image her, you'll see what I mean. She doesn't look like a slick politician, she looks like a physics teacher. Her hair is always pulled back in a neat no-nonsense pony tail, glasses perched at the top of her nose. She looks unassuming but also unflappable. While tensions were still running high in Soopikada people gradually started to calm down; they stopped packing up and fleeing. If the health minister had come to the village, then it couldn't be that bad, could it? If she wasn't scared to be there, then why should they be? By June 2018, less than six weeks after the identification of the first case, the areas affected by the virus were declared to be free from Nipah. Seventeen people were dead; a tragedy, but nowhere near the full-scale disaster it could have been without Shailaja and her associates' quick response and trust-building. 'She was there at the epicentre, with senior members of the health department,' Arunkumar, director of the Manipal Centre for Virus Research, later told the *Indian Express*.[5] 'Decisions were taken swiftly. She was open to suggestions, took technical advice seriously and put in place a system of transparent communication. That gave confidence to the system.' Her efficiency was combined with empathy; she made sure to check in on people and see how they were doing. When, in 2020, a rival politician with a long history of misogynistic remarks tried to claim that Shailaja Teacher hadn't been in the village as much as it was made out, some of the villagers rushed to her defence. 'Shailaja Teacher was very much with us like a family member, always keeping in touch and taking care of things,' the husband of Lini Penthussery, the young nurse who died, wrote on Facebook.[6] And Shailaja Teacher had, indeed, taken care of things: the World Health Organization described Kerala's handling of the virus as a 'success story'. And Mollywood (the nickname for the film industry in Southern India) released[7] a movie called *Virus* celebrating the response. Shailaja was flattered; although she wasn't too impressed that the actress playing her looked worried all the time.

Shailaja, who is in her sixties, probably thought she might get a little breather from killer viruses; she probably hoped she'd get to spend more time with her grandchild. But less than two years after the Nipah outbreak she started reading about something called the coronavirus, which was spreading in China. On 23 January 2020, long before places like the UK and the US started to take the virus seriously, she set up a special Covid-19 control room and held a meeting with a rapid-response team.

As one of her first steps, Shailaja ordered Kerala's four international airports to start screening passengers; anyone with Covid-19 symptoms was taken to be tested and isolated at a government facility. It didn't take long before three medical students travelling back to Kerala from Wuhan became the first positive cases reported. Shailaja and her team were ready for this: the government of Kerala issued a 'state calamity warning', initiated contact tracing and placed contacts of the medical students under quarantine. By February Shailaja had assembled a state response team to coordinate with public officials across Kerala and ensure the public was kept informed.

While Shailaja was doing all this, Narendra Modi, the prime minister of India, seemed to be in a state of denial about the severity of the coronavirus. He was putting all his energy into wooing Donald Trump instead: towards the end of February, Modi packed a stadium in Ahmedabad, the largest city in the state of Gujarat, with over 125,000 people[8] to welcome the US president on his first visit to India. The rally was dubbed 'Namaste Trump' but it might as well have been called 'Namaste Coronavirus': the Gujarat Congress later alleged[9] that the event was responsible for the spread of the virus in the state. Even on 12 March, the day after the WHO described the outbreak as a pandemic, Modi seemed reluctant to acknowledge the extent of the crisis: India's national health ministry announced that it wasn't a 'health emergency'.[10] Then, just twelve days later, Modi dramatically changed tack and ordered one of the strictest lockdowns in the world. He went on TV and gave Indians just four hours' notice to prepare for the three-week lockdown. It was a typically Modi move: a big, dramatic gesture that was poorly thought out. While the nationwide lockdown came as a shock to many, Keralans had already been in an unofficial lockdown and people were largely prepared. 'There was so much confidence in the state government,' one resident told the MIT Technology Review[11] in April 2020, 'that there was no resistance to modifying one's behavior by staying in.' People knew that Shailaja Teacher had delivered for them before; they knew she had a plan they could trust.

To begin with, that plan worked. Kerala aggressively flattened the curve: by 10 June 2020 it had managed to keep the R0, or basic reproduction number, at 0.45;[12] far lower than the Indian average (1.22) and the world average (3). The R number is a way of calculating a disease's ability to spread: if it's higher than 1, then cases increase exponentially and you're in real trouble. There were days that cases in Kerala were brought down to 'zero' and Shailaja was praised as 'the Coronavirus Slayer'.

Kerala, of course, did not come out of the pandemic unscathed. Despite the cool nickname, Shailaja is a human being, not a superhero. After flattening the curve at the beginning of the year, Kerala saw a surge in cases in July. To some degree the state was a victim of its own early success: complacency set in, leading people to drop their guard. The R rate crept above 1 and stayed there; in early 2021 it surged again. Nevertheless, things in the state of 35 million people could have been far, far worse. Kerala is hugely vulnerable to infectious diseases: it has the largest proportion of elderly[13] people in India, it's highly urbanized and has a migrant workforce estimated at between 2.5 and 3 million. The general consensus amongst policymakers around the world is that Kerala did an exceptional job with the resources it had. While Shailaja obviously did not fight the coronavirus single-handedly, her leadership, and the trust people put in that leadership, has been seen as a key factor. In November 2020 *Vogue India* paid tribute to Shailaja by putting her on the cover of the magazine and giving her the magazine's Leader of the Year award. The *Financial Times* listed her as one of the most influential women in the world in 2020.

Getting plaudits from the international media is all very well, but what really counts is what your own constituents think of you. 'Shailaja definitely won the people's trust,' Dr K. Srinath Reddy, president of the Public Health Foundation of India, told me over the phone, pointing to Shailaja's party gaining votes in recent local elections. Reddy works on India's overall public-health strategy, so he wasn't in the trenches with Shailaja as she worked to lead Kerala through the pandemic – however, he has worked with her before and notes how he was struck by her down-to-earth demeanour. 'She's not a know-all politician who believes that she must only pass orders; she's hands-on without being authoritarian,' he explains. Rather than controlling things from a distance, she goes and talks to people. In order to trust someone, you need to feel like they're on your side: that they're willing to show up for you, and they're not concealing things from you. Shailaja did both of these things, explaining things to people clearly and in person rather than issuing jargon-filled government directives. She's got the 'right balance of efficiency and empathy'. And that combination has won her what has eluded a lot of politicians: trust.

There has been a lot of hand-wringing about 'the crisis of trust' in recent years. 'Our world is suffering from a bad case of "Trust Deficit Disorder",' United Nations Secretary-General António Guterres announced as he opened the

General Assembly in 2018. 'Trust is at a breaking point. Trust in national institutions. Trust among states. Trust in the rules-based global order. Within countries, people are losing faith in political establishments, polarization is on the rise and populism is on the march.' Since then, things have only got worse. The 2021 Edelman Trust Barometer,[14] a respected annual study of trust around the world, found that public trust had eroded even further in social institutions (government, business, non-governmental organizations and media) thanks to the pandemic, the global outcry over systemic racism and the rise of misinformation.

It's not exactly surprising that people have lost faith in traditional institutions, is it? Why would you trust the people in charge? I remember marching on the streets of London as an idealistic university student back in 2003 to protest against the Iraq War. It was the largest protest in British history and there were similar protests around the world. At the time I naïvely thought that the powers would be would have to listen. But, of course, they didn't: Iraq was invaded under the pretence of finding 'weapons of mass destruction'. It's hard to overstate how much the Iraq War undermined faith in democracy and trust in government. People felt lied to and deceived; manipulated by an elite who had concealed information and spun a scary story to justify doing whatever they wanted while facing no consequences for their actions. A few years later, the global financial crisis happened. Again, people felt lied to and deceived. Most people had no idea what the hell a derivative or a subprime mortgage was; they lost jobs and homes because of a system nobody seemed to understand, created by people who once again faced no consequences for their actions.

In short, there is no 'crisis of trust'. There is a crisis of leadership. People were attracted to Donald Trump, a billionaire who railed against the 'elite' from his private jet, because it felt like he said what he meant and meant what he said. That was nonsense, of course, but his election demonstrated a desperate desire for a different sort of politician. Shailaja Teacher is a case study in what a different (and actually effective) sort of politician sounds like: throughout both virus crises she communicated clearly and shared information in an accessible way, while making it clear that she cared about what she was saying. She communicated, in short, like a teacher. After all, what are the key skills a teacher needs? They need to explain complex information in a clear and simple way to people with different levels of understanding. If they fail at that, then the kids fail their tests and the teacher fails at their job. Politicians, on the other hand, are not incentivized to communicate clearly. Quite the opposite. Politicians speak in deliberately vague, and often emotionally charged, language because they want to appeal to as many people as possible and they want to avoid being held to specific promises. Businesspeople similarly avoid clear language because the goal is often to persuade people, not inform people. One of my first jobs in advertising was on a shampoo brand; I had to test a bunch of claims with focus groups. We'd make up bullshit like 'new and improved hydra-oils' and see how people reacted to the language. If we were honest about the product, we'd just say: contains the same old chemicals as every other shampoo out there, just in a different bottle. But honesty is not really a profitable policy.

Trust is built in a variety of different ways and, to some degree, every single lesson in this book is a lesson in how you build trust. This chapter, however, focuses on how you build trust through language. While actions always speak louder than words, words matter enormously. If we are to rebuild trust in institutions, it starts with changing the language of leadership. We need our leaders to communicate less like politicians and businessmen, and more like teachers. Teaching, of course, is an overwhelmingly female profession, which means it's undervalued. Once again, instead of pathologizing 'female' skills we desperately need to be elevating them.

Use clear language to create accountability

If Shailaja Teacher is The Coronavirus Slayer, Katie Porter may well be The Bullshit Slayer. Like Shailaja, Porter has a background in teaching; the law professor turned California congresswoman only became a politician in 2018, but she's already built up a formidable reputation and taken down a number of smug CEOs. Porter's name may not be immediately familiar to you – she's not internationally famous the way Alexandria Ocasio-Cortez is – but there's a good chance you've seen one of the many viral clips of the forty-five-year-old questioning (or more appropriately, eviscerating) a powerful figure during congressional hearings. Porter, like Shalija, doesn't really look like a slick politician. However, as a number of politicians and businessmen have painfully realized, you underestimate her at your peril.

Power props itself up with layers of bullshit; it uses puffery to escape accountability. George Orwell said that rather more eloquently in his famous essay 'Politics and the English Language'. Political language, Orwell said, 'is designed to make lies sound truthful and murder respectable, and to give an appearance of solidity to pure wind'. Powerful people use vague, meaningless language because they're often not interested in telling the truth, but hiding it. 'The great enemy of clear language is insincerity,' Orwell wrote. 'When there is a gap between one's real and one's declared aims, one turns as it were instinctively to long words and exhausted idioms, like a cuttlefish spurting out ink.'[15]

Porter's superpower is her ability to cut through that bullshit. Perhaps because of her background in teaching, she's good at efficiently reducing complex information into easily absorbed bullet points. She's good at eliminating ambiguity and holding powerful people accountable to specific promises. Nothing quite compares to watching her do this on film (I recommend you watch every single one of her YouTube clips), but let's zero in on her questioning of Tim Sloan, CEO of Wells Fargo, about the bank's business practices. Wells Fargo, to give you some background, has a history of doing jaw-droppingly immoral things. Employees were encouraged to aggressively cross-sell and, during the early 2010s, the bank opened millions of savings and checking accounts and ordered new credit cards on behalf of its clients without their consent. Their clients only realized this when they started getting unanticipated fees. And it wasn't just clients who suffered: non-management employees were so stressed about meeting their sales targets that many suffered mental-health problems. One former employee, speaking to the *New York Times*[16] in 2016, said that the stress was so intense she used to go the bathroom and drink the hand sanitizer to calm her nerves. Wells Fargo was fined heavily for these scandals and replaced its chief executive with Sloan in October 2016. But had the bank actually changed? Sloan was summoned to Capitol Hill in March 2019 to convince the House Financial Services Committee that people could trust Wells Fargo again.

Sloan was questioned for hours by members of Congress, during which he said vacuous things like 'Wells Fargo is a better bank than it was three years ago, and we are working every day to become even better.'[17] The lawmakers questioning him were sceptical, but Sloan repeatedly took cover from the questioning with more vague statements like 'I can't promise you perfection, but what I can promise you is that the changes we've implemented since I've become CEO will prevent harm the best we can.' There was so much hot air in the room it is a surprise no one fainted. It's highly unlikely that the average person would have had any idea that the hearing even happened, let alone what was said in it, had it not been for Porter and her whiteboard.

Each congressperson gets five minutes for questioning in hearings like this. When Porter's time came, she started by quoting statements that Sloan had made in 2016 and 2017, including: 'I'm fully committed to taking the necessary steps to restore our customers' trust' and 'We've already made progress in restoring customers' trust.'

'Those statements to me sound pretty vague,' Porter said. 'They sound like they might be obscure, empty promises. Do those statements really mean something to you, Mr Sloan?'

'They do,' Sloan replied.

'Why should we have confidence in those promises?'

Sloan waffled for a little bit until Porter cut back in.

'So it's safe to say that the statements you've made mean something to you, and that customers and investors can rely on those statements?' Porter asked.

'That's correct,' Sloan said.

Porter slowly reached under the table and pulled out a whiteboard, which had a piece of paper taped on it.

'Then why, Mr Sloan,' Porter said, 'are your lawyers in federal court arguing that those exact statements that I read are, quote, "paradigmatic examples of non-actionable corporate puffery, on which no reasonable investor could rely"?'

The whiteboard Porter was holding had an image of that court document. The quote she read out was enlarged on that document and easily legible. 'Corporate puffery' was highlighted in yellow. Sloan was trapped.

'Uh uh uh, I don't know why our lawyers are arguing that,' Sloan said and waffled defensively.

'It is convenient for your lawyers to deflect blame in court and say your rebranding campaign can be ignored as hyperbolic marketing, but when you come to Congress you want us to take you at your word,' Porter replied. 'I think that's the disconnect. It is why the American public is having trouble trusting Wells Fargo.'[18]

Two weeks later, Sloan abruptly resigned from Wells Fargo without any severance.[19] It is, of course, impossible to say with certainty that Porter's questioning was solely responsible for this, but it clearly played a role. Not only did Porter catch Sloan out in an untruth, she made it impossible for him to easily escape that untruth. Pictures of her whiteboard were all over the news, the phrase 'corporate puffery' jumping out of it. Without Porter's questioning – and her whiteboard – there wouldn't have been anything particularly newsworthy about the hearing; nobody would have paid attention.

It's not just Sloan who has been taken down by what has been dubbed the mighty whiteboard of truth.[20] Porter, who used to be a law professor, makes liberal, and very tactical, use of the visual prop.

'I see the whiteboard as a tool to help both the witness and those in the audience stay focused, which is exactly the way I used the whiteboard in my classroom,' Porter once explained[21] to *New York Magazine*'s *The Cut*. 'If the students were not following, or I thought there were too many details, or the subject was really complex, I would turn to the whiteboard and try to map out what I was explaining. It also helps convey to the witness that you know what you're talking about and that you've done the research, so there's no room for waffling here.'

Crucially, the whiteboard doesn't just help people in the room stay focused. It also makes complex political hearings more digestible for everyone else.

'[I]t helps Americans who are watching later to follow along, because they probably haven't watched all four hours of the hearing, nor should we expect them to,' Porter explained.

Making politics accessible and engaging, which Porter's whiteboard interrogations do, is an essential part of rebuilding trust in the political system.

There are endless whiteboard stories, but one of Porter's finest moments may have been in March 2020, when she used her whiteboard to secure free coronavirus testing for all Americans. You'd have thought that free testing during a pandemic would be a no-brainer, but this is America we're talking about: when it comes to health care, profits always come before people. The situation around testing in March was very unclear: some insurance companies had said they'd cover testing for certain policyholders but people who weren't insured risked being on the hook for a small fortune. Or $1,331 to be exact: Porter did the maths on her whiteboard at a congressional hearing and demonstrated exactly how much it would cost an uninsured American to be tested.

Porter also demonstrated that she did her homework: there was a federal statute the government could use to ensure coronavirus testing was free for every American. Porter turned to Robert Redfield, the director of the Centers for Disease Control and Prevention (CDC), and asked him whether he could commit to 'using that existing authority to pay for diagnostic testing free to every American, regardless of insurance?'

'Well,' he replied, 'I can say we're going to do everything to make sure everybody can get the care they — '

By now you know how this goes, right? Porter doesn't tolerate equivocation. As Redfield attempted to waffle, she cut back in and kept on pressing him until he said, 'Yes.' That still wasn't enough. She turned around and summed up the exchange to ensure that his commitment was crystal clear: 'Everybody in America hear that? You are eligible to go get tested for coronavirus and have that covered regardless of insurance.'

During Kerala's Nipah crisis, Shailaja Teacher knew that people wouldn't listen to the government's health guidelines unless she physically showed up in the village that was ground zero of the outbreak and talked to people directly. And she couldn't show up, take a few photos, say a few words, then rush back to safety: she had to show people that she cared and that she was committed. Porter's whiteboard is analogous to that. She can't show up in every living room in America and have a chat with people, but she can ensure that hours of congressional hearings get boiled down to one key point, written on a whiteboard, that everyone can understand. She can build trust by reducing the distance between government waffling and people's everyday lives. She can build trust by stopping powerful people from escaping into ambiguity and forcing them, instead, to say exactly what they mean. Redfield's promise made headlines across America. And that made it very hard for Redfield to renege on his commitment. In the end, coronavirus testing was free, regardless of what insurance you had.

Say what you mean

Katie Porter and K. K. Shailaja excel at clear, buzzword-free communication. Are they exceptional, or are women in general more likely to avoid buzzwords? I couldn't find definitive research on this, so I decided to think outside the box and touch base with a female-led data company called First & First Consulting to see if there were synergies in our thinking and whether we could ideate together. They circled back and said this sort of thing was right in their wheelhouse and they'd drill down into some data for me and analyse the Twitter activity of 179,000 male and female executives. 'Executive' was defined as people that have C-Suite titles in their bio (e.g. CEO, CFO, etc.) and share relevant business content that validates that they are in fact a leader in a business organization.

The bottom line? It seems male business leaders use buzzwords 17% more often on Twitter than women leaders. They also used slightly different buzzwords. Women were more likely to reach for more touch-feely buzzwords, while men were more likely to use sales-focused buzzwords.[22]

BUZZWORDS MORE COMMONLY USED BY FEMALE LEADERS	BUZZWORDS MORE COMMONLY USED BY MALE LEADERS
Customer journey	Freemium
Hyperlocal	Drill down
Unpack	Quick win
Touchpoint	Retargeting
Sustainability	Big Data
Impact	Content is King

This obviously doesn't serve as definitive proof that men are more likely to use buzzwords. It's also worth noting that a recent study on buzzwords didn't find a significant gender difference in office jargon; rather, it found you're more likely to use buzzwords when you're insecure and have a lower professional status. Nevertheless, there is plenty of evidence that shows men and women use language differently. One big difference is that men are more likely to use abstract language, while women are more likely to speak in concrete terms and say exactly what they mean. A study published in 2020[23] by researchers from San Francisco State University, for example, analysed[24] over 500,000 transcripts of text delivered by more than 1,000 US Congress members from congressional sessions spanning 2001 to 2017 and found men used significantly more abstract language in their speeches than women. They define abstract speech as language 'that focuses on the broader picture and ultimate purpose of action rather than concrete speech focusing on details and the means of attaining action'. This was true regardless of political affiliation.

Not only do men tend to use more abstract language, there is also evidence that suggests they are more likely to use sensationalist language. One analysis of titles and abstracts in more than 100,000 scientific articles, for example, found that female-authored papers were about 12% less likely than male-authored papers to include bombastic terms[25] such as 'unprecedented', 'novel', 'excellent' or 'remarkable'.

To make all of this a little less abstract, I think it's worth looking at the language world leaders used during the pandemic. Specifically, the way in which men were more likely to reach for military metaphors (about as abstract and sensationalist as you can get) than women.

'We are at war,' Emmanuel Macron said in a televised address on 16 March 2020 that marked his first big coronavirus speech to the French people. 'We are at war . . . we are at war . . . we are war . . . we are at war . . . we are at war.' Macron used that phrase six times overall, along with other battlefield imagery. 'We're not up against another army or another nation. But the enemy is right there: invisible, elusive, but it is making progress.' Macron's wartime rhetoric was echoed by pretty much every other male leader. China's Xi Jinping called for a 'people's war' against the virus.[26] Donald Trump, famous for dodging the Vietnam draft, labelled himself[27] 'a wartime president'. Indian Prime Minister Narendra Modi said that every Indian complying with lockdown was 'a soldier in this fight'.[28] Andrew Cuomo similarly called health-care workers 'soldiers'. Boris Johnson said that 'we must act like any wartime government' to support the UK economy. Everywhere you looked, armchair generals were puffing out their chests and reaching for military metaphors.

Female leaders were not entirely exempt from this. However, they used war metaphors far less than men according to a study published in the *BMJ Global Health* journal,[29] which analysed speeches made by twenty heads of government around the world between 26 February and 6 April 2020. The study, 'Words matter: political and gender analysis of speeches made by heads of government during the COVID-19 pandemic', found that seventeen of the twenty leaders used war metaphors to describe the virus and response. 'In the 19 speeches made by women who used war metaphors, they average 6.1 references to this rhetoric. In the 40 speeches made by men with this language, they average 25.4 references to war metaphors.' Women were also more likely than men to use empathetic language that focused on compassion and cooperation. So when war metaphors were employed by women they were used in a way that emphasized unity rather than division. In the two instances that Taiwan's Tsai Ing-wen used the war metaphor, for example, it was to describe the necessity for 'full international cooperation [as] the only way to ensure that the international community can win this battle'.[30]

Does it sound awfully stereotypical to say women urged cooperation while men played at being soldiers? Absolutely. But have you looked around a toy store lately? As soon as kids are born, boys are encouraged to be boisterous while girls are encouraged to cooperate. It's socialization, not biology. Indeed, there was one female outlier when it came to war rhetoric: Jeanine Áñez, who served as Bolivia's interim president from November 2019 to November 2020, was the only female leader to use war rhetoric in double digits. 'On average, for speeches that did employ war rhetoric or aggressive language, it constituted 3.5% of each speech made by men, and 2.8% for the women (1.9% without Áñez).' Áñez was installed by a coup, so it's not particularly surprising that she's a fan of military language. She's a reminder that the qualities discussed in this book aren't unique to women or men, but are what we traditionally describe as 'masculine' or 'feminine'.

War metaphors aren't intrinsically bad. In some instances, they can be useful. They can help solidify an intangible threat. They can quickly and efficiently convey how serious a situation is. However, war is also inherently divisive and the language around it can be the same. Military language can spread fear and be used to justify authoritarian actions. It can also be used to victim-blame. Look, for example, at recent pushback against characterizing cancer as something to be 'battled'; that sort of language implies that if you don't beat the disease it's somehow your fault. You just didn't fight hard enough.

There are times when military metaphors are appropriate, there are times when they're not. The lesson here isn't that 'battle' is a bad word, it's that sowing fear isn't a good way to build trust. Playing the general and invoking an enemy is a lazy, unimaginative and often ineffective way to get people to fall into line. You may get people to follow your orders out of fear – but isn't it better if they do what you say because they trust you? You don't built trust by scaring people into subjugation. Nor do you do it through grandiose abstract language. You build trust by giving people the information they need clearly and calmly.

Angela Merkel's first big coronavirus speech, a televised address on 18 March 2020, is a very clear example of this. The speech is well worth reading in its entirety: it's a masterclass in crisis management and trust-building. And that's not just my opinion: it was selected as the 'Speech of Year' for 2020 by a panel of rhetoric experts[31] from Germany's Tübingen University, who argued Merkel's address 'directly influenced the German population in a way that almost no other speech of the past years has done'.

The first notable thing about Merkel's speech was that she decided to give it in the first place. Unlike some politicians, Merkel isn't in love with the sound of her own voice; when she speaks it's because she's got something to say. This was the first unscheduled television address Merkel had given in almost fifteen years of leadership; she didn't need to use war metaphors to communicate how serious things were, her presence was enough to get people to sit up and pay attention.

Merkel started her speech by calmly acknowledging the gravity of the situation and explaining the importance of transparency. 'I'm addressing you in this unconventional way today because I want to tell you what guides me as Federal Chancellor and all my colleagues in the Federal Government in this situation,' she said. 'This is part of what open democracy is about: that we make political decisions transparent and explain them; that we justify and communicate our actions as best we can, so that people are able to understand them.' Merkel didn't just avoid using military metaphors, she avoided metaphor in general and spoke in clear and simple language. Instead of calling the coronavirus a 'war' or a 'battle', she described it as 'this situation,' 'a historical task', and a 'great challenge'.[32]

While Merkel invoked scientists and experts, noting that everything she was saying was underpinned by consultations with experts, she also grounded what she was saying in her personal experience. The chancellor famously grew up in East Berlin; she grew up under a sort of lockdown. 'Allow me to assure you that, for someone like me, for whom the freedom of travel and the freedom of movement were a hard-fought right, such restrictions can only be justified if they are absolutely imperative,' Merkel said. 'These should never be put in place lightly in a democracy and should only be temporary. But they are vital at the moment in order to save lives.' There was no abstract or flowery language about war and duty, she spelled out what was happening in simple and non-alarming terms. It was quite the contrast to the authoritarianism that ran through Macron's speech and his warnings that 'all [lockdown] infractions will be punished'.[33]

Merkel's no-nonsense speech is a good reflection of her no-nonsense political style. The chancellor is not known for her oratory; indeed, her public speaking style has been compared to watching paint dry. She says what's necessary when it's necessary without any embellishment. People don't adore her, but they trust her. In October 2020[34] a Pew Survey of fourteen countries found that more people trust Merkel than any other world leader. A median of 75% across the surveyed countries say they have confidence in Merkel to do the right thing regarding world affairs. The scores for other world leaders? Macron (63%); Johnson (50%) Vladimir Putin (23%); Trump (17%). A majority of adults across every country surveyed said they had confidence in the German Chancellor. Perhaps more leaders should focus less on trying to play the role of the heroic army general and more on saying exactly what they mean and meaning what they say.

Mean what you say

Want to know what the worst word in the English language is? It's not 'moist'. It's not 'smegma'. It's not 'empowerment' – although that's definitely a runner-up. The worst word is 'electability'. It's a flimsy concept that is often wielded by people who want to protect the status quo and who don't think very much of the electorate. Back in 2008 a lot of pundits and pollsters thought Barack Obama was unelectable, for example, because they superimposed their own prejudices onto America as a whole. Mark Penn, a renowned political strategist famous for getting Bill Clinton into power and getting Tony Blair a third term, told Hillary Clinton that she'd win easily against Obama. He was unelectable, Penn said in a memo to Clinton, whose campaign he was working on, 'except perhaps against Atilla the Hun'. Why was he so unelectable? Oh, you know why. In the same memo Penn sneered: 'All of these articles about his boyhood in Indonesia and his life in Hawaii are geared towards showing his background is diverse, multicultural and putting that in a new light. Save it for 2050.'[35]

The fact that one of the world's most renowned political strategists thought it would take decades for Obama to become palatable shows how ridiculous the entire concept of 'electability' is. (Not to mention what it says about Penn's own biases.) The fact that nobody thought a reality TV star with zero political experience could win the White House in 2016 shows how ridiculous the idea of 'electability' is. And yet there's still an obsession with the concept. It was one of the biggest buzzwords of the Democratic 2020 primaries.

You know who else wasn't thought to be electable? Katie Porter. One reason Porter may be such an effective politician is that she never really wanted to be a politician. (I'm not sure you ever trust anyone who started life actually wanting to be a politician.) She was very happy being a law professor until she was radicalized by Donald Trump's 2016 electoral victory and felt a burning desire to do something to change the status quo. Her boyfriend suggested she run for Congress and, as she turned the idea around in her mind, she Googled how many points her current congressperson had won by. Porter, a Democrat, is from Orange County, California, a district that has always leaned Republican; the congresswoman at the time was Mimi Walters, an investment banker turned Republican politician who had won re-election against a Democrat by seventeen points in 2016. That's a lot of points. People told Porter running as a Democrat was hopeless, but she decided to do so anyway.

Porter's first challenge wasn't beating a Republican, it was beating Dave Min, a fellow Democrat and UC Irvine law professor, in the primary. If you're in a state that leans to the right the conventional wisdom is that you should also lean to the right and parrot what you think the average voter wants to hear. That's what all the Clever Centrist Pundits love to tell us anyway, and that's what Min was doing. Min, who was backed by the Democratic establishment, was a firm centrist who thought pushing universal health care was way too far left for Orange County. Min made it very clear what he didn't stand for (wild lefty ideas like ensuring people don't die because they can't afford health care), but it was less clear what he did stand for. 'He answers a lot of questions with an apology about how nerdy he's about to get,' a reporter for *Vox*[36] noted in a 2018 piece. 'When I ask him about automatic voter registration, he begins with the ancient Greeks.'

Min, in short, was the sort of politician that Clever Centrist Pundits and the establishment adore. A guy who stands firmly for the status quo. A guy who worships incrementalism. A guy with a handy stockpile of Heraclitus quotes to distract you from the fact that he has no real ideas. A guy who, conventional wisdom dictated, was the safest choice for beating an incumbent Republican in a district that leans Republican.

Porter, on the other hand, was very clear that she stood for progressive policies like Medicare-for-all. She refused money from corporate PACs. She didn't focus on trying to be 'electable', she focused on communicating exactly what she stood for and why. She didn't pander to voters by telling them what she thought they wanted to hear. Rather, she argued her case treated them as smart enough to make up their own mind about what they wanted. And, in the 2018 elections, she ended up flipping the Republican seat and winning, making her the first Democrat to represent the electoral district since it was created in 1953. In the 2020 elections she won again. (Members of the House of Representatives serve two-year terms and are considered for re-election every even year.)

It's hard to trust someone if you have no idea what they believe. With Porter, you know exactly what she believes and, more importantly, you know why she believes it. I think one reason Porter is so effective at what she does is that she's not a militant ideologue or a devoted party politician. She's not out there preaching socialism, nor is she a fervent member of the Democratic establishment. She's a bankruptcy lawyer and a teacher, and she presents herself first and foremost as an advocate for consumer rights. Her stance on everything is basically 'you shouldn't be getting ripped off'. Which is a simple message anyone can get behind, no matter their political persuasion.

The 'crisis of trust' is often discussed like it's an incredibly complex problem. It's not. When leaders hide information from you, when they speak in vague meaningless language and don't believe a word they say, then you're obviously not going to trust them. You solve the crisis of trust with leaders who communicate like teachers; leaders who use clear language that creates accountability, leaders who say what they mean and mean what they say. The language you use should reflect the person you are, not the image you want to project. Otherwise, it's almost inevitable you'll look like a hypocrite.

3

Don't be a Hypocrite

Seventy-two hours

That was the amount of time[1] between Justice Ruth Bader Ginsburg dying in September 2020 and Donald Trump offering Amy Coney Barrett, a conservative judge who once served as a 'handmaid' in a Christian community called People of Praise, the nomination to the US Supreme Court.

Thirty-five days

That was the amount of time between Barrett's nomination and the 2020 election. It was the shortest period of time between a Supreme Court nomination and an election in US history.

Eight days

That was the amount of time between Barrett's confirmation to the Supreme Court and the election. Just over a week before America went to the polls Barrett was given a lifetime appointment, shifting the Supreme Court from a 5–4 conservative majority to a 6–3 super-majority. Well, 'given' is something of a misnomer. Barrett was confirmed without having the support of a single member of the minority party (the Democrats): it was the first time in 151 years that that had happened. Only one member of the Republican party broke rank and voted against her confirmation. Her appointment was a hugely partisan affair.

It was also a hugely hypocritical affair. In 2016 the GOP had blocked Barack Obama's nomination of Merrick Garland to the Supreme Court because it was nine months before the end of Obama's term. Notably, Barrett herself went on *CBS News* and said that a nomination in an election year would be completely inappropriate and she didn't support nominations that would 'dramatically flip the balance of power on the Court'.[2]

Lindsey Graham, the Republican Senator for South Carolina, was even more adamant that filling a vacancy during an election year was *verboten*. 'I want you to use my words against me,' Graham said at the time. 'If there's a Republican president in 2016 and a vacancy occurs in the last year of the first term, you can say Lindsey Graham said let's let the next president, whoever it might be, make that nomination.'[3]

Graham doubled down on this promise two years later. In a recorded interview with the *Atlantic*'s editor-in-chief, Jeffrey Goldberg, he declared: 'I will tell you this, if an opening comes in the last year of President Trump's term, and the primary process has started, we'll wait to the next election.' To underscore just how serious he was, he added, 'Hold the tape.'[4]

We all know what happened next. RBG died in the last year of Trump's term and Graham suddenly decided his previous comments didn't matter any more. He justified his about-face by invoking what he considered to be the Democrats' partisan treatment of Supreme Court nominee Brett Kavanaugh. 'The rules have changed as far as I'm concerned,' he told *NBC News*.[5] Despite the fact that thousands of Americans were dying from Covid-19 each week, Republicans made confirming Barrett their highest priority. They dragged their feet on passing a pandemic relief bill, but they jumped straight into action with Barrett: demanding that the judiciary committee convene in person (and indoors) to push her nomination through.

Hypocrisy and politics go hand in hand. 2020, in particular, was a bumper year for political hypocrisy, with endless examples of politicians skirting the lockdown rules they'd imposed upon others. Nevertheless, Barrett's Supreme Court appointment stands out as a particularly egregious example of political hypocrisy. Except, of course, it was only egregious to people who disagreed with Barrett's politics. For anti-abortion activists it was a massive win. Getting Barrett confirmed and shifting the Supreme Court to a conservative super-majority gave them enormous control over the future of America. They could rationalize the hypocrisy because the end more than justified the means.

Hypocrisy thrives in hyper-partisan times: Barrett's appointment is a clear example of this. Sticking it to the other side was more important than being able to claim the moral high ground. It's not just the right who are guilty of hypocrisy, it should be said; liberals are equally culpable. During the pandemic, endless Democratic leaders who tut-tutted about how Trump wasn't taking the crisis seriously flouted laws they had told everyone else to follow. A maskless Nancy Pelosi got her hair styled in a San Francisco salon, breaking rules that only allowed service outdoors. California Governor Gavin Newsom told people not to socialize and was then caught celebrating his lobbyist friend's birthday at the very fancy French Laundry restaurant. There are endless examples of liberal hypocrisy and, when they're called out, they're often justified with cries of 'Well, look at what your side did!'

Why are we living in what seems to be a golden age of hypocrisy? I called up Jay Van Bavel, associate professor of psychology at NYU's Social Identity and Morality Lab – and something of an expert in hypocrisy – to get his view. Here's how he explained it:

> The context of political tribalism means that people are more motivated than ever to be loyal to a party position. People are paying a lot of attention to politics, and they're updating their beliefs in line with party leaders and moment-to-moment world events rather than thinking about what they believe and trying to have some internal consistency in their own value system. So when the party leader does something that violates their values or previous beliefs they quickly modify their beliefs and seemingly update their value system.[6]

In other words? Tribalism has turned us into sheep. Rather nasty sheep at that. 'We're in a period of history where people's dislike of the other party is just as important, if not more important, than how much they like their own party,' Van Bavel explains. Social media has amplified this. You get clicks and likes for calling out the bad behaviour or a member of the opposite side. 'LOOK WHAT THEY DID!!!' 'BUT LOOK WHAT YOU DID!!!' 'BUT WHAT ABOUT WHAT YOU DID!!' Hatred for the 'other side' hasn't just caused us to become nastier, it has caused the average citizen to exercise less critical thinking. Misinformation is fuelled by partisanship: according to a series of experiments Van Bavel worked on,

Democrats are more likely to believe negative fake-news stories featuring Republican politicians, whereas Republicans were more likely to believe negative fake-news stories featuring Democratic politicians. What we choose to believe is now fuelled by who we hate.

The depressing conclusion to all this? If you want to get ahead in these polarized times, being a hypocrite can be more of a help than a hindrance. The other side might loathe you, but your side will make excuses for your behaviour. And if what you're doing furthers your side's agenda then your hypocrisy will be completely excused. Bearing all that in mind, 'don't be a hypocrite' may not be the best advice if all you care about is getting ahead. But a leader isn't someone whose only concern is personal advancement. Being a leader doesn't mean having a fancy title and lots of power – that's a boss or a dictator. A leader is someone who doesn't take an easy path to self-advancement but instead works towards a greater good.

Women, I want to make clear, are obviously very capable of hypocrisy; there are plenty of hypocritical female politicians out there. However, hypocrisy is fuelled by self-interest and women have traditionally been socialized to be caregivers and put others before themselves. Studies show that women are more generous[7] than men. One study even found that men and women's brains process generosity differently: female brains trigger a stronger reward signal for generous behaviour than men's brains. This probably isn't innate; rather, the researchers note that empirical studies show girls are praised for prosocial behaviour from a young age.

Because women are trained to put the greater good over themselves, female politicians seem more able to avoid blind party loyalty; global studies show that women are more likely than men to work across the aisle to get things done. One example of this is when the US government shut down for sixteen days in 2013 after partisan bickering over health care left Congress unable to agree on a budget for the new fiscal year. Between 1 and 17 October 2013, nearly 800,000 federal employees were furloughed without pay and more than a million other working employees had their paychecks delayed. The shutdown was a big, expensive mess that cost America $1.5 billion a day. You know what ended that mess? Women putting partisan differences aside and working together. Maine Republican Susan Collins came up with a three-point plan she thought everyone could agree on and asked her colleagues to come together and legislate in good faith. Both Republican and Democratic women took her up on this and the group, which eventually grew to include a few token men, eventually came up with a framework that allowed government to reopen.

'I don't think it's a coincidence that women were so heavily involved in trying to end this stalemate,' Collins later said.[8] 'Although we span the ideological spectrum, we are used to working together in a collaborative way.' (Collins enjoyed a great deal of respect from liberals and a reputation as an independent thinker for her part in ending the shutdown. Then, in a move which angered many liberals and somewhat sours this example, she toed the Republican party line to confirm Brett Kavanaugh.)

Similarly, a 2015 study[9] by a research company called Quorum found female senators co-sponsored (a fancy word for 'supported') an average of 171.08 bills with a member of the opposite party. For the average male senator, that figure was 129.87. By putting ideological differences aside and collaborating, female senators got more laws passed. The study found that female senators moved an average of 4.88 bills out of committee (a key step in the bill becoming law) and had on average 2.31 bills enacted over a period of seven years compared to the 3.24 bills their male counterparts got out of committee and 1.57 bills enacted. While working across the aisle doesn't mean you can never be hypocritical, it does mean you're better able to focus on the big picture rather than just yourself.

Corporate feminism has taught us that female selflessness is a weakness and we should focus on self-advancement; selfishness has been recast as empowerment. However, the last thing the world needs is more leaders who act purely out of self-interest and see nothing wrong with hypocrisy as long as it serves them. The world is stuck in a vicious circle of cynicism and distrust: we expect the 'elite' to play by different rules from the rest of us and this normalization of hypocrisy means leaders don't even seem to bother trying to hide their double standards any more. This rampant hypocrisy has undermined trust in the system. So, please let's stop telling women that doing whatever it takes to get ahead is empowering. Rather, we need to encourage a model of leadership that is driven by solidarity rather than individualism. We need leaders who don't think they belong to an elite that doesn't have to play by the same rules as the rest of us. And we need leaders who are more concerned about doing their job properly rather than their career progression.

Focus on doing your job, not keeping your job

When Mary Robinson became the UN High Commissioner for Human Rights in 1997, a friend of hers told her she shouldn't expect to stay in the job for very long. 'If you're too popular in the job you're not doing a good job,' Robinson remembers her saying.[10] It didn't take long for Robinson to realize her friend was right. Robinson's job was to stand up for the human rights of ordinary people – and that often meant speaking uncomfortable truths and annoying a lot of powerful politicians. Like George W. Bush, for example, with whom Robinson famous feuded. 'Are you not afraid of losing your job or not getting a second term?' journalists would ask her. 'I'm here to do a job, not keep a job,' she would repeat.[11]

Robinson didn't keep that job; she was pushed out at the end of her first term after publicly criticizing America's war on terror after September 11. She was routinely attacked by the likes of John Bolton and praised by human-rights organization: evidence, if ever there was any, that she very much did her job. In 2009 Barack Obama awarded her the Presidential Medal of Freedom, the highest civilian honour, describing her as 'an advocate for the hungry and the hunted, the forgotten and the ignored'.

We hear a lot about the art of compromise when it comes to leadership. How you can't always be true to your values if you want to get things done; how 'purity politics' will get you nowhere. And, of course, compromise is important. But so is being able to tell the difference between constructive compromises and compromises that mean that you're simply not doing your job. Speaking to me from her office in Dublin, Robinson notes that when it comes to the UN system, the Secretary-General inevitably has to compromise a lot; that's his job.

'But I think the important thing is that you have voices that don't compromise and who speak truth to power.'[12] Robinson's job as Commissioner for Human Rights was to amplify marginalized voices. The first three words of the United Nations Charter (the foundational treaty) are 'we the peoples', Robinson stresses. She was accountable to ordinary people, not member states. Ignoring that wouldn't have been merely hypocritical, it would have gone against the entire premise of her job.

Nadia Whittome is another example of how sometimes the only way to do your job properly is to be unafraid of potentially sabotaging your career. In September 2020 she, along with some other Labour MPs, voted against a new law that would make it harder for military veterans to be prosecuted for past actions. The Overseas Operations (Service Personnel and Veterans) Bill was, the government said, meant to protect the armed forces from 'vexatious prosecutions'. However, a number of Labour MPs worried that it would make it harder for veterans to sue the government and violated rule-of-law principles. Labour MPs were ordered to abstain in the vote; anyone who wanted to vote against the whip was told they'd have to resign from positions they held on the front bench. Whittome, along with the Labour MPs Beth Winter and Olivia Blake, chose to resign from her position as Parliamentary Private Secretary (PPS) to vote against the bill. A PPS is an MP who serves as an unpaid assistant to a government minister. While their duties are fairly thankless, it's a highly coveted role as it's often the first step in becoming a minister yourself. So if climbing as high as you can in government is your biggest priority in life, then going against your party and forfeiting your PPS gig isn't a great idea.

Going against the party line wasn't easy, Whittome told me. 'That might be hard to believe given that I've broken the whip several times now. But it's not a decision I take lightly. I was elected as a Labour MP, not an Independent MP. I was elected to represent my constituents and to vote with Labour.'[13] But, she says, she wasn't going to 'abstain on a bill that effectively decriminalizes torture. I don't believe my constituents would have wanted me to abstain on that either.' Whittome didn't just listen to her conscience, she listened to the views of members of the military, who raised grave concerns about the bill. Her vote was deeply considered.

Being a member of a political party means occasionally having to suck it up and support something you're not thrilled about for the sake of unity. However, there's a difference between compromise and compromising your integrity. There are times when you need to speak up – even if it comes at a personal price.

Timnit Gebru is one example of the sort of toll that speaking up can take. If you're in the tech world, you'll already be familiar with Gebru. She's done ground-breaking work in the field of AI and Ethics. One of the reasons why there are now mainstream discussions about the problems of facial recognition is thanks to a 2018 research paper called 'Gender Shades' that Gebru authored with computer scientist Joy Buolamwini. The study revealed[14] that commercial facial-analysis software was significantly less accurate[15] for darker-skinned women than for lighter-skinned men: it misidentified dark-skinned women as much as 35% of the time, but worked almost perfectly with white men. This paper is widely credited[16] with sparking mainstream criticism of facial recognition and spurring attempts to rectify bias in the technology. It led to cities like San Francisco banning facial-recognition technology and companies like IBM, Amazon and Microsoft disavowing the tech or promising not to sell it to police departments pending federal regulation.

It's hard to overstate the impact of Buolamwini and Gebru's work in the field of AI ethics. 'I've lost track of the number of times I've heard someone say Timnit Gebru is saving the world recently,' a June 2020 Venturebeat article stated.[17]

When I called up Gebru to interview her on Zoom, it was still November 2020 and she was still the technical co-lead of Google's Ethical AI team; one of the few Black women in a senior role in the AI space. She sounded pretty exhausted during our chat. Her work is full on. The other day, she told me, she'd answered the door and got served a subpoena: it demanded she provided all communication related to a paper she wrote on facial recognition. A lot of companies are being sued for misusing the technology and because Gebru's work is seminal, it's being cited in all these lawsuits. I'll go into why her work is so important, and how it directly affects your life, in Chapter 7, 'Think Long and Wide'. But the point here is that working in AI and Ethics at a place like Google has its challenges. Sometimes you uncover uncomfortable truths that your bosses don't want to hear. Google had just called her up and told her she wouldn't be able to publish a research paper she had recently co-authored. It pointed out flaws in an important part of Google's business, she said, which didn't make them happy.

Gebru was hired by Google to point out issues like this. Her job was supposed to be about ensuring that Google was using AI in a way that doesn't hurt people; that the company was thinking carefully about the wider ramifications of their technology on society. And yet, she told me, they didn't seem keen on her actually doing her job.

'It's like, you bring me in, you parade me around, and then, in the most disrespectful manner possible, you have someone come in and tell me to retract my paper?' she says incredulously. 'There wasn't even a conversation or anything. Someone just told me to do it.'[18]

When Gebru told me this, I was a little surprised that she was being so candid and hadn't frantically told me 'this is off the record'. You don't fuck with Google. In one of my previous jobs I was tasked with putting together a marketing email for an event my company was putting on. At the time there had been headlines about how Gmail reads your email to target you with ads and I made an innocuous little joke in my email, which went out to all our clients, about that. Very big mistake. Google was one of our clients and I later heard that they'd called up the company in a rage and threatened to pull their business over that very innocuous joke. (And, by the way, nothing about that joke was inaccurate. Google was reading your emails. In 2017 Google announced that it had stopped scanning people's inboxes to personalize ads. However, if you're not careful about granting permissions in Gmail to third-party apps then third-party developers might be reading your emails without your informed consent.) Google does not like bad PR and they have a whole machine in place to stop it. If they got so upset about my silly joke, I couldn't imagine they'd be thrilled at Gebru talking about this paper. During my chat, I made a note to follow-up on the status of that research paper.

Turns out that reminder wasn't necessary. A couple of days after our Zoom conversation, Gebru wrote a withering email[19] to an internal group for women at Google, calling out the way she'd been treated and the way she'd been silenced. Shortly after that, she was very publicly ousted from Google. The company maintains it didn't fire her; she maintains they did. Popular opinion was very much on Gebru's side: her departure made headline news and caused an enormous PR disaster for Google. '[L]eaders in the field of AI ethics are arguing that the company pushed her out because of the inconvenient truths that she was uncovering about a core line of its research – and perhaps its bottom line,' the MIT Technology Review reported.[20]

The story didn't fizzle out. Gebru made the news day after day and spurred a conversation about issues of corporate influence in research, bias in AI, and the lack of diversity at Big Tech. In December 2020 over 2,600 Google employees and 4,300 other people in academia, industry, and civil society had signed a petition[21] denouncing Gebru's dismissal, which they described as 'unprecedented research censorship' and 'retaliatory firing'. Computer scientists began to refuse[22] to review Google AI research, in support of Gebru.

Even the US government got involved. On 16 December 2020 nine members of the US Congress, including Elizabeth Warren, sent a letter[23] to Google, asking for clarification on Gebru's dismissal. 'Artificial intelligence is perhaps the most transformative technology of our time,' the letter said. 'To ensure America wins the AI race, American technology companies must not only lead the world in innovation; they must also ensure such innovation reflects our nation's values.' The letter called out the impact of Gebru's work on improving AI accountability, and expressed alarm at the circumstances of her departure. It noted that the incident may have a 'chilling effect on researchers, particularly on issues relating to algorithmic bias'.

In the wake of Gebru's firing, workers at Google and other Alphabet companies created a union. 'This is historic – the first union at a major tech company by and for all tech workers,' said Dylan Baker,[24] a software engineer who used to report to Gebru. 'We will elect representatives, we will make decisions democratically, we will pay dues, and we will hire skilled organizers to ensure all workers at Google know they can work with us if they actually want to see their company reflect their values.'

Gebru made a bigger impact being fired than some people do in their entire careers. Without people like Gebru fearlessly agitating for change, there will never be any change. And I want to stress that Gebru didn't do this for fame or money. Do you know how easy Gebru could have it if she decided to just toe the line and do the sort of work that would make Google look good? She'd probably be getting a promotion instead of getting kicked out; she'd be pulling in a big pay cheque and sitting by a pool right now. Instead, she's being harassed on Twitter by right-wing trolls. When women speak out, they're always accused of making a fuss or having ulterior motives. Speaking out often comes at a heavy personal price and it's often just easier to stay silent. But when it comes to the business world, staying quiet in the face of something unconscionable isn't leadership: that's hypocritical careerism.

While Gebru, Whittome, and Robinson are all examples of women who put their conscience ahead of their career, I want to be very clear that 'following your conscience' isn't exactly simple. Most things in life aren't straightforwardly 'good' or 'bad', they're nuanced. Avoiding hypocrisy doesn't mean rigidly sticking to a fixed set of principles and beliefs, it means being able to update your thinking as new facts come in. Indeed, the easiest way to be a hypocrite is thinking that you are the authority on what's right and wrong and never changing your mind as new information comes in.

Don't be afraid to change your mind – just explain why

There's bad hypocrisy and there's good hypocrisy, Van Bavel, the NYU Professor who specializes in hypocrisy, told me. Good hypocrisy is when you're not afraid to update your thinking. Scientists do this all the time, after all; they are constantly looking at the data and changing their opinions as new evidence comes in. 'Great leaders should be doing the same,' Van Bavel says. 'But ideally what you want from them is some honest acknowledgment of that and a clear explanation of why they changed their thinking. Unfortunately, politicians don't talk like that much.'[25] Indeed, politicians often seem to go out of their way to boast about how they'll never change their mind. 'You turn if you want to. The lady's not for turning,' Margaret Thatcher famously said.[26] When politicians do change their minds on big issues – gay marriage for example – they often talk vaguely about how they've *evolved their thinking* on the matter rather than acknowledging that they were wrong. And, funnily enough, a lot of powerful people only seem to evolve their thinking when it becomes politically expedient to do so.

It would be hypocritical of me to suggest that there's overwhelming evidence demonstrating that female politicians are remarkably better at updating their thinking and clearly explaining the rationale behind it than their male counterparts. Politicians seem to be uniformly bad at this. However, I think some of the most egregious recent examples of politicians refusing to change their minds come from men with fragile egos who are desperate to be liked. (Hi, Boris Johnson!) I'll expand on that in the next chapter.

73

Elizabeth Warren came frustratingly close to showing how a clearly communicated change of opinion can make you seem like a more thoughtful and authentic politician. Warren used to be a Republican; she has explained that she joined the party because she believed in its conservative approach to markets and was against government regulation. As a student, she sided more[27] with corporations than consumers. She left the Republican party in 1996 when she was in her mid-forties. This wasn't a snap decision. Bankruptcies had been increasing in the 1980s and Warren started researching why. In her 2014 memoir, *A Fighting Chance*, Warren admitted that she'd approached the research thinking consumers were to blame. 'I might not have said so at the time, but I think I was on the lookout for cheaters and deadbeats as a way to explain who was filing for bankruptcy,' she wrote. However, after extensive research she learned 'that nearly 90% were declaring bankruptcy for one of three reasons: a job loss, a medical problem, or a family breakup'. It shook her beliefs in untrammeled capitalism. 'I did the research, and the data just took me to a totally different place,' she said in a 2007 interview. [28] That data then informed her policy positions.

While Warren has talked about this story on multiple occasions, she largely tried to avoid it while running in the 2020 Democratic primaries. Clearly she thought it was a weakness and would hurt her chances. A few people agreed with this analysis. '*I was stupid and then I became educated* isn't a great political narrative,' an executive vice president of Third Way, a centrist Democratic think tank, told the Atlantic in January 2020. On the whole, however, the media embraced her political journey. Her metamorphosis reveals 'a woman who searched for answers and found something she had never expected, then altered her thinking accordingly,' the *New York Times* wrote in a 2019 profile. The subtext to that being: 'isn't this exactly the sort of person we should want as president?' (*The Times* later endorsed Elizabeth Warren and Amy Klobuchar for the Democratic Party's presidential nomination.) A *Washington Post* columnist similarly opined that Warren shouldn't hide her Republican past: 'Her story of moving from right to left is, in many ways, as good a case for "capitalism with rules," as she describes her beliefs, as any policy paper or proposal.'[29]

Politicians should give us all more credit: it's patronizing to think that people will automatically mark someone down for updating their thinking. That said, I think the media ought to work harder to reassure politicians that they won't be judged for changing their minds. Flip-flopping on issues or being morally inconsistent is very different from learning new facts and adjusting your behaviour and beliefs accordingly. The former should be condemned, the latter should be encouraged and celebrated.

Fight hypocrisy with solidarity

Ultimately the best way to avoid hypocrisy is by rejecting our individualistic model of leadership and elevating the sort of prosocial behaviour that is drummed into girls at an early age. It's a lot easier to focus on doing a job than keeping a job when you're not driven by self-interest. It's a lot easier to update your thinking when you're less concerned about your image than your impact. When you see yourself as a representative of the people rather than a demi-god, then you're far more likely to play by the same rules that you impose on everyone else. Real leaders don't think they are more special than everyone else, they demonstrate solidarity. Nadia Whittome, for example, did that by taking a pay cut when she became an MP. When the coronavirus pandemic hit, Whittome once again made headlines by choosing to stand with ordinary workers and live by the principles she espouses: she went back to her old job in a care home in her hometown of Nottingham. *We're all in this together,* celebrities and politicians were all saying at the time. However, while many of them were tweeting platitudes from their holiday homes, Whittome was actually standing for normal people and speaking up about the conditions they were working under. About a month after returning to work, she publicly complained about the lack of personal protective equipment (PPE) faced by workers on the front line; her employers, she alleged, told her not to come back. She was on a zero-hours contract, but she'd effectively been sacked. Whittome used the media attention around that to draw more attention to conditions in the care sector and advocate for a 'new deal for social care'.

Jacinda Ardern, New Zealand's prime minister, also put substance behind the idea that *we're all in this together* when the pandemic hit. In April 2020, Ardern said she and other ministers would take a 20% pay cut lasting six months, to show 'leadership and solidarity' with people suffering from the pandemic in New Zealand. 'If there was ever a time to close the gap between groups of people across New Zealand in different positions, it is now,' Ardern said.[30] 'I am responsible for the executive branch and this is where we can take action.' You know what sort of action the UK government took? In October 2020 the Independent Parliamentary Standards Authority recommended that a £3,300 pay rise for MPs should go ahead; MPs were given an extra £10,000 expenses allowance to meet home-working costs[31] at the beginning of the pandemic.

The pandemic, of course, isn't the only example of leaders telling us 'we're all in this together' while demonstrating the exact opposite. Real solidarity is fairly rare in leadership, so I want to introduce you to a woman called Pia Klemp, who embodies what the opposite of hypocrisy looks like. Back in 2017 Klemp, a German biologist, human-rights activist and ship captain, was skippering a rescue vessel called the *Sea-Watch 3* in the Central Mediterranean, the deadliest strip of sea in the world. As they patrolled the Mediterranean, they got a routine call about a boat in distress: an inflatable pontoon carrying around 150 migrants trying to flee from North Africa and reach Europe had started to sink. By the time the *Sea-Watch 3* reached the migrant boat, the Libyan Coast Guard (LYCG) was already there. This wasn't a good thing. The LYCG are part of the Libyan Navy and are supported by the UN and EU – however, the group has come under scrutiny from human-rights organizations for funnelling money to militias. The people in LYCG are rarely there to help migrants: they either take them back to Libya where they'll be thrown in a detention centre, or they'll sit by and watch as the migrants drown. Which, at that particular moment, was exactly what the LYCG were doing. Half a dozen migrants were already in the water in desperate trouble, but the LYCG just stood by, radioing the *Sea-Watch 3* to stay away.[32]

Klemp didn't listen. The *Sea-Watch 3* lowered its two dinghies and began to rescue terrified people from the freezing water. A video of the scene analysed by Forensic Architecture[33] shows the LYCG trying to stop them, hurling potatoes at the rescue dinghies. Klemp's crew pulled fifty-nine people from the water that day, including a mother and her two-year-old son. The mother survived but her little boy couldn't be resuscitated. European authorities would not let the *Sea-Watch 3* into port and the boat didn't have a morgue; they were forced to store the toddler's body in the ship's freezer. Klemp, seething with anger and despair, didn't know what to say to the traumatized mother. How do you rationalize a situation like this? How do you reconcile the fact that the EU, which had been awarded the Nobel Peace Prize for the advancement of peace and human rights in Europe, branded people like this distraught mother 'illegal' and blocked the ships trying to save their lives? There were no words that were adequate. For days the boat was adrift in international waters; no European country wanted to take responsibility for the living migrants or the dead child. The boat had nowhere to go, so, for days, it bobbed up and down with the tiny body of a two-year-old boy lying dead in its freezer.

The ships that Klemp has worked on are estimated to have rescued about 14,000 migrants from drowning; she has personally assisted in the rescue of more than 1,000 people.[34] Except, according to the Italian government, Klemp hasn't actually saved 'people', she's criminally aided illegal immigrants. A couple of months before the horrors of the mission with the drowned two-year-old, Klemp had been arrested by Italian authorities and the ship she was working on, the *Iuventa*, was impounded. The crew on the *Iuventa* hadn't realized it, but while they were saving lives they were also being spied on. But by whom? Investigative journalists have, disturbingly, found evidence which appears to show[35] that the surveillance wasn't government-mandated to begin with, but was orchestrated by a private security agency and the far-right anti-immigrant political leader Matteo Salvini. Ten members of the *Iuventa* crew, including Klemp, were accused of collaborating with smugglers. In March 2021 an Italian prosecutor brought charges of 'aiding and abetting illegal immigration to Italy' against twenty-one individuals and three NGOs[36]—including four members of the *Iuventa*. If convicted, they face up to twenty years in jail and fines of 15,000 euros per person rescued.

The *Iuventa10* (as the collective of crew members are now known) deny ever working with smugglers. The case is very clearly politically motivated. It is, as the human-rights group Amnesty International has noted, part of 'a dangerous pattern of criminalizing people helping migrants and refugees in Europe.' Immigration is a complex issue, but saving people from drowning shouldn't be. Some on the right have argued that humanitarian ships rescuing refugees in the Mediterranean act as a 'pull factor' increasing refugee crossings. However, that theory has been debunked by a number of reports, including one from the Forensic Oceanography department at Goldsmiths, University of London. 'The evidence simply does not support the idea that rescues by NGOs are to blame for an increase in migrants crossing,' an author of the report noted. Desperate people will always try to flee dire circumstances in search of a better life. Letting them die at sea is unconscionable.

But this isn't a treatise on the ethics of immigration policies. I wanted to talk about Klemp here because she's an extraordinary example of someone who follows their conscience and refuses to tolerate hypocrisy in any form. In 2019, for example, the council of the City of Paris announced that Klemp, along with activist and captain Carola Rackete, would receive the Grand Vermeil Medal for their bravery in saving lives at sea. The Grand Vermeil Medal is Paris's highest civilian honour. However, Klemp turned it down, arguing that it was fundamentally hypocritical.

'We do not need authorities deciding who is a "hero" and who is "illegal",' Klemp said in a Facebook post addressed to Paris Mayor Anne Hidalgo. Klemp noted the City of Paris was giving her an award for rescuing 'migrants from difficult conditions on a daily basis' while simultaneously making life harder for homeless people, migrants and asylum seekers. She attached an image of an article from a French newspaper showing 'anti-migrant rocks' the city had installed under a bridge where people slept while waiting to be seen by a humanitarian centre.

'You want to give me a medal for actions that you fight in your own ramparts,' Klemp wrote in the scathing post. 'It is time we call out hypocrite honorings and fill the void with social justice.'[37]

Klemp's rebuttal of the Grand Vermeil Medal made international news and, in doing so, sent an important message about institutional hypocrisy. How can you give medals to people helping migrants when you are simultaneously creating policies that hurt migrants? Hypocrisy comes in many forms and some of them are so insidious and normalized we barely pay them any attention. Klemp made people pay attention.

One of the people paying attention, it turned out, was Banksy. In September 2019, shortly after Klemp turned the Parisian medal down, she got an intriguing email.

'Hello Pia, I've read about your story in the papers. You sound like a badass,' the email said.

'I am an artist from the UK and I've made some work about the migrant crisis, obviously I can't keep the money. Could you use it to buy a new boat or something? Please let me know. Well done. Banksy.'[38]

Klemp thought she was being pranked at first. But it really was Bansky and he really did want to help. And so, on 18 August 2020, a boat named after a nineteenth-century French feminist anarchist, financed by a British street artist and captained by a German anti-Fascist, set sail from a Spanish seaport. The *Louise Michel*, a bright pink motor yacht, departed in secrecy: the crew didn't want the attention a mission funded by Banksy was inevitably going to get. That sort of attention would backfire. European authorities would find a way to stop the boat from doing what it was meant to be doing: saving people's lives. And it didn't take long before the *Louise Michel* saved hundreds of people's lives. Banksy documented some of the mission, posting a video on his Instagram. (Note: Banksy is widely presumed to be a man but could certainly be a woman – as Virginia Woolf once said, 'for most of history, Anonymous was a woman'.) The video began with footage of the auction of Banksy's *Girl with Balloon* painting at Sotheby's in October 2018. The painting sold for £860,000 before being shredded by a mechanism hidden in the bottom of the frame. Then the video cuts to people screaming as they attempt to stay afloat in the Mediterranean. 'Like most people who make it in the art world, I bought a yacht to cruise the Med,' a voiceover says. 'It's a French navy vessel we converted into a lifeboat. Because EU authorities deliberately ignore distress calls from "non-Europeans".' Banksy's video ends with the phrase: 'All Black Lives Matter'.[39] It's a dig at the governments trying to claim they care about racial equality while simultaneously taking a hard – and deadly – line against immigration.

The moral of this story isn't that we should all go out on boats rescuing migrants. I, for one, would love to think I could be like Klemp but I will never be that brave. But we can all try and channel some of the moral fortitude, the intolerance for hypocrisy, that she has. We can all try to put the greater good ahead of individual glory. Corporate feminism has taught women that self-promotion and self-advancement are the noblest of goals. Corporate feminism would have told Klemp she deserved that medal the City of Paris was trying to give: yasss, queen, slay! You earned it! True leadership, however, means thinking about what other people deserve. Ultimately one of the best ways to avoid hypocrisy is to practise solidarity. And that means thinking less about your ego, and more about your impact on others.

4

Embrace Imposter Syndrome

You know how the old saying goes: when life gives you lemons, rob a bank. That was McArthur Wheeler's plan anyway. On April 1995 Wheeler, a portly middle-aged guy from Pittsburgh, robbed two banks in broad daylight. He didn't wear a mask or any form of disguise, he just strolled up to the bank tellers, shoved a gun in their faces and demanded money.

Wheeler was caught on surveillance cameras and his picture was put on local TV. It wasn't long before he was identified and arrested. Which, it turns out, wasn't something he had been expecting. 'But I wore the juice!' he reportedly protested when police turned up at his house.

Did you think Wheeler was an idiot who had made no attempt to hide his identity? Wrong. He'd squeezed lemon juice over his face before going on his robbing spree. You can make invisible ink with lemon juice – you probably did so as a kid – so surely you can make a kind of invisibility cloak out of it? Wheeler experimented at home: he covered himself with squeezed citrus and took a selfie with a polaroid camera. *Voilà*, his face didn't appear in the polaroid! Which may have been because the lemon burned his eyes and he wasn't able to direct the camera lens at his face. Or . . . it might have been because the lemon juice made him invisible! Wheeler decided it was the latter and headed off to rob a couple of banks.

That's how the story goes anyway. To be honest, I'm not sure how much of it is true. The legend of McArthur Wheeler stems from an article in the *Pittsburgh Post-Gazette*[1] ('They had larceny in their hearts, but little in their heads') but I can't find evidence that backs it up, just numerous retellings of the original article. Here's the important thing, though: a Cornell psychology professor called David Dunning read about Wheeler and he had something of a Eureka moment. He realized that there are a lot of people like Wheeler in the world: people are too incompetent to know that they're incompetent. People who are absurdly confident in their abilities because they lack the ability to realize that, in fact, they don't have any abilities. Dunning teamed up with a graduate student called Justin Kruger to investigate, publishing their results in a 1999 paper 'Unskilled and Unaware of It: How Difficulties in Recognizing One's Own Incompetence Lead to Inflated Self-Assessments'. The phenomenon is now known as the Dunning–Kruger effect.

The Dunning–Kruger effect wouldn't really matter if the guys suffering from it didn't get into positions of power. But we've been conditioned to conflate confidence with competence: the world is largely run by overconfident men whose egos vastly eclipse their abilities. There are women like that, of course, but the majority of people suffering from Dunning–Kruger are men. Numerous studies show that men tend to rate their own intelligence and attractiveness higher than women[2] do. A certain type of man is told they are a master of the universe from a very young age and they believe it. David Cameron, for example, was once asked why he wanted to be prime minister and replied: 'Because I think I'd be rather good at it.'[3] He was, in fact, one of the worst prime ministers that Britain has ever had.

'Historians of the future may refer to ours as the Dunning–Kruger era,' Oliver Burkeman mused in a 2016 piece in the *Guardian*. Forget historians: I'm calling it now. Pretty much every fiasco of recent years is down to guys with big egos taking on challenges they don't recognize are way beyond their capabilities. Here, for example, is a little selection of things that Boris Johnson and other leading Brexiteers said about how easy Brexiting would be:

'Brexit means Brexit and we're going to make a titanic success of it'
(Boris Johnson, 3 November 2016, as he collected a Comeback of the Year award at the *Spectator* awards[4])

'Well, the Titanic *exhibition in Northern Ireland is the single most popular attraction in the province. We are going to make a colossal success of Brexit'*
(Boris Johnson after George Osborne, who presented him with the *Spectator* award, reminded him the *Titanic* sank[5])

'It doesn't seem to me to be very hard to do a free trade deal very rapidly indeed'
(Boris Johnson, Treasury Select Committee meeting, 23 March 2016[6])

'There is no plan for no deal, because we're going to get a great deal'
(Boris Johnson, 11 March 2017, Johnson was Foreign Secretary at the time)

'[W]e will bang it through. We'll get Brexit done very, very fast and avoid another infinite period of dither and delay'
'We've got a deal that's oven-ready. We've just got to put it in at gas mark four, give it 20 minutes and Bob's your uncle'
(Boris Johnson, 3 November 2019, interview with the *Sun*)

'And if you say "Can I absolutely guarantee that we will get a deal?" I think I can'
(Boris Johnson, 5 December 2019, responding to a question from *Sky News*'s Beth Rigby)

'The day after we vote to leave, we hold all the cards and we can choose the path we want'
(Michael Gove in a campaign speech, April 2016)

'The free trade agreement that we will have to do with the European Union should be one of the easiest in human history'
(Liam Fox, 2017 radio interview in his capacity as International Trade Secretary)

'To me, Brexit is easy . . . We have back British passports, we have control of our fishing waters, and our companies are not subject to EU law through the single market'
(Nigel Farage in a 2016 interview with the BBC)

'If Brexit is a disaster, I will go and live abroad, I will go and live somewhere else'
(Nigel Farage, 27 March 2017)

'A trade deal with the EU could be sorted out in an afternoon over a cup of coffee'
(Gerard Batten, the former UKIP leader in February 2017)

Brexit, of course, didn't get sorted out over a brisk cuppa. After four years of bitter wrangling, the European Union and the United Kingdom came to a last-minute trade deal on Christmas Eve 2020, narrowly averting the hardest possible Brexit. While the very worst-case scenario possible may have been averted, the deal was still full of uncertainty and short-term measures. Just one month after the agreement came into force, the EU threatened to override it following a fight over the supply of coronavirus vaccines. But this is not a book on Brexit – God knows there are enough of those around – the key point here is that the entire thing was a disaster. Or, as Johnson might say, a titanic oven-ready disaster. And the worst thing of all is that Nigel Farage did not make good on his promise of going to live somewhere else.

Brexit is far from the only cautionary tale of what can happen when you put unqualified men with wildly inflated egos in charge of important things. I won't bother mentioning Donald Trump here – I think we all know how that story ends – but I do quickly want to introduce you to a twenty-two-year-old called Andrei Doroshin who was put in charge of efforts to administer coronavirus vaccines in the city of Philadelphia.

Doroshin does not, as you may have wondered, have a background in public health. He was not some kind of prodigy. He was a graduate student in psychology at Philadelphia's Drexel University. But he was also a go-getter: when the pandemic hit, he teamed up with a bunch of friends and started a non-profit, Philly Fighting Covid, to help out. They used 3D printers to make face shields and even opened a testing site in a neighbourhood without one. Really commendable stuff. The problem is, Doroshin had ambitions that wildly outweighed his abilities. On 7 October 2020, two months before the FDA issued the first emergency authorization for a vaccine, the grad student gathered a bunch of volunteers together and livestreamed a PowerPoint presentation he'd put together which laid out his plans to secure a contract to vaccinate between 500,000 and 1.5 million people in the city.

'This is a wholly Elon Musk, shooting-for-the-heavens type of thing,' Doroshin said as he unveiled his plans.[7] 'We're gonna have a preemptive strike on vaccines and basically beat everybody in Philadelphia to it.'

The kicker? Just like Musk, they were going to help the world but get rich doing it.

'This is the juicy slide,' said Doroshin as he got to the financing section of the PowerPoint. 'How are we gonna get paid?'

He explained that the vaccine doses were free, provided by the federal government. But Philly Fighting Covid could bill insurance companies $24 a dose for administering it.

'I just told you how many vaccines we want to do – you can do the math in your head,' he announced.

I actually can't do the math in my head but, according to my iPhone calculator, they stood to make between $12 and $18 million. All while making the world a better place! Not bad work if you can get it. And Doroshin was determined to get it: a month or so after he laid out his plans for vaccination domination, he managed to get in front of the Philadelphia City Council to pitch his plans. With a projected budget of $2.7 million, he said, Philly Fighting Covid would build out five vaccination sites that could take up to 10,000 patients a day.

But why should the city of Philadelphia trust a ragtag bunch of students without a medical background for something as important as administering coronavirus vaccines? Precisely because they didn't have a medical background. As Doroshin later explained to NBC's *Today* show: 'We're engineers, we're scientists, computer scientists, we're cybersecurity nerds. We think a little differently than people in health care do.'

What do people in health care know about public health, eh? Nothing worth worrying about, according to Doroshin. 'We took the entire model and just threw it out the window,' Doroshin boasted. 'We said to hell with all of that. We're going to completely build on a new model that is based on a factory.'

He reiterated this in a later interview.[8] 'We said all right if in America our health-care system is not built for doing high volume, let's build one that can. And so we hired engineers that have built factories; we've hired cyber security experts who, you know, secured stuff in the military; we've hired engineers who've done all kinds of process engineering up, down and sideways; physics people who've done, you know, flow mathematics and basically built this model.'

That plan apparently sounded great to Philadelphia. The city didn't sign a contract with Philly Fighting Covid but they gave the group part of the vaccine allotment and shared lists of residents who were eligible for the vaccine. On 8 January 2021 Doroshin stood alongside Mayor Jim Kenney at a press conference launching the first mass vaccination centre. 'What you see here is the problem that we've been solving for six months,' Doroshin announced loftily. 'This is the problem of vaccinating an entire population of people on a scale that has never been seen before in the history of our species.' Rhetoric straight out of the Trump handbook.

Things did not get off to the best of starts. Philly Fighting Covid was supposed to be ensuring that vaccine recipients would reflect the city's racial make-up: 44% of Philadelphia's residents are Black. However, after the first vaccination event, Philly Fighting Covid managed to lose all the racial and ethnic data for the patients. It was 'a glitch' in Amazon's cloud, they said.

The city of Philadelphia didn't see this glitch as anything worth cutting ties with Philly Fighting Covid over. Local reporters, however, started investigating the group. And what do you know? A ton of red flags turned up. Just before Philly Fighting Covid began its vaccination work, for example, it became a for-profit company[9] called Vax Populi without informing the city of this change of status. It also abruptly dropped the community testing it was previously involved with, leaving communities and partner organizations in the lurch.[10] By the end of January, the scandal had got so big that the group was making national headlines: it turned out that Doroshin had been vaccinating his young friends while turning vulnerable patients away. The Philadelphia Department of Public Health ended its relationship with Philly Fighting Covid, expressing regret it had ever worked with them. The whole thing was a hugely predictable shitshow.

If Doroshin had been an aberration, that would have been one thing. But the episode was just one in a series of endless examples of how devalued experience and competence have become. The world is in thrall to overconfident, underqualified dudes (and the occasional #girlboss) who want to *disrupt* things. And they generally do end up disrupting things: just not in a good way. You know what the worst thing is? We've been telling women that if they want to get ahead, they should be aiming for this sort of delusional self-assurance. They should be doing power poses and leaning in and channelling the confidence of a mediocre white guy. Here's a thought: why don't more mediocre white guys aspire to the competence of a middle-aged woman who is far too qualified for her job?

How do we stop future Doroshins? We change what leadership looks like. We start elevating humility and recognizing the benefit of self-doubt. And we move from an authoritarian style of leadership to a more democratic one. In the past, some people have argued that authoritarian leadership get results and that 'well-intentioned' dictators drive economic growth. (How many people supported Trump, for example, because they thought he would be good for the economy?) An abundance of evidence shows that to be wrong. Yes, there are authoritarian regimes with strong economic growth such as China and Singapore, however that's not the norm. A 2019 study published in *Leadership Quarterly*,[11] for example, analysed the governments of 133 countries between 1858 to 2010, and found that strongmen are generally bad for the economy.

And we're not just talking leaders of nation-states; the same is true when you look at leaders of companies or cities or organizations. Authoritarians are ego-driven and hire yes men instead of the brightest talent. They remove themselves from the checks and balances that stop them making bad decisions. They lead through fear rather than instilling real respect. They may provide a mirage of control, but in the long term they rarely get great results.

Don't believe your own hype

A case in point? Andrew Cuomo, the former Governor of New York. Or, as he was known in the early months of the pandemic: America's Governor, America's Boyfriend, the future President of America, the Hero We Need, The Second

Coming. Cuomomania was everywhere for much of 2020. And you can understand why: the pandemic was ravaging America, New York was at the epicentre of the outbreak, and presidential leadership was nowhere to be seen. Donald Trump veered between denial ('one day, like a miracle, coronavirus will disappear!'); blame ('the China virus'); and extremely weird theories ('perhaps try injecting bleach?'). People were panicked and desperate for leadership. Cuomo stepped into a leadership vacuum: between 2 March and 19 June he delivered 111 consecutive daily TV briefings. Unlike Trump, Cuomo was tough and to the point. It was what people desperately needed at the time and, for a while, he was a national hero. The comedian Randy Rainbow came out as a 'Cuomosexual'. There was speculation he could be president. The guy even got a special Emmy Award for his TV briefings.

Cuomo also got a book deal. Writing a book while governing New York, a state of 19 million people, would have been tough at the best of times; most mere mortals wouldn't even consider taking something like that on during a once-in-a-century pandemic that was killing their constituents in enormous numbers. But Cuomo, of course, is not a mere mortal. He dashed off a self-congratulatory book in record time; *American Crisis: Leadership Lessons from the COVID-19 Pandemic* was released on 13 October 2020. Which, just to remind you, wasn't when the pandemic was over. It was actually just as coronavirus cases started surging back up in New York again.

Cuomo defended the timing of his book with some sporty spin: he wasn't bragging, he said, it was 'a halftime review' of the crisis. The point of the book, he told NPR, was to 'look back at the first half of the game',[12] and figure out where he'd gone wrong, where he'd gone right, and how best to move forward. Which sounds like a very sensible thing to do – it's just the sort of thing you normally do in internal meetings rather than via a book. Cuomo didn't reveal how much he got paid for the book until his mandatory financial disclosures were due in May 2021. Turns out he got a whopping $5.1 million for his musings.[13] Monetising a crisis you are supposed to be managing? It really isn't a good look. Still, Cuomo seemed to get away with it. He got a lot of flack from the right-wing press, but liberals largely treated him with kid gloves. Liberal anger was reserved for the guy in the White House.

When I say we need to raise the bar when it comes to leadership, Cuomo is exactly what I mean. The man was treated like the second coming just because he told people what was going on. He was lauded for doing the bare minimum. Cuomo is good on TV, I don't dispute that. But the hype around him reflects the way in which style has triumphed over substance in politics. It reflects the same problems that got us Donald Trump. And it's the sort of adulation that only a man would get. Can you imagine a female leader publishing a self-congratulatory book in the middle of a crisis? She would be torn apart. She wouldn't even think about doing it for a second. Then again, a woman wouldn't have been offered a book deal just for projecting an air of authority on TV.

And that's really all Cuomo did, by the way. He may have seemed like he had everything under control when he was speaking on TV, but it was a completely different story on the ground.

In the early stages of the pandemic, for example, Cuomo downplayed the severity of the coronavirus; American exceptionalism, he presumed, would be enough to shield the country. On 2 March a Manhattan health-care worker who had recently returned from Iran became the first positive coronavirus case in New York. The next day, Cuomo held a news conference saying there was nothing to worry about. 'Excuse our arrogance as New Yorkers,' he said,[14] 'I speak for the mayor also on this one – we think we have the best health-care system on the planet right here in New York. So, when you're saying, what happened in other countries versus what happened here, we don't even think it's going to be as bad as it was in other countries.' He was right: it was much worse.

Cuomo could be forgiven for underestimating the coronavirus to begin with if he'd stepped up his leadership later on, but he didn't. Instead, he let his famous ego get in the way. Instead of coordinating with Bill de Blasio, New York's mayor, he fought with him. This wasn't unusual; the two men were famous for fighting over everything. They once even feuded over a white-tailed deer called Jackie Robinson that had been captured in Harlem; for a couple of days the two men issued competing and contradictory statements about what should be done with the deer. (The feud was so ridiculous it made headlines.[15] It also seems to have made poor Jackie Robinson lose the will to live: the deer died moments before it was supposed to be driven to the countryside and released.) But there was far more than a deer at stake this time. A virus was raging across New York and the two most powerful men in the state were more concerned about looking like they were the one in control than actually managing the crisis at hand.

On 17 March, for example, de Blasio announced that New York may need a 'shelter-in-place' order; a few hours later, Cuomo told the press that he had absolutely no intention of quarantining the city. 'For any city or county to take an emergency action, the state has to approve it,' Cuomo said in a podcast interview on 18 March. 'And I wouldn't approve "shelter in place".' It was an assertion of his authority. A 'fuck you' to de Blasio. He underscored it by then barring local officials[16] from issuing their own executive orders to fight the coronavirus without getting approval from his health department first.

Three days later, Cuomo announced that, actually, New York was going to shut down – although he rebranded it as going 'on pause'. (It turned out to be an extremely long pause.) When 'New York on Pause' took effect at 8 p.m. on 22 March, around 25,000 New Yorkers had tested positive for Covid-19. If Cuomo and de Blasio had worked together and locked down earlier, thousands of lives could have been saved. According to Columbia University researchers,[17] 'If everybody had done exactly what they did one week earlier, more than 50% fewer people would have died by the end of April.'

Once again, the two men who were supposed to be leading New York let their egos get in the way of effective governance. 'The mayor and the governor were in a constant pissing contest. The people in the middle get urinated on,' Gustavo Rivera, a New York state senator later said.[18]

It might have taken even longer for New York to go into lockdown had a woman not stepped in to manage Cuomo's fragile ego and fix things. On 19 March New York's attorney-general Letitia James organized a call with community leaders, elected officials and business representatives to garner support for a lockdown.[19] Working behind the scenes,[20] James tried to figure out how they could get Cuomo to initiate a shutdown without making it seem like he was following de Blasio. Familiar story, isn't it? A woman working hard in the background to get things done, while simultaneously trying to manage a guy's ego and make him think everything is his idea. James's intervention was analysed by the *Wall Street Journal*, but she stayed behind the scenes in the article and didn't comment. Few people realize her role in getting Cuomo and de Blasio to agree on a lockdown. Her intervention undoubtedly saved lives but, unlike Cuomo, she didn't feel the need to get applause for her actions.

James didn't end up staying behind the scenes for long. In early 2021, Cuomo's leadership started to get some much overdue scrutiny. With Donald Trump out of the White House, there were fewer distractions; you couldn't get away with so much by waving your hands and saying *'Look at the bad Orange Man!'* Cuomo had been dealing with controversy around his administration's former policy of requiring nursing homes to accept coronavirus patients discharged from hospitals – leading to preventable deaths – for a while; however, it had largely escaped mainstream attention. In January 2021, though, James released a bombshell report stating nursing-home deaths were 50% higher than Cuomo's administration had claimed. Things got worse: it transpired that Cuomo's aides had rewritten a report stating how many nursing-home residents – 9,000 by June 2020 – had died in New York during the pandemic. The *New York Times* later noted: 'The extraordinary intervention, which came just as Mr. Cuomo was starting to write a book on his pandemic achievements, was the earliest act yet known in what critics have called a months long effort by the governor and his aides to obscure the full scope of nursing home deaths.'[21]

You know what that is? It's an extremely complicated way of saying Cuomo didn't want to ruin his book deal or tarnish his shiny new image, so he got his lackeys to cover up data that made him look very bad.

That wasn't the only problem Cuomo was dealing with by then. Several women, including a number of former aides, had come forward to accuse him of sexual harassment. James had hired an outside law firm to investigate Cuomo's workplace conduct. Cuomo was also facing allegations of workplace bullying, with a number of former employees coming forward to say he created a toxic work environment.

At the same time, it was also becoming a lot harder to try to pretend that New York's response to the pandemic was in any way commendable. In March 2021, a year after the pandemic started, New York City had the highest number of deaths per capita than any other metropolitan area: 294 deaths per 100,000 people.[22] Which area in the US did the best? Seattle. It only had 64 deaths per 100,000.

There are a number of reasons why Seattle did better than New York, but one of them was leadership. Instead of feuding and trying to undermine each other with mixed messaging, the governor (Jay Inslee) and mayor (Jenny Durkan) worked together to present a united front. 'We could not afford to have mixed messages,' Durkan told the *New York Times*[23] in March 2021. I wish Cuomo had realized that.

Alas, critical self-reflection has never been Cuomo's strong suit. For a few months in 2021, Cuomo refused to acknowledge that he was anything other than God's gift to New York: the Governor stubbornly clung to power despite repeated calls for him to resign. And, for a little while, it looked like Cuomo might be able to weather the storm and run for another term like nothing had ever happened. Then, in August, the state attorney general released a damning report concluding that Cuomo had sexually harassed 11 women. Establishment support for the Governor began to collapse and acolytes that

Cuomo had surrounded himself with began to distance themselves from him. Eventually, Cuomo was forced to resign. Even
as he resigned, however, he didn't express any real remorse for
his action which he continued to deny. Rather, he framed
himself as the victim of a 'politically motivated' controversy.
He also minimised the sexual harassment allegations against
him, almost suggesting that young people today were just too
damn sensitive. 'There are generational and cultural shifts that
I just didn't fully appreciate,' he said in his resignation speech.

But, of course, Cuomo wasn't a victim of some kind of
woke takeover; he was very much the architect of his own
downfall. Speaking to the *New York Times*, Congressman
Ritchie Torres, who represents the Bronx, likened Cuomo's
demise to a Greek tragedy. 'It's the most precipitous collapse in
the history of gubernatorial politics,' he said. 'And as with all
Greek tragedies, at the heart of it all is hubris.'

Whether Cuomo will ever have a political career again
remains to be seen. But I'm not here to speculate about his
political future. The reason I've spent so long on the man is
because I think his fall from grace provides a very important
leadership lesson: don't believe your own hype. The media can
build you up and it can tear you down. If you stay focused and
do what's right rather than getting distracted by trying to protect
your image, history will judge you kindly. Perhaps Cuomo may
be able to hang on to power, but I think he's made it very clear
that he's not a leader, he's a power-hungry narcissist.

Use self-doubt constructively

Do you know what Cuomo absolutely does not have? Impostor
syndrome: the psychological phenomenon where you feel that

you've only succeeded because of dumb luck and are going to be found out any day; the constant nagging feeling that you're not good enough even if there's plenty of evidence that shows you most certainly are. Women tend to be plagued with impostor syndrome because, from a very early age, we're bombarded with messages that tell us that we're not as good as men. We're bombarded with messages that tell us we shouldn't take up space, we shouldn't be too loud, we shouldn't be too clever. And so we internalize those messages and learn to doubt ourselves.

Getting rid of a lifetime of insidious social conditioning is tough: even some of the world's most powerful women admit to still feeling impostor syndrome. In 2018, for example, Michelle Obama told an audience of British schoolgirls that she still had feelings of self-doubt and impostor syndrome.[24] Finland's Sanna Marin, who became the youngest serving prime minister in the world in 2019, has also admitted to feelings of inadequacy.[25] As has Jacinda Ardern. In a December 2020 interview[26] with John Kirwan, a former All Black and mental-health advocate, Ardern said she suffers from impostor syndrome, but tries to channel it into something that drives her to be better. 'Some of the people I admire the most have that self-consciousness and that slight gnawing lack of confidence,' Ardern said. When she starts to doubt herself, she asks why that is. 'Does it mean I need to do a bit more prep, do I need to think more about my decision making?' Instead of allowing feelings of self-doubt to undermine her, she uses it to propel herself to be better.

The traditional thinking around confidence is that the more you have of it, the better. Women have been told to take up space, speak up and act like men. You've probably seen a frequently cited statistic which shows men apply for a job when they meet only 60% of the qualifications, but women apply only if they meet 100% of them. That statistic isn't actually based on a study, it's completely speculative. Nevertheless it is frequently used to tell women that they should have more faith in themselves and apply for positions for which they are underqualified. Perhaps the more important lesson from that study, however, is that we should be encouraging more men to be competent rather than confident. Again, instead of telling women to act like men, we should be telling men to act more like women.

There's a balance with all of this, of course. Too little self-confidence is obviously not a good thing. I'm obviously not saying you should only apply for jobs when you perfectly fit the advertised criteria – not to mention, there's also a much larger conversation to be had here about the gendered way in which many companies advertise their jobs. What I am saying is that we need to stop fetishizing confidence. Indeed, studies show that encouraging women to be over-confident might stop them being effective leaders. According to an analysis of thousands of 360-degree reviews,[27] women outscored men on seventeen of the nineteen capabilities that differentiate excellent leaders from average or poor ones. But even though women scored better on their capabilities, they didn't rate themselves as highly as men, until the age of forty. 'It's highly probable that those women are far more competent than they think they are, while the male leaders are overconfident and assuming they are more competent than they are,'[28] the researchers noted. 'It's possible that these lower levels of confidence at younger ages could motivate women to take more initiative, be more resilient, and to be more receptive to feedback from others, which in turn makes them more effective leaders in the long run.'

Another study, published in the *Leadership Quarterly* journal,[29] similarly shows that lower levels of confidence can enhance leadership by encouraging self-criticism. If you're not overly confident then you're better able to see faults that could be improved or to anticipate problems on the horizon.

Again, the lesson here isn't that confidence isn't important: it's that self-doubt isn't necessarily a bad thing. In my chat with Mary Robinson, she said she found self-doubt a 'complete asset' during her career. A lot of women in leadership, she'd noticed, were full of self-doubt.

'This is actually a positive. When women leaders meet, we tend to talk about the things we didn't do well and what we've tried to learn from them,' she told me. 'I don't hear men having those conversations. But those conversations are very valuable.' The sort of self-doubt Robinson is referring to, she clarifies, isn't the type that undermines you, it's the type that improves you. 'I find that any woman leader who's leading as a woman, tends to have that constant self-correction going on internally, because of the desire to do it as well as possible.'[30]

Studies back that up: a 2019 study[31] from researchers at the University of California, Berkeley, found that doubt piques our curiosity and drives us to learn more. The study challenged the notion that curiosity is the primary driver of learning. According to researchers, it's uncertainty; it's that moment when you think you know something and discover you don't that leads to the most curiosity and learning. One practical application of this, the study suggests, is tailoring classroom learning to misconceptions. So instead of just explaining what causes climate change, you'd ask students what they think causes climate change. When they realize that they don't have the full picture, they're more stimulated to learn.

Robinson, it should be noted, may have self-doubt but she's not exactly short of confidence. One of the most important years of her life, she tells me, was when she did a Master's in Law at Harvard Law School in the Class of '68.

'Most of my American contemporaries were criticizing an immoral war in Vietnam and trying to avoid the draft. Martin Luther King was assassinated in April, Robert Kennedy was assassinated just after I graduated. That year, I saw young people were doing things and they were taking responsibility. They were going into civil-rights programmes. And I came back to Ireland full of what my future husband called my "Harvard Humility".' She stood for the Irish Senate the following year and got elected at the age of twenty-five. 'I would never have been able to do that without the sense as a young person of why not have my voice heard?'[32]

So, again, confidence is important. But, like Goldilocks and the porridge, you need the amount to be just right. Too little confidence paralyzes you. Too much intoxicates you. The best sort of confidence is quiet. This sort of confidence is very different from 'ego', which is loud and attention-seeking. Quietly confident people don't need to be the centre of attention, they don't need to win every argument or have the last word, and they aren't desperate to be liked. When you're driven by ego, you worry about how your actions will make you look, rather than their impact: that invariably leads to poor decision making. Boris Johnson is one example of that. Johnson, it's worth remembering, once allegedly said that he wanted to enter politics because 'no one puts up statues to journalists'. He may be arrogant, but a frequent observation of people who have worked with him is that he's desperate to be liked. This means he finds it difficult to make tough decisions and ends up catastrophically zigzagging as he tries to evade responsibility. In December 2020, for example, Johnson promised the UK a five-day reprieve from coronavirus restrictions over Christmas. This was obviously a bad idea and, just three days after he said it would be 'inhuman' to cancel Christmas, he ended up cancelling Christmas.

If Boris Johnson exemplifies loud confidence, Angela Merkel is the very understated embodiment of quiet confidence. She doesn't pander or try to appeal to the masses through simplistic patriotism – which is, after all, the last refuge of the scoundrel. When *Der Spiegel* asked her about speaking lightly about her homeland and being insufficiently patriotic, she refused to rise to the bait. 'I don't think the Germans are particularly bad or outstandingly wonderful,' she said curtly. 'I am fond of kebabs and pizza, I think the Italians have a nicer alfresco cafe culture, and I think there is more sunshine in Switzerland.' At the end of the interview she returned to the subject, saying: 'I use the term fatherland not to mean that we are the hub around which the world revolves. I use it in the sense that this is my language, these are my trees, that is my lake, I grew up here, I like living here. I am part of its history, with all the pain and all the good things.'[33] It's a very far cry from the sort of patriotic bluster that comes from populists like Johnson. One of Johnson's favourite phrases during the pandemic, for example, was 'world-beating'. Britain certainly beat much of the world when it came to the highest Covid-19 death toll.

Johnson, by the way, was wrong about people not putting up statues to journalists: there are several around the world, including a statue of George Orwell that is outside the headquarters of the BBC. The wall behind it has an inscription from an unused preface to *Animal Farm*: 'If liberty means anything at all it means the right to tell people what they don't want to hear.' I think that if leadership means anything all it might mean having the confidence to do the right thing even though you know it won't make you popular in the short term. Merkel's approach to migrants is a case in point. In 2015, Germany took in more than 1.7 million asylum seekers; Germany was a strong country and would be able to handle it, Merkel famously said at the time. '*Wir schaffen das!*'[34] At the time, critics predicted she'd regret those words. 'The worst decision a European leader has made in modern times,' Nigel Farage told Fox News.[35] 'She's finished.' Farage, along with Merkel's other critics, was wrong. The policy became an integration success story: more than half of the refugees who came to Germany had found jobs and were paying taxes within five years.[36] More than 80%[37] of refugee children and teenagers said they felt a strong sense of belonging to their German schools. The German economy and Merkel's approval ratings are at all-time highs.

Merkel is obviously not perfect. And nobody could call her progressive: she's staunchly against gay marriage, for example. But she's a highly effective Chancellor who demonstrates the sort of quiet confidence all leaders should be aiming for. Unlike many politicians, she's not swayed by short-termism and doesn't let her ego get in the way of long-term planning. She also doesn't have the desperate need to control everything and take credit for everything that leaders like Cuomo have. Rather, she realizes that collaboration and cooperation are essential to effective leadership.

5

Collaborate Ruthlessly

One of the defining features of New York City is trash. There are rubbish bags everywhere, which means there are rats everywhere, and, in the summer, you are treated to the sweet smell of hot garbage. Leaving rubbish piled up on the street is a pretty gross way of handling sanitation but the city doesn't seem to have come up with a better solution. We can put men on the moon, but I guess we can't figure out urban logistics for one of the most important cities in the world.

Things used to be just as rubbish in Taiwan. In fact, people used to call the place Garbage Island. There were overflowing dumpsters and loose trash on every street; nobody recycled. So, starting in 1998, the government implemented a sweeping new 'trash doesn't touch the ground' system. Yellow trucks would appear at pick-up points nightly playing music – popular tunes include Beethoven's 'Für Elise' – to alert people to their arrival. Like ice-cream vans, basically, but not quite as pleasant. A new community ritual began: when you heard the musical garbage truck, you, along with all your neighbours, would run out to the collection point with your bag of waste and your recycling and stick it in the truck yourself. Making people responsible for disposing of their rubbish themselves incentivized them to produce less.

Taiwan went from Garbage Island to one of the world leaders in recycling.

While Taiwan's sanitation system may be efficient, it's not super-convenient. Miss the truck and your trash piles up, stinking out your apartment. Howard Wu, an engineer in his thirties based in the city of Tainan, wasn't a big fan of sitting around waiting for the truck to arrive. So, in his spare time he made a garbage tracker: you'd look at an app and see where the nearest truck was and when it would be at your corner. Wu loves making useful tools like this; he's a 'civic hacker', someone who collaborates with others to create open-source solutions to social issues. So, when the pandemic hit, he naturally started to think of ways to hack the coronavirus. On 2 February, a couple of weeks after Wuhan had gone into lockdown, he turned his attention to the problem of mask availability. People in Taiwan were spooked by what was happening in China, which was only 100 miles away, and had started panic-buying masks. Shops everywhere were sold out. So Wu made a tool similar to his garbage tracker but for masks. The app crowdsourced information as to where masks were available and pinpointed all 10,000 convenience stores in Taiwan on Google Maps. Stores with masks available were marked green, stores where they were out-of-stock were marked red.

Wu's map became hugely popular pretty much overnight. Which also meant it got incredibly expensive to run overnight. Putting Google Maps into an app isn't free: the more people who access the map, the more the developer has to pay. Around twenty-four hours after the site went live, Wu got a bill for $2,000. Fine, he thought, if it's helping people I'll shell out two grand. But the next day he got a bill for $26,000. Wu didn't have unlimited supplies of cash; there was no way he could continue like this.

If I found myself in a situation where I was getting surprise bills for $26,000 from Google, I think I might turn off the app I'd made, find myself a new identity immediately, and flee the country. Luckily Wu is a little calmer than I am. He kept the app up, even though it was getting increasingly popular and the bills were racking up, and went on the messaging platform Slack[1] to talk to a bunch of his civic-hacker friends about the pickle he was in. Wu was in a group called g0v (pronounced 'gov zero'), a decentralized tech community that is committed to using technology in the interest of the public good. Audrey Tang, Taiwan's digital minister, was also in this Slack group. Don't worry, Tang told Wu. She'd pitch in for the bill and talk to Google for him. More importantly, however, she loved what he was doing and she was going to work with the Taiwanese government to find a way to take his project to the next level.

The major problem with Wu's map, apart from the cost, was that it relied on crowdsourced data, meaning it wasn't completely accurate. What the app really needed was access to real-time information about mask supplies. And you know who had that data? The government. In response to mask shortages the government had implemented a name-based rationing system[2] which went into effect on 6 February. Masks were only sold at pharmacies affiliated with Taiwan's govern-ment-run health-care system. You were only allowed to buy masks on a day determined by the number on your National Health Insurance Administration (NHI) card and each person was allowed to buy two masks per NHI card a week. What's important here is that the NHI had a database of all the products that are in stock in these pharmacies: they could see in real time how many masks were available at a specific location.

The day after her chat with Wu, Tang had a meeting with President Tsai Ing-Wen. Here's an idea, she said, why don't we share all this data we have with people like Wu? Instead of hoarding the data and making our own version of Wu's website, we can give it to civic hackers and they can do whatever they want with it. Ing-Wen gave the proposal the green light and the pharmacy mask inventory data was shared almost immediately. A thousand hackers joined a virtual hackathon to find ways to improve the tool: adding features like voice control for people with visual impairments, for example. Just six days after Wu improvised a mask map, Taiwan had thrown the government's weight behind him and opened up access to resources that could help others improve and build on his idea. Google also temporarily waived Maps charges to help out.

It's not just what the government did that was important, it's what they didn't do. As Tang explained to me in a chat over Skype[3], what they didn't do was offer Wu a contract to lead the map project. They didn't decide his solution should be the only solution. Under an authoritarian style of leadership there's an assumption that there is only one solution, Tang notes. 'We're much more pluralistic.' The government amplified Wu's idea but they also gave civic hackers information and resources to build on that idea.

Let's recap. Engaged civilian makes useful tool that ends up costing them a lot of money; engaged civilian asks government's digital minister for help in a Slack group; the next day digital minister sorts everything out and gets authorization from the Taiwanese premier to hand over a bunch of useful data to civic hackers to do whatever they want with; six days later, Taiwan has a real-time mask map. It's mind-boggling how efficient and organic it all was. Can you imagine something like that happening in the UK or US? I certainly can't. I can imagine someone in the government giving their mate at McKinsey millions of dollars to come up with game-changing ways that tech people could work in conjunction with government officials. I can imagine lots of PowerPoint presentations and lots of task groups. I can't imagine this sort of seamless back and forth.

Just compare Wu's project to an analogous project by a similarly enterprising civic hacker in New York, for example. In February 2021 Huge Ma, a thirty-one-year-old New York-based software engineer, built a bot called TurboVax that compiled vaccine availability from the three main city and state New York vaccine systems. The vaccine appointment system in New York was a complete mess: if you didn't have a lot of patience and digital literacy, there was no way you could get an appointment. So Ma made a better solution; TurboVax cost him $50 and took him a few days. Ma got written up in the *New York Times* and city councilmen tweeted about how great his website was, but the city didn't find a way to work with him to scale his idea. TurboVax got so popular[4] Ma's server couldn't handle all the traffic and he had to temporarily close the service. All across America, other engaged citizens with tech skills were cobbling together similar solutions. In New Jersey, for example, a team of volunteers crowdsourced information as to where vaccines were available on a site called vaccinatenj.com. You had government efforts and citizen efforts on two parallel tracks. Imagine just how much better each state's response would have been if there had been the same sort of agile back and forth that happened with Wu's mask map? Imagine if we had more leaders who truly valued collaboration?

Collaboration has become something of a buzzword. However, while we pay it a lot of lip service, it's not a trait we really associate with leadership. And that, in part, is because leadership is coded male and collaboration is coded female. Numerous studies show that women tend to be more collaborative than men. We have, after all, been socialized that way. We've been taught not to be 'bossy'. We've been taught it's rude to take credit for things. We've been taught that our main purpose in life is to nurture and help others. And if we don't conform to those social norms we get penalized. In a study led by NYU psychologist Madeline Heilman,[5] a man who stayed at the office late to help coworkers was rated 14% higher than a woman who did the same. When neither stayed late to help, the woman was rated 12% lower than the man.

Corporate feminism has told us that one way we should respond to this unfair state of affairs is for women to put themselves first and refuse to help out. I remember sitting in a female leadership training session early on in my career and being told that if I was asked to take notes on a whiteboard during a meeting I should say: *I'd rather not.* (Honestly, my own strategy for getting out of tasks like this has been developing such terrible handwriting that nobody in their right mind would ask me to take notes.) Again, telling women to act more like men isn't helpful. What's really required is a new leadership paradigm that values the collective over the individual. We also need to recognize that collaboration isn't an airy-fairy soft skill; it's not holding hands and singing 'Kumbaya'. Effective collaboration doesn't mean relinquishing control completely and succumbing to the wisdom of the crowd. Rather, it means leveraging collective intelligence efficiently. How do you do that? First and foremost, to go back to the point made in the previous chapter, you need leaders who realize they don't have all the answers and aren't desperate to control everything. Then you start to build processes and platforms which allow great ideas to rise to the top and get executed.

Create space for people to participate

The seamless back and forth around Taiwan's mask didn't happen overnight; like everything that looks easy, it took a lot of hard work. A significant amount of which was done by Tang, who had dedicated the previous few years to building bridges between engaged citizens and Taiwan's government. Tang, it is an understatement to say, is not your typical politician. While I don't want to play into the leader-as-genius trope, Tang is certainly a prodigy. When she was eight, she wrote a computer game for her little brother to help him with fractions. When she was fourteen, she dropped out of school to start a search-engine company. When she was nineteen, she left Taiwan to become an entrepreneur in Silicon Valley. She became a digital advisor to Apple and helped develop some of the software used in Siri; in a very prescient move she asked Apple to pay in her in Bitcoin, which was worth around $400 back then. (In 2021 it hit $62,000 a Bitcoin.) As well as being a tech genius, Tang is also a self-described 'conservative anarchist' and activist. In 2014, seeing what was happening in her country, she quit her job and headed back to Taiwan, where she was one of a few hundred young activists who occupied Taiwan's parliament building for months as part of what became known as the Sunflower Movement. The trigger for the movement was a controversial trade agreement deal with China, but this was really just the tip of the iceberg: young people were fed up with Taiwan's relationship with China. While older generations largely accepted the idea of 'one country, two systems', millennials in Taiwan wanted a country and identity of their own. For twenty-four days, young activists occupied the parliament, until the ruling party, the pro-China Kuomintang (KMT) agreed to more transparency.

The Sunflower Movement didn't end when activists left the legislative buildings. The non-violent occupation of the legislature, and the positive international coverage it had received, energized people and propelled pro-democracy efforts. In 2016 the ruling KMT party were defeated and Tsai Ing-Wen, who led the Democratic Progressive Party (DPP), became Taiwan's first female president. One of Ing-Wen's first moves as president was headhunting Tang and inviting the thirty-five-year-old to become the island's first minister without a portfolio. (Tang then became digital minister a couple of years later.) Tang is one of eight 'horizontal ministers' whose remit is building common values and consensus.

Tang doesn't see her job as working for the government or working for the people: she sees her job as breaking down barriers, promoting transparency and finding common values. These aren't just nice buzzwords, she ensures she lives these principles: every single conversation she has in an official capacity (including the one I'm having with her) is recorded and a transcript is released. She doesn't have any access to classified information and she reserves an entire day a week for open-office hours. She's described herself as a moderator or editor: someone who works with others to create consensus. In some ways, Tang's entire life has a been a rejection of binaries. Tang changed her name, and began taking female hormones when she was twenty-four. Transitioning, she says, made it easier for her to see things from different perspectives. While she adopted female pronouns when she first transitioned she no longer minds what pronouns people use to describe her and, when she went into government, wrote 'not applicable' in the gender field. She also wrote 'not applicable' in the party affiliation field. 'This is basically a transcultural outlook that's applied to both gender and political ideology and many other things as well,' she explains. 'This is taking all the sides.'

Tang excels at finding and using digital tools to foster collaboration and build trust – which isn't exactly easy in a world where everyone has started to look at technology with suspicion. She is often asked how she does this and her answer is pretty much always the same: stop talking endlessly about it and start giving people opportunities to participate in government decision-making. If you want to tap into collective intelligence and surface great ideas, then you need to do two key things: give people safe spaces to participate and develop a quick response cycle.

Those spaces don't need to involve complicated technology. In January, for example, Taiwan activated something called the Central Epidemic Command Center (CECC) to help manage the pandemic. Anyone could pick up a phone, dial a toll-free number (1922) and ask questions or share ideas; every day there was a press conference and some of these questions would be answered. One day in April, a young boy called up[6] to say that, thanks to mask rationing, he hadn't been able to pick the colour of his mask and had wound up with pink ones. He was worried that the kids at school would make fun of him. The next day, everyone in the daily livestreamed CECC press conference wore pink masks. Suddenly famous people started turning their avatars pink. Pink became the coolest colour. This little kid called up, voiced his concerns, and was actually listened to. 'This fast iteration cycle, this agile response, that makes the social sector more strong and more robust because everybody, instead of waiting for the command from the command center, they can actually just participate in the code making,' Tang said in an interview.[7]

This sort of participation was a very different approach from what happened in a lot of places. In many countries around the world, the pandemic response was characterized by borderline authoritarianism and distrust. Governments and health authorities delivered orders, people questioned the validity or motive behind those orders. In Taiwan, the pandemic response was a lot less *shut up and listen while we tell you what to do* and a lot more *we're working together on this and we're going to help you participate in a united response.*

And that approach worked: Taiwan is a standout case study in how to manage a pandemic. It went for over 250 days between April and December 2020 without recording a local infection. As of April 2021, Taiwan, which has a population of 23.8 million, has had ten deaths from the coronavirus. There are, of course, a number of reasons for this. Taiwan has a universal health-care system with sophisticated digital capabilities, for example. People's travel histories could be linked to their National Health Insurance card, so hospitals could identify potential cases in real time. Taiwan is more community-minded then the Western world and had an established culture of face-mask use. It had also been burned by the SARS scare of 2003 and subsequently put together a comprehensive play-book to make sure nothing ever got as bad again. The CECC was set up to be activated when it looked like a serious disease was imminent. Legislation called the Communicable Disease Control Act was passed that enabled the CECC to direct resources to control outbreaks. Taiwan had trained for the coronavirus for years.

However, let's not forget that Taiwan also went into the pandemic with some disadvantages. It is very close to China and has a high population density. It has also been excluded from the World Health Organization because China claims Taiwan as a province with no right to its own representation on the global stage. (If Taiwan had been part of the WHO, it might have helped the rest of the world.) In short: Taiwan's incredible response to the pandemic was not inevitable. The key to Taiwan's success, Ing-Wen has said,[8] was creating a shared sense of purpose among people and inspiring unity. Ing-Wen isn't one to toot her own horn, but leadership was also crucial. Effective collaboration doesn't just happen automatically. You need leaders like Tang and Ing-Wen who work to create consensus and manage collaboration efficiently.

Remember the need for speed

You know which Western leader has done a really good job of using digital tools to encourage participation and inspire unity? Barack Obama. In 2007, his campaign developed an internal social network, which enabled people to connect with each other and organise on behalf of Obama. It was a groundbreaking use of new technology and has become a case study in how you engage and empower voters with digital tools. People felt involved; like they were part of a movement. That sort of enthusiasm, that feeling that you matter and that you're being listened to, is essential to both collaboration and a thriving democracy.

However, while Obama's campaign serves as a stellar case study in tech-driven participation, his presidency leaves rather more to be desired. Which is a shame because Obama started off with big ambitions to forge a more collaborative model of government . On 21 January 2009, his first full day in office, he issued a statement[9] announcing that his administration was committed to 'creating an unprecedented level of openness in Government' and would establish a 'system of transparency, public participation, and collaboration.' A major part of this initiative was an online petitioning tool called We the People that launched in 2011. You could petition the government to do something and, if enough people signed your petition (the original threshold of 25,000 signatures in thirty days eventually became 100,000), the White House was required to respond. It sounds simple but it was a pioneering way to bring people closer to government. Or at least that was the idea, anyway. In the end We the People turned out to be little more than an expensive PR exercise: millions of petitions were filed but few got substantive responses or led to legislative change. Responses were also often painfully slow. A Pew Research Center analysis conducted in 2016[10] found that the average length of time from when a petition reached the signature threshold to when the White House issued their response was 163 days—that's more than five months. Some serious petitions took substantially longer to be answered; it took the White House two years, for example, to respond to a We the People petition asking for Edward Snowden to be pardoned[11]. (The response was basically 'nah, screw him.') Meanwhile, it took the administration just two months to issue a jovial response to a tongue-in-cheek petition asking the administration to build a Death Star like the one in *Star Wars*. (The response was basically 'nah, we don't support blowing up planets.')

'There's a lot of frustration,' J. H. Snider, an expert on politics and public policy told NPR in a 2013 discussion about We the People[12]. Snider noted that rather than fostering transparency, a lot of the White House responses to petitions were 'sort of political responses, where you're not quite sure what the person is saying. They say, on the one hand, we support and recognize your concerns. But on the other hand, nothing is really happening.'

We the People ran for five years before year Donald Trump took power and temporarily shut it down. In that time, the only meaningful success story was a 2013 petition asking the White House to overturn a decision by the Library of Congress that seemed to make it illegal for Americans to unlock their cellphones so they could use them on other networks. The White House responded to that petition quickly and a law was passed making it clear that consumers could unlock their phones. I suppose you could also call the success of a petition to release the White House beer recipe a win, but it's a far cry from the original aims of the program.

I don't want to imply that fostering seamless civic participation in a country with over 300 million people is a breeze and Obama should have been able to pull it off. Nevertheless, I think there are a couple of important lessons to be taken from the failures of We the People. First, the Obama administration created a place for people to participate but it didn't build in effective mechanisms to cut through the noise; very quickly the White House found itself inundated with an unmanageable number of petitions, many of which were inane time-wasters. 'If you had told me a year and a half ago that the White House would be devoting time writing [an official statement] on how Lord Vader could fix our economic woes, I would have just laughed loudly at you,' one White House staffer told the media outlet Mother Jones in the early days of the initiative. 'Sometimes, I find myself thinking, "My God, what have we done?"' another staffer said.[13]

Remember Tang's two main rules about fostering civic participation? You need a safe space where people can partici-pate and you also need a rapid response cycle. We the People had the former but the lack of focus meant it didn't have the latter. It took months or years to respond to petitions; instead of feeling included people felt ignored. We the People was an ambitious initiative with a lot of potential. Alas the United States wasn't quite ready for it.

Cut through the noise and develop 'rough consensus'

We the People is an example of how creating spaces for people to participate can quickly turn into chaos if you don't find ways to efficiently manage collaboration. vTaiwan ('virtual' Taiwan), on the other hand, is a case study in how you manage that noise. The platform, which brings together people from the public, private and social sectors to debate policy issues and recommend legislation, was launched after Jaclyn Tsai, a government minister focused on digital technology (Tang's predecessor), went to a g0v-sponsored hackathon in December 2014 and suggested building a neutral platform where policy ideas could be exchanged. VTaiwan was launched the following month and functions like a massive town hall where you can go to input your views on important national issues. Topics that have been debated include: 'Should Uber be allowed?' and 'Should alcohol be available to buy online?' A platform like this could very easily be hijacked by trolls and descend into unproductive chaos, but it has proved useful and effective. While the government isn't obliged to follow vTawian's recommendations, it has been used to craft at least twenty-six pieces of legislation. And it's helped to resolve deadlocked issues such as how best to regulate Uber.

vTaiwan has proved useful because it has been designed to build 'rough consensus'. The concept comes from the software developer community and Tang has defined it as consensus that you can live with. The focus isn't on wasting time fine-tuning language but on agreeing a view that minimizes disagreement. So something isn't pushed through if 60% of people love it and 40% absolutely hate it; it's pushed through when the smallest number of people possible hate it. Topics are framed in the least polarizing way possible and solutions are crowdsourced. You can't reply or comment on people's proposals, you simply vote on them. Removing the 'reply' button serves as a major disincentive for trolls. Unlike most social-media platforms, vTaiwan is designed to ensure you don't lock yourself into a filter bubble or echo chamber; an artificial intelligence (AI) tool called Pol.is[14] visualizes participants' views on a map so you can quickly see where there is divide and where there is consensus. In the Uber debate, for example, the map showed that opinion coalesced into four distinct groups: taxi drivers, Uber drivers, Uber passengers and other passengers. People then compete to draft comments that these different groups can agree on: you're rewarding agreement rather than disagreement. By the end of the Uber exercise there were seven comments that had pretty much unanimous approval from all groups. These included 'The government should set up a fair regulatory regime' and 'Private passenger vehicles should be registered'. Tang then used those suggestions in offline talks with stakeholders and the government eventually adopted regulation inspired by vTaiwan's suggestion.[15]

VTaiwan and Pol.is are nifty tools, but great technology is useless without people who can apply it in the real world. Colin Megill, the founder of Pol.is has noted that the tool he created is just a hammer without someone who wants to bring those kind of participatory practices into government. Tang, Megill said, is 'the carpenter'.

Alicia Garza, who is one of the co-founders of Black Lives Matter, is another sort of carpenter: she excels at rallying people around common concerns and building movements. Garza stepped away from BLM a few years ago and has been putting her energy into an organization called Black Futures Lab, launched in 2017, which aims to make Black people powerful in politics. How's it doing that? Through the power of rough consensus. In 2018 the Black Futures Lab initiated the largest survey of Black people conducted in the United States in over 155 years. Over 30,000 people were surveyed about their political views and concerns. That data was condensed into the Black Agenda, a policy platform reflecting the most common concerns within the Black community across the political spectrum. One policy demand, for example, is making college affordable. The 2020 version of the Black Agenda notes that 8% of Black Census respondents 'see rising college costs as a problem in the community and a similar percentage favour making college affordable for any person who wants to attend'.

Having developed a clear policy platform around areas of consensus, Garza's next stop was getting voters to pledge to support the agenda and use it to make decisions about who they vote for. It provides something you can use to hold politicians accountable to.

Sounds pretty straightforward, doesn't it? Finding issues people agree on and then developing a clear agenda that a diverse group can rally behind. But like many things that sound simple, it's a lot harder in practice than it is in theory. Just look at the infighting between centrist Labour supporters and leftists in the UK. Or the infighting between progressives and centrist Democrats in the US. Garza is focused on building the broadest coalition possible by moving away from divisive labels and ideology and focusing instead on shared values. One of the reasons that a progressive didn't become the 2020 Democratic presidential nominee, Garza told me in an interview I did with her for the *Guardian*, was because the people who supported Bernie Sanders and Elizabeth Warren focused more on what they disagreed on than the many things they did agree on. Instead of arguing about details they should have been building rough consensus.

Ego is the enemy of collaboration

I've spent a lot of time talking about the processes that effective collaboration requires. Ultimately, however, the most important component of collaboration is humility. Great leaders aren't people who lock themselves away in corner offices and reckon they have all the answers. They're people who genuinely value outside opinion and find ways to bring others closer to the decision-making process. Even if, sometimes, that means spending hours sorting socks.

Have you ever sorted socks? You don't realize just how many different types of socks there are in the world until you're landed with the unenviable job of organizing them. Crew socks, short socks, tall socks, thin socks, men's socks, women's socks: there are endless varieties in many different sizes. Stacking them was a job that nobody at REI, a popular American sporting goods store, ever jumped at doing. But it was something Sally Jewell always made a point of helping out with when she was CEO of REI (2005–13). Jewell would regularly visit store branches and, while there, would help employees with some of the more frustrating bits of grunt work.

Gestures like this can be cringey if they're simply one-off stunts: *quick, take a photo of me spending thirty seconds doing menial work so I look like I understand the common man!* But, for Jewell, spending time alongside the people who kept REI's stores running was an important part of being a good CEO. When you're working alongside someone, when you're treating them as an equal, they often start to open up to you. They tell you about all the things that are happening on the ground that are bothering them, she tells me over Zoom from her home in Washington state. 'They're frustrated about the amount of plastics that everything comes wrapped and they're feeling guilty about having to put that plastic in the dumpster, for example. As a company committed to sustainability, isn't there something that we can do about this?'[16] You get insights that help you do your job better. And Jewell did her job very well: during her tenure at REI, she took sales from $1 billion to nearly $2 billion, added seventy-one stores and expanded online business.

People don't just automatically open up to the CEO, of course. 'Consistency is incredibly important; it takes a long time to build trust,' she told me when I called her up for a chat. Authenticity is also important. You have to be genuinely interested in the people you're talking to and the point of view they bring. 'It's not about manipulation,' Jewell stresses. 'Like I'm going to pretend to stock socks because I really want to pick your brain about what it's like working in the store. That's not authentic.'

Jewell didn't always get great insights from her chats in the sock department, but she did build a culture of trust and respect. Part of that came from the fact that Jewell was very clear about what she didn't know. She might have been the CEO, but at that particular moment she was just someone who had absolutely no idea where the smart wool socks were supposed to go. She didn't fire lofty operational questions at her employees, she didn't kick off a conversation by asking them broad questions about issues they might have with company policies, she just commiserated about the process at hand. 'Wow, this is frustrating. Where do these smart wool socks go? This seems pretty inefficient. What could we do to be more helpful?' Jewell was never going to pretend that she knew what it was like to walk in a store employee's shoes, but she made it clear it was important to her to get a glimpse of what their day was like. She wanted to let them know their work was appreciated and that it was difficult. 'That shows respect. And when people feel respected, I think there is a greater safety and the ability to speak up.'

We often think leaders are supposed to have all the answers. But a great leader is someone who knows how to ask the right questions and creates an environment where people feel comfortable giving honest answers. Ego can get in the way of both those things. And, as discussed earlier in the book, impostor syndrome can actually be an advantage. 'It can help create situations where you're not afraid to ask questions that you wouldn't otherwise have.'

Jewell started her career as an engineer in the oil fields of Southern Oklahoma and Colorado. It wasn't exactly the career a woman born in 1956 was encouraged to do, nor was it something Jewell ever knew to aspire to. If you look at her high-school yearbook it says that she wanted to be a dental hygienist. 'As a teenager you strive to fit in, and fitting in as a female meant going into a traditional profession.' She only ended up in engineering because she met a guy in her college dorm – who turned out to be her future husband – whose mechanical engineering homework looked a lot more interesting than her own. So she was always something of an outsider in the profession; she didn't go into it having been told all her life that this is what she'd be great at, this is what she was born to do.

In a sense that was an advantage. Jewell didn't go into her first job as a test engineer in a manufacturing plant that was making gear for the Alaska pipeline thinking she had all the answers. 'I went in thinking: have no idea what I'm doing,' she laughs. 'I learned then the power of asking questions and listening to the people that are closest to the action on the ground.' She didn't lord it over people who were doing more blue-collar jobs, the people on the installation and manufacturing line, for example; she realized that they knew things she didn't know. She treated them with respect. 'I came in saying, "I know this, but I know nothing about your core work. Will you help me?" I recognized that if I was nice and respectful to people, that they would go to the ends of the earth to help me,' she said. 'And I also realized that they were frustrated about things that were happening in the organization above them, that they would share with me.'

The idea that leaders should respect their employees and try to find ways to involve them in the decision-making process should be painfully obvious. However, this sort of collaboration isn't actually integral to our traditional model of leadership. Instead, the individual reigns supreme: their vision matters more than their values. If they act like a tyrant to achieve their vision, then so be it. Take Elon Musk, for example: he's been described[17] as the most inspirational leader in the tech industry but is widely acknowledged as being a horrible boss. Former employees have said Musk never bothered learning their names and didn't give employees any autonomy. 'There was only one decision-maker at Tesla, and it's Elon Musk,' one former employee said.[18] Employees simultaneously adore and fear Musk. 'Everyone in Tesla is in an abusive relationship with Elon,' another former Tesla executive said.[19] People put up with it because they feel that Musk is a genius who is changing the world.

Musk may be changing the world but it isn't always for the better. During the pandemic, Musk seemed to think that this expertise in electric vehicles meant he was also an epidemiologist: he repeatedly downplayed the virus and tweeted misinformation to his more than 40 million followers. He promoted a widely discredited paper on the benefits of chloroquine,[20] Trump's favourite drug. He called panic about the coronavirus 'dumb'. On 19 March 2020 he predicted that the US would see close to zero new cases by the end of April; 350,000 died of Covid in the US in 2020. In a September 2020 interview with journalist Kara Swisher, Musk said he wouldn't take a

Covid-19 vaccine. 'I'm not at risk for Covid, nor are my kids,' he said. And so on. These sorts of statements are incredibly reckless: millions of people listen to Musk and hang on his every word. Straying out of his lane and proclaiming him an expert on Covid isn't just arrogant, it's deadly. It could stop people getting vaccinated, make them take more risks; it could get them killed. When we treat leaders like demigods then they act like demigods. And that can have disastrous consequences for the rest of us.

6

Rethink Risk

Want to ensure you're not inadvertently committing incest? In Iceland there's an app for that: users can bump their phones together and the app trawls[1] an online genealogical database to check if they're related. *Bump in the app before you bump in bed,* the tagline declares.

'People may think it's funny, but (the app) is a necessity,' one Icelander told the Associated Press back in 2013. 'Everyone has heard the story of going to a family event and running into a girl you hooked up with some time ago. It's not a good feeling when you realize that girl is a second cousin.'[2]

I wouldn't go so far as to say accidental incest is an epidemic in Iceland, but it's certainly more of a risk than it is in most other countries. One reason for this is naming conventions: unlike other Western countries, there aren't family names. Instead, Icelandic surnames are usually derived from the first name of their father (or occasionally mother), followed by *son* ('son') or -*dóttir* ('daughter'). There are also, by the way, some fascinating rules when it comes to first names. Unless both parents are foreign, the law dictates that you've got to choose a first name that is on a recognized list of 1,853 female and 1,712 male names.[3] If it's not on the list then the parents need to get approval for the name from an organization called the Icelandic Naming Committee which ensures names are, amongst other things, 'capable of having Icelandic grammatical endings'. It's illegal to call your kid Harriet, for example, because it can't be conjugated in Icelandic.[4]

The second big incest risk factor in Iceland is the size of the country. It's got 350,000 people; its population is 1/26th that of London. So your dating pool is limited. Which has absolutely nothing whatsoever to do with this chapter except to underscore the fact that Iceland is very small. Still, that didn't stop some Icelanders from having oversized ambitions. During the early 2000s Iceland's financial sector, buoyed by deregulation and access to lots of cheap money thanks to low interest rates, boomed. The country's three main banks – Glitnir, Kaupthing and Landsbanki – grew exponentially; one economist called it 'the most rapid expansion of a banking system in the history of mankind'.[5] By 2006 the three main banks, which had very little experience of international finance, counted themselves among the top 300 biggest banks in the world. By 2008 the country was basically one big hedge fund: the big three accounted for about 85% of the financial system and the total assets of those banks were almost ten times Iceland's GDP and twenty times the state budget.

You know what happened next: the bubble spectacularly burst. In October 2008 Iceland's three main banks collapsed leaving debts far too big for the state to bail out. 80% of the stock market was wiped out overnight. A quarter of Icelanders lost their savings. The currency collapsed. Unemployment was at record levels and young people left the country in droves. Things were so bad someone jokingly put Iceland for sale on eBay; the starting price was 99 pence.

While much of Iceland was in ruins, one investment firm

came out of the crisis not just unscathed but having made a profit. The firm was called Audur Capital and it was founded by two women, Halla Tómasdóttir and Kristín Pétursdóttir, with the aim of incorporating feminine values into finance. I probably don't need to tell you that all the banks that collapsed were run by men.

Halla and Kristín (Icelandic naming conventions mean you refer to people by their first name) came up with the idea for Audur Capital in 2006, and founded it the following year. 'We founded our investment firm, because we felt like something was terribly off in the financial sector,' Halla tells me over Zoom.[6] She was the CEO of the Iceland Chamber of Commerce at the time and Kristín had just left her role as one of the only female executives at Kaupthing, one of the three big banks. Both women felt disturbed by the 'highly testosterone-driven culture' and the myopic focus on short-term profits and endless growth. The entire sector, Halla says, felt like 'a great big penis competition'. It just didn't feel sustainable.

In 2006 and 2007 the idea that there was something rotten in the state of Iceland's economy wasn't exactly a popular opinion domestically. The IMF, the international media and a number of economists had started to sound alarm bells about Iceland; the government and Icelandic bankers did not want to listen. The real problem, they decided, wasn't their business practices, it was the way those practices were communicated, and they went on a PR blitz. Rather than reining in the big bankers, the government encouraged them: shifting the tax burden from the rich to the poor and slashing corporate taxes[7] in order to strengthen 'incentives for risk taking'.[8] Arthur Laffer, the American economist who inspired Ronald Reagan's tax cuts in the 1980s, was invited to Iceland to reassure everyone that rapid growth and eyewatering debt were the keys to success: 'Iceland should be a model to the world,' he declared in November 2007.[9] (Iceland's economy tanked soon after and Laffer went on to become an economic advisor to Donald Trump's campaign and get awarded the Presidential Medal of Freedom.)

We tend to think of risk-taking as maverick, as fearlessly going against the grain. However, the sort of reckless risk-taking that was going on in Iceland in the early 2000s wasn't brave, it was greedy and incredibly stupid. 'I think excessive risk-taking is another word for herd behaviour,' Halla tells me. 'You don't understand the risks that you're taking, you just follow the herd. This is true for teenagers and it's true for the financial markets.' When you looked around, it was very clear that there wasn't actually any real value creation going on at the time. 'It was young excessively risk-taking egoistic leaders on a growth journey that was hugely leveraged.'[10]

Instead of taking the same course as the Icelandic banks, Audur Capital took a more risk-aware approach. They invested in state-backed bonds rather than corporate bonds. They didn't put all their money into the stock exchange because it was full of financial services and, if you have a financial crisis, those are the companies that get hit hardest. Everything they did, Halla explains, was guided by a few simple rules. First, never invest in something you don't understand; if you can't explain it in simple language to a client, that means you don't understand it. Second: profit with principles, never invest in something when the evidence doesn't convince you there is both economic and social value to be created. Third, maintain your independence: never leverage your balance sheet from someone that can then own you.

Being risk aware doesn't mean you don't take risks, Halla stresses. In finance you always have to take risks. Being risk aware simply means you don't rush into things; it means you take intelligent risks. For Audur Capital, that meant ensuring that you didn't just do financial due diligence when it came to investments, but you also did what Halla describes as 'emotional due diligence'. When Audur Capital assessed companies, they didn't just focus on the metrics you could put into an Excel spreadsheet, they looked at the corporate culture and thought about how much they actually believed in the direction the company was going. They asked themselves whether they were being tempted by short-term profits or if the company really had what was needed for long-term sustainable success. When the crisis hit, they weathered the storm. The guys who used to make fun of them didn't find their approach to risk-awareness quite so hilarious any more; Halla ended up having the last laugh.

Ardur Capital is far from the only case study that shows a 'female' approach to risk literally pays off. There are endless studies that show women tend to be better investors than men because they follow the same sort of rules that Ardur Capital set themselves. Women tend to take a more long-term, rational, approach to investing while men are more drawn to specula-tive stocks and the thrill of investing. (And yet women are still considered the emotional ones, eh?) One seminal study, by researchers at Cal-Berkeley, *Boys Will Be Boys: Gender, Overconfidence, and Common Stock Investment*, analysed the common stock investments of men and women from over 35,000 households from February 1991 through January 1997. They found men traded 45% more frequently than women, but women outperformed men by 0.94% per year. (Which might not sound like a lot, but adds up massively over time.) Single men traded less sensibly than married men; married men traded less sensibly than single women. Just being in proximity to a woman seemed to make men better at making rational decisions. Similarly, in 2016, the Warwick Business School surveyed 2,456 investors and found the 450 women in the group outperformed males in the study by about 1.8% per year.

This obviously isn't to say that men are not good investors – however, the best male investors seem to have more of a 'female' investing style. Just look at Warren Buffett. A book about his investing style by financial writer LouAnn Lofton, *Warren Buffet Invests Like a Girl,* argues that he is successful because he has a calm temperament, a long-term outlook, does a lot of research, trades less, and remains steady under pressure. What does Buffet think about the idea that he invests like a girl? According to Lofton: 'he said he pled guilty'.

There are lessons to be learned here beyond investing. First, we need to recognize that 'risk' isn't a neutral term, but is strongly associated with masculinity. A 2017 study led by the University of Exeter,[11] for example, notes that 'the current measures of risk-taking are biased toward identifying risk-taking in men'. Taking risks is associated with acting in a macho way: riding a motorbike without a helmet, for example, or betting lots of money on a football game. The researchers found that when you ask people how likely they are to engage in risky behaviour that isn't so associated with masculinity (e.g. confronting someone about sexism; going horseriding) then women can be just as risk-taking as men, or even more so. 'We've been overlooking female risk-taking because our measures have been biased,' the study noted. All of this isn't just academic: the way we think about and measure risk matters immensely. First, because we associate risk with financial and occupational success, arguing that women just don't take enough risks can be a way of justifying the lack of women in leadership. Second, because our definition of risk is so steeped in macho behaviour, we confuse recklessness with risk. And that results in things like the financial crisis. Instead of over-looking female-risk taking, we should be encouraging men to emulate it. From investing to politics to science, there's evidence that a more feminine approach to risk-taking results is more effective. And that's largely because women seem to take a more long-term approach to risk. When you're calmly looking at the big picture rather than reacting to the moment, then it stands to reason that you're going to make better decisions. I'm going to follow Audur's example and suggest three simple rules for how we should be redefining risk.

Don't mess with things you don't understand

Who's afraid of a novel coronavirus? Not a strong, masculine, manly man! During the early days of the pandemic, some of the world's male leaders seemed to think that taking the coro-navirus seriously was a sign of weakness. Brazil's Jair Bolsonaro dismissed the virus as nothing more than a common cold and pointedly mingled with crowds of supporters. Donald Trump refused to wear a mask for months. Boris Johnson boasted about shaking hands 'with everybody'[12] at a hospital with confirmed coronavirus patients.

This axis of idiots all got Covid-19, of course. Bolsonaro got it twice. Johnson was incredibly sick and ended up wearing an oxygen mask in an intensive care unit; arrangements were made for his death. In the end, he was out of action for about a month. We'll probably never know exactly how sick Trump was, but the general consensus seems to be that he was far sicker than he acknowledged. Even while in hospital he was terrified of being seen as 'weak'. He apparently had a stunt planned for his exit: when he left the hospital he wanted to rip off his button-down shirt and reveal a Superman T-shirt to the cheering masses. Thankfully someone dissuaded him from doing this. Instead he just went home and tweeted an incredibly irresponsible video saying 'don't be afraid of Covid',[13] and 'don't let it dominate you'.

It's easy to take shots at Johnson, Bolsonaro and Trump. However, a lot of guys seemed to think that admitting the pandemic was serious would undermine their masculinity. Influential podcaster Joe Rogan, who has an army of mostly male followers, suggested that only 'bitches' wear masks. A number of studies, meanwhile, found that men were less likely than women to wear masks – largely because they found them embarrassing. Men were more likely than women to agree with the idea that wearing a mask is 'shameful, not cool, a sign of weakness and a stigma'. Similar attitudes are behind why men are 10% less likely than women to wear seat belts: they think it makes them look weak. This, again, feeds into our masculine ideas of risk. Being reckless is coded as 'macho' and something to boast about.

While there are plenty of female anti-maskers out there (we've all seen the 'Karen' videos), women are less likely to take risks with things we don't understand and be reckless with our health. When you are traditionally the caregiver, you simply can't afford to be reckless; too many people depend on you. This attitude towards risk seemed to translate to managing the coronavirus. In the early stages of the pandemic, an interesting trend emerged: countries led by women seemed to be doing a far better job of managing the crisis than countries led by men. A million memes celebrating female leaders were born and there was a flurry of articles asking whether women really were doing a better job.

An analysis of 194 countries by economists from the University of Liverpool and the University of Reading dug into the issue further to see if this claim stood up to scrutiny. Female-led countries were matched with their closest neighbour based on socio-demographic and economic characteristics considered important in the transmission of coronavirus. New Zealand was matched with Ireland, for example. Bangladesh, which has a female prime minister,[14] was compared with Pakistan. Serbia, which has a female and openly gay[15] prime minister, was compared with Israel. Germany was matched with the UK.

Turns out the memes, while simplistic, were right: women were doing a better job. 'Nearest neighbour analysis clearly confirms that when women-led countries are compared to countries similar to them along a range of characteristics, they have performed better, experiencing fewer cases as well as fewer deaths,' the study's authors declared.[16] (The study, it should be noted, analysed differing policy responses and subsequent total Covid-19 cases and deaths until 19 May, so it only covers the early part of the pandemic.)

So what were women doing differently? Taking action, for one thing. 'Our results clearly indicate that women leaders reacted more quickly and decisively in the face of potential fatalities,' the authors noted. Female-led countries locked down significantly earlier; 'i.e. when they were seeing fewer deaths (twenty-two fewer) than male-led countries'.

Researchers suggest one explanation for earlier lockdowns in female-led countries was a gendered approach to risk: 'Women leaders seem to have been significantly more risk averse in the domain of human life, but more risk taking in the domain of the economy.' Their priority was saving lives, not saving the stock market. There was, after all, less uncertainty when it came to the economy. There had been recessions before. They were not easy to manage, but there were tried-and-tested ways to do it. Covid-19, on the other hand, was completely novel. There were still far too many unknowns. Could you catch it multiple times? Could you infect people if you were asymptomatic? Where exactly did it come from? What kind of long-term effects were there? Remember rule number one of Audur Capital? Don't invest in things you don't understand. By the same token, you should never underestimate things you don't understand. That's a lesson Bolsonaro, Trump and Johnson learned rather too late.

Don't follow the herd

Her throngs of Reddit admirers call her Cathie Bae or Mama Cathie. In South Korea, retail investors (non-professional stock market traders) call her 'Money Tree'. In early 2020 Bloomberg[17] called her the 'best investor you've never heard of'. In 2021, the *Economist* called her the 'investment manager of the moment'. Her real name is Cathie Wood, and she's a sixty-six-year-old devout Christian with three kids and a Midas touch. She has a very mild-mannered demeanour but inspires intense emotion: a lot of Wall Street money men can't seem to stomach her success. A lot of rivals are rooting for her to fail.

Before I get into why Wood inspires such passion, a quick word about ETFs for those who may not be familiar with them. Exchange-traded funds (ETFs) are not exactly the sexiest things in the world: they're baskets of securities (stocks, bonds, commodities, etc.), typically organized around a theme, that you can exchange like a stock; their main advantage is that's a very easy way to diversify your portfolio. There's an ETF that trades under the ticker $MAGA, for example, that invests in companies that have recently donated to Republicans. There's an ETF called $YOLO that invests in cannabis shares. There are two types of ETFs: passive ETFs and active ETFs. Passive ETFs track a benchmark like the S&P 500; active ETFs attempt to outperform a benchmark, and a fund manager actively picks and chooses different stocks.

Wood runs a company called Ark Investment Management (it's a biblical name, referring to the Ark of the Covenant, a gold-covered wooden chest containing Aaron's rod and a pot of manna which was described in the Book of Exodus). She has a bunch of funds which specialize in disruptive technology. She looks at companies with a long-term horizon, trying to find the players that will dominate the future. 'Innovation is causing disruption and the risks associated with the traditional world order are rising,' the website reads. 'We strive to invest at the pace of innovation.'[18]

It is buzzwordy, sure, but the approach has paid off. If you had put money in the Ark Innovation ETF (ARKK), which invests in disruptive-technology companies, a few years ago then you would have done very well indeed. As of October 2020, ARKK averaged a +31% YoY return since 2014. As of 12 December 2002 it was up 147%. It's done the best of all firms offering actively managed ETFs.

I'll be quite honest: my politics are about as different from Wood's as you can get. She has talked about[19] 'being on the right side of change' when it comes to investments but she doesn't seem too concerned about being on the right side of social change. A lot of the 'disruptive' innovations she's invested in are problematic in ways we'll get into in the next chapter. Wood also supported Donald Trump's re-election because she thought a Biden presidency might stifle innovation; again, not sure that's being on the right side of change. Politics aside, however, there are a few really enlightening lessons in why she has done so well so far.

What's most important, I think, is that Wood doesn't follow the herd. When she first entered the male-dominated finance world in the 1980s she was something of an outsider. She wasn't welcomed into the boys' club so, she has said, she had scrape around and look for 'the companies that fell through the cracks'. Being on the outside made her think more creatively. She began to specialize in companies that were still growing, or didn't easily fit into specific industries. 'I learned that when analysts and portfolio managers dismiss something as being too small or something that isn't going to fit neatly into any port-folio, those are usually real opportunities to surprise on the upside,' Wood has said.[20] When Wood worked at AllianceBernstein she became the first manager at the firm to buy Amazon.[21] At the time the company had a market capitali-zation of around $5 billion and her colleagues thought she was an idiot for buying it. 'People literally laughed,' she has said. Now Amazon is a valued at over a trillion dollars.

One of Wood's most controversial bets is Tesla. 'She's a rare breed,' Daniel Ives, a tech analyst who has covered Wall Street for twenty years, told Coindesk.[22] 'So many on Wall Street just go with consensus, and are afraid to deviate. But if you go back over the last decade with Tesla, she was bullish when 99.9% of the street was bearish.' In May 2019 Tesla was trading at around $200 a share. Wood suggested it could eventually rise to as much as $6,000 a share over the next five years. Her case for that is that Tesla outpaces its rivals when it comes to battery technology and she thinks Tesla will develop a fleet of a fleet of autonomous-driving taxis. Pretty much everyone in the business laughed at her. Morgan Stanley's Adam Jonas even suggested that Tesla could go down to $10 a share. 'I'm probably the most trolled portfolio manager on the internet, certainly when it comes to Tesla,' she said in a 2019 interview.[23] Still, Wood had the last laugh yet again. Shares in Tesla rose more 700% during 2020 to become the world's most valuable car company. They, along with other technology stocks, dropped at the beginning of 2021 in a sharp correction, but Wood was unfazed. What has made Wood successful so far is she's got her eye very much trained on the long-term prize. The ups and downs of a particular stock don't faze her if she truly believes the company has a future. She doesn't follow the herd, she forges a new path.

Wood was also bullish in Bitcoin much earlier than the rest of Wall Street; she started investing heavily in it in 2015. As with Tesla, her focus was on the long-term potential not the short-term ups and downs (of which there have been many). Again, Wood was laughed at by her peers. In 2017 Jamie Dimon, CEO of J. P. Morgan famously said that Bitcoin is 'just not a real thing, eventually it will be closed.' Again, Wood had the last laugh. Bitcoin was the best-performing asset of 2020. It passed $50,000 a Bitcoin in early 2021 and some people reckon it could eventually reach $1 million a coin.

Another way Wood has resisted following the herd is in her attitude to information sharing; she stands out for her willingness to share ideas and information. A lot of traditional investment firms see transparency as a risk and actively fight having to disclose their holdings. Wood, on the other hand, embraces information sharing. You can sign up to get an email every time she makes a trade, for example. And she credits a lot of her firm's success to their use of social media. 'As we're putting our research out, we'll get the innovators in that space DM-ing us and saying "Hey, what about us?" or "Hey, have you thought of this?"' or "Hey, you're wrong." I think the collaborative research ecosystem that we have keeps fresh ideas flowing through.'[24] Sharing your ideas doesn't have to be risky, Wood has realized. The biggest risk is not being open to new ideas. The biggest risk is being too comfortable with the status quo.

Don't be complacent

NYC IS DEAD FOREVER,[25] a former hedge-fund manager called James Altucher declared in a LinkedIn post in August 2020 that went viral. Altucher proceeded to lay out exactly why he thought the Big Apple was never ever coming back from the pandemic: his favourite restaurant had shut down, his friends were all moving elsewhere, remote work was here to stay, etc. He included a lovely little chart on bandwidth speed to make it clear this was an analysis you should take very seriously. Anyway, said Altucher, he'd had enough. He was getting the hell out of Dodge and going somewhere with a future. He was relocating his family to Miami.

Altucher wasn't the only rich guy starting a new life in Florida. During the pandemic Miami (along with Austin,

Texas) became a magnet for finance folk and tech types fleeing New York and California. 'I've been buying real estate in Miami for over twenty years, and it has been a great flight. Since Covid started, it's a rocket ship,' developer Alex Rodriguez, a former Major League Baseball superstar, told CNBC in December 2020.[26]

The benefits of living in Miami are obvious: sun, sea, sand and very low taxes. But the downsides should also be obvious: Miami is literally sinking into the sea. It is the 'the most vulnerable major coastal city in the world', according to recent modelling[27] by Resources for the Future, a nonpartisan economic think tank. We're not talking hundreds of years until the climate crisis disrupts everyday life, catastrophe is around the corner. Nearly half a million Floridians living less than three feet above current high-water levels could experience regular flooding, threatening $145 billion worth of real estate in the next twenty years.[28] By 2030 there will be fifty days of sunny-day flooding per year in Miami, according to projections by the Union of Concerned Scientists.[29] By 2045, there will be 250 per year. Sunny-day flooding, also known as tidal or nuisance flooding, happens when tides are high rather than when it storms. City sewers and storm drains get clogged and water rises up into the streets, causing disruption and damage. Some people are forced to live in precarious flood zones because they can't afford to move out; rich dudes, meanwhile, are flocking to them.

Miami is a fascinating case study in risk perception. Luxury waterside condos are still being built – ironically the city needs the taxes from these places to fund climate-change protection. Despite all the risks, guys like Altucher are still happily moving to Miami. The real-estate market is booming. It feels like Iceland back in 2006: people are in complete denial about the risks that are right around the corner. To some degree, that's just human nature. We respond to immediate threats and are bad at abstract projections. But there's also another phenomenon at play: the White Male Effect.

Coined in a 1994 study, the 'White Male Effect' is the tendency for white men to downplay risks compared to women and racial minorities. Researchers analysed the results of a national US survey looking at the public's perception of a variety of different health, environmental, and lifestyle risks: they found white men were always less likely to rate a hazard as 'high risk'. Take a look at this chart from that 1994 study.[30] The difference is striking:

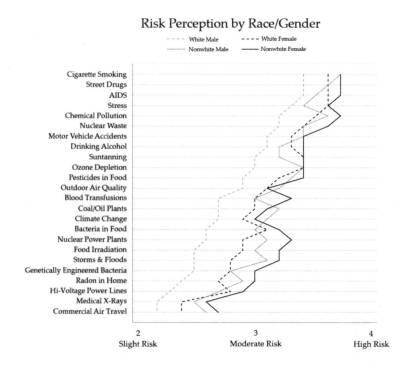

Risk Perception by Race/Gender

To be fair: it's not all white men who are fearless. The data is skewed by a well-defined subset of educated, affluent, conservative white men. (Sound like any politicians you know?) These guys don't think about risk. They don't worry about things the way other people do. And why would they? They're at the top of the pecking order. Bad things don't happen to people like them. When their recklessness causes the economy to crash, they get bailed out. When sea levels rise, they buy a house further away from the ocean. When a global pandemic hits, they go and quarantine on their superyacht or in their luxury New Zealand bunker. They can afford to be complacent.

You might think that, at least it when it comes to the climate, the White Male Effect might have diminished somewhat since 1994. There is so much evidence when it comes to the climate crisis now, how can this group of well-educated guys not take it seriously? Alas, it seems they are still in denial. Scores of studies show that conservative white males in America are more likely than other Americans to endorse climate-change denial.[31] A 2011 study of people's attitudes toward climate change found that 48.4% of conservative white men[32] who self-report a high understanding of global warming – the study dubbed these 'confident' conservative males – don't think climate change is real. That's compared to 8.6% of all other adults.

How about the impact of 2020? Has a year full of record-breaking wildfires done anything to cancel out the White Male Effect? It doesn't look like it. Looking at data from GlobalWebIndex, you can see that high-earning men are the least likely to believe that the environment is going to get worse in the future and low-earning women are the most likely.

Belief that the environment will get worse in the future

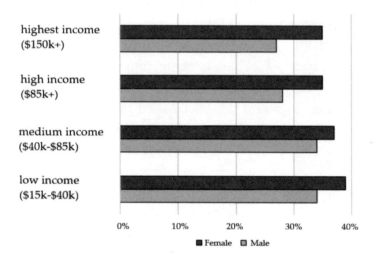

Similarly, data from GlobalWebIndex[33] shows that white men are the least likely demographic to agree climate change will have an impact on their lives in the next thirty years, while Black females are the most likely to think it's going to impact their lives.

One reason that white males are less afraid of various risks is because they're more afraid of something else. According to Yale Law School professor Dan Kahan,[34] an expert in risk perception, what really scares these guys is the 'loss of status they experience when activities symbolic of their cultural worldviews are stigmatized as socially undesirable'. They're invested in the status quo not just because it works well for them but because it's part of how they think about their own cultural identity.

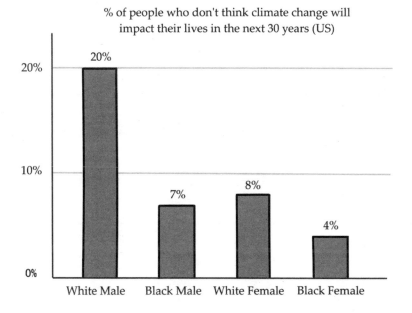

% of people who don't think climate change will impact their lives in the next 30 years (US)

In 2012[35] Kahan ran some numbers and found that there are certain risks that white men are a lot more worried about. When you ask how much risk high tax rates for business pose to human health, white men were the most likely to rate the risk highly, minority females were more likely to rate the risk as low. In conclusion, Kahan noted, risk is relative. 'Men are more risk tolerant than women' *only* if some unexamined premise about what counts as a 'risk' excludes from assessment the sorts of things that scare the pants off of white men (or at least hierarchical, individualistic ones).

The psychological aspect of the White Male Effect explains why so many middle-aged men are terrified by Greta Thunberg. Australian columnist and conservative climate-change denier Andrew Bolt, for example, has called her 'deeply disturbed'. 'I have never seen a girl so young and with so many mental disorders treated by so many adults as a guru,' Bolt wrote[36] in a *Herald Sun* column. A very reasonable and normal thing for a grown man to write. *Sky News* commentator Chris Kenny has similarly described Thunberg as a 'hysterical teenager' who needs to be cared for.[37] Donald Trump famously tweeted that 'Greta must work on her Anger Management problem'. These guys took Thunberg's warnings about the climate crisis deeply personally. 'At a deep level, the language of climate denialism is tied up with a form of masculine identity predicated on modern industrial capitalism,' Camilla Nelson, an associate professor of media at the University of Notre Dame has noted.[38] 'By attacking industrial capitalism, and its ethos of politics as usual, Thunberg is not only attacking the core beliefs and world view of certain sorts of men, but also their sense of masculine self-worth. Male rage is their knee-jerk response.'

It's not unfair to say that what happened to Iceland in 2008 was also a result of the White Male Effect: macho male bankers with a stubborn world view led the country. Afterwards, however, women stepped in to clear up the mess. The male prime minister was replaced by Johanna Sigurdardottir, the country's first female prime minister. Banking executives were removed and, in some cases, sent to jail. Women were put in as the new CEOs. The country made a shift from short-term thinking to sustainable growth. 'What we have learnt since [2009] is that if we want to stay out of crisis and build, we all know now we have to think in terms, not of the immediate future, but of the next ten or twenty years,' Minister Katrin Jakobsdottir told the *Independent*[39] in 2012. 'That is not the way a male-dominated government would be thinking; that is a female way of thinking.'

Iceland wasn't the only country that suffered a financial crisis in 2008, of course. People around the world suffered the consequences of Wall Street's greed and unrestrained risk-taking. However, Iceland is probably the only country that really tried to fix the roots of the crisis. It's certainly one of the only countries, along with Ireland, to have put banking executives in jail for their role in the crisis. In most places the executives who caused the financial crisis escaped serious punishment. It was the taxpayer who paid for their mistakes.

The financial crisis should have served as a reset button in the economic system. But over a decade later it seems that we have simply returned to business as usual. All the banks that were 'too big to fail' are even bigger now. J. P. Morgan has over $3.2 trillion in assets now, compared with $1.5 trillion in 2007. Wells Fargo has over $1.9 trillion in assets now, compared with $575 billion in 2007. Big banks have larger capital buffers now than they did in the 2008 recession, but they're still engaged in risky and opaque practices.[40] Wall Street bonuses are at record highs. It feels very much like we've seen this movie before.

We can't continue like this, Halla tells me with a frustrated sigh. We can't continue with this style of capitalism; we can't continue with a style of leadership that only values financial profit for shareholders. 'That model has left us with a burning planet and a broken social contract and a global pandemic. It's left us in a mess. We need a new model of stakeholder capitalism.' Halla has left Audur Capital now and leads a company called the B-Team, designed to 'confront the crisis of conformity in leadership'. Risk is often associated with trying new things. But it has become very clear that the riskiest thing to do right now, as the climate crisis grows more urgent and inequality gets more entrenched, is continue with the status quo.

7

Think Long and Wide

Deep inside a limestone mountain in West Texas, a very fancy cuckoo clock is being built. When it's finished, the clock will be hundreds of feet tall and will tick for 10,000 years. Instead of counting hours, there is a century hand which advances every 100 years. Every now and again the clock will chime. Not just any chime, mind you: the musician Brian Eno has built a melody generator that produces a different chime sequence every day for 10,000 years. The *pièce de résistance*? A cuckoo that pops out on the millennium. This thing which is known as 'The Clock of the Long Now' or the '10,000 Year Clock' has cost $42 million to build so far. God knows what the final cost will be.

What fresh hell is this, you ask? It's a billionaire's vanity project of course. While the clock was dreamed up by an American inventor called Danny Hillis, the project is largely being funded by Amazon founder Jeff Bezos. The clock is supposed to be a symbol of the importance of long-term thinking; a prompt for us to all imagine what the world will look like in 10,000 years and act accordingly. It's attached to a foundation called The Long Now that believes the world is plagued by a dangerous short-sightedness. This is a trend, the website[1] notes, that 'might be coming from the acceleration of technology, the short-horizon perspective of market-driven economics, the next-election perspective of democracies, or the distractions of personal multi-tasking. All are on the increase'. The Long Now wants to counter these trends with projects intended to make long-term thinking more common, fostering responsibility and patience.

The Long Now's diagnosis of the problems the world is facing is spot on. Our political and economic systems are set up to reward short-term thinking and disincentivize the long view. CEO and executive pay, for example, is often tightly linked to the stock price incentivizing strategies that boost short-term profits instead of long-term growth. Hillary Clinton once described this as 'quarterly capitalism'. Political leaders are similarly incentivized to focus on quick wins that will help them get re-elected instead of building a solid foundation to tackle long-term problems. Unless this sort of thinking changes soon, we're headed to disaster. Look, for example, at the changing nature of work. Research[2] from Oxford University predicts 47% of jobs are likely to be automated within a decade or two; that doesn't necessarily mean they'll be destroyed; many will be redefined. The implications of automation are enormous: we will need to re-skill people to fill new roles. If there isn't enough work for people to do, then we will need something like a universal basic income. And yet, despite the fact that this is all basically around the corner, too many politicians are barely paying automation any attention. The issue is 'not even on our radar screen', US Secretary Treasury Steve Mnuchin said when asked about automation in 2017, 'I'm not worried at all.' Even politicians who do pay the issue lip service aren't adequately preparing for the policy challenges automation poses.

So, to reiterate: The Long Now is absolutely correct in its assessment of the problem. However, I can't say I agree on their solution to it. Indeed, the fact that a billionaire is fiddling with an expensive 10,000 year clock while the world burns makes me go mildly cuckoo. (Yes, to be fair, Bezos isn't just thinking about clocks, he's also building rockets and dreaming about space colonies.) I have a very hard time seeing the clock as a symbol of long-term thinking. Rather, I see it as a symbol of the dangerously narrow form of long-term thinking practised by some of the world's most powerful people. The question you always need to ask when thinking long term is: _whose long term are we talking about here? How is this going to play out in the long term for people who don't look and act like me?_ And yet a lot of the big names we associate with long-term thinking don't seem to do that. (Incidentally, as of March 2021, there were twenty people on the board of The Long Now: fifteen white guys, four white women, one Asian woman.) Rather, they practise a very narrow form of long-term thinking that seems to envisage a future designed by and for a very particular type of person. It is informed by a homogenous, and very alpha male, philosophy which sees growth as unambiguously good and a certain type of human as expendable.

Let's take a look at Bezos, for example. 'It's all about the long term,' Bezos said in a manifesto[3] issued in 1997 when Amazon went public. From the very beginning, Bezos positioned Amazon as a counterpoint to quarterly capitalism. 'We will continue to make investment decisions in light of long-term market leadership considerations rather than short-term profitability considerations or short-term Wall Street reactions,' his manifesto stated. The plain English translation of that? 'We're not going to bother making a profit for a while because our goal is to put all our resources into growth so that we crush the competition and dominate the market. Once we've done that, then everyone else will be out of business and we'll be raking it in.' That strategy has paid off handsomely. Amazon's focus on the future has made Bezos the richest man in the world and the company's shareholders very rich. Amazon is now America's second-largest private employer. Its web-services division helps power large parts of the internet. It has gone from an online bookstore to a global behemoth.

Before I go onto criticize Bezos, I want to put my hand up and admit that I am a complete and utter hypocrite when it comes to Amazon. I signed up to Amazon Prime in 2004 when I started buying books on the platform. I got addicted to the convenience and I've been using it ever since. I keep meaning to quit (and I promise you I will!) but it's hard. Things like one-click ordering, two-day shipping and the cheap prices make it the easiest place to shop. I'm hooked.

A lot of people are. Amazon's long-term commitment to making things as easy as possible for the customer has got it a devoted customer base, but this has come at a cost to the environment and to its workers. We've all seen the reports about Amazon employees being forced to pee in bottles because they don't have time to take break. We've all read the articles about how Amazon gamifies warehouse work so its fulfillment-centre employees improve their efficiency. A benevolent employer it is not. And then there's the environment impact. In 2019 Amazon, after a lot of pressure, finally released data on its climate emissions. According to this, the company emitted 44 million metric tons of CO_2 equivalent in 2018, including indirect sources; that's about the same as the annual emissions of Norway. Along with those issues, Amazon has also been accused of copying bestselling items made by small businesses and putting them out of business.

Let's go back to that clock Bezos is building, shall we? What do you think the world is going to look like in 10,000 years? If we continue to do what we're doing now, then I reckon the world is going to be a massive Amazon warehouse where a subclass of human beings live. They'll deliver products to their overlords in Bezos-branded space colonies via Uber Rocket and communicate via Facebook chips implanted into their brain. I've got a feeling that vision isn't too far removed from the sort of future Silicon Valley wants to see anyway. The digital economy is turning into a winner-takes-all market dominated by a few big players. The sort of narrow long-term thinking practised by Amazon is now standard practice for tech start-ups. Look at Uber and Lyft: they haven't made any money at all. They make a loss on every ride. But that's OK, because the long-term plan is to dominate the market and eliminate competition.

The sort of long-term thinking that pervades Silicon Valley is great if all you're concerned about is maximizing profits for your company down the line. But what about everything else? What are the knock-on effects on workers' rights, on the environment, on people trying to run smaller businesses? What are the long-term consequences for people who aren't shareholders? When your long-term view is so narrow then you're not concerned about these wider ramifications. You're not concerned about thinking about things from other people's points of view. Your eye is firmly on the prize. In a winner-takes-all world, no one cares about the losers.

How do we solve this? With leaders who think long *and* wide. In politics, this means a different approach to decision-making: one which prioritizes long-term impact over short-term wins. In Silicon Valley, it means a less narrow form of long-term thinking, one which considers social impact, not just profit. Across every sector and industry, thinking long and wide requires skills that we traditionally consider 'female'. It requires empathy; it requires looking at things from a wide range of different perspectives and asking ourselves who we are designing the future for. Are the most vulnerable factored into our long-term planning or are we designing a future for a small and privileged sector of society?

Because women have traditionally been caretakers, we've been socialized to think long and wide. What does that mean in politics? It means, a huge amount of evidence shows, that female politicians are more concerned about social-welfare issues and the greater good than their male counterparts; they spend more on traditional areas such as education, health care and social assistance. Research has found that a higher share of women in government is associated with a higher fraction of government spending being allotted to education and health.

Studies also show that women tend to define success more broadly than men. One study that looked at gendered differences is defining success tracked a group (1,037 males, 613 females) of mathematically talented teenagers for forty years.[4] By middle age the group had a dizzying amount of achievements to their name: collectively they had published eighty-five books and 7,572 peer-reviewed academic articles and had secured 681 patents and $358 million in grants. They were all successful in various ways but thought about it differently. The men prioritized spending time on challenging careers while the women had a wider definition of success that included family and community investment. While both men and women said they were proudest of their family, men tended to invest in their family through tangible contributions (making money) while women more highly prioritized investing their time and emotional energy. That includes making sacrifices for their family. Studies show mothers, for example, are more likely than fathers to report experiencing significant career interruptions in order to attend to their families' needs.

It's worth reiterating that women are not inherently less selfish than men; we're not angels. Society just expects us to put other people's needs before our own and think about the impacts of our actions on others. Wouldn't it be nice if society expected men to do the same? Instead of holding up Bezos and his billionaire friends as paragons of long-term thinking, we need to be elevating a wider and more inclusive model of long-term thinking. That starts by rethinking how we measure success.

Think wide by moving away from narrow measurements of success

In order to look at how we might go about changing our measurements of success, allow me to transport to you to the M4 relief road in Wales. I don't know if you're familiar with Wales, but it seems that the traffic is a nightmare. Back in 1991 the Welsh government decided that something needed to be done to relieve the congestion faced by drivers around Newport by building a new fourteen-mile stretch of motorway. There was a lot of hemming and hawing and for the next twenty years various government departments argued over the project. In 2017, it looked like the road was finally going to be built, at the cost of £1.1bn. Environmentalists were not impressed. As one activist put it: 'Building a motorway to bypass a motorway is like loosening your belt to fight obesity.'

Despite the opposition, the motorway might have been bull-dozed through had it not been for the fact that Wales is the only nation in the world where the need to protect future generations is integrated into the law. In 2015 it introduced the Wellbeing of Future Generations (Wales) Act,[5] which the UN has described as a role-model[6] for other countries to follow. It 2016 Sophie Howe was appointed the world's first future generations commissioner with statutory powers; her job is to represent unborn Welsh citizens. Howe has limited powers – she can't prevent certain decisions from being made – but she acts as an important watchdog. Howe was legally obliged to consider the impact of the new road on future generations and, after looking at the plan, she advised against it. 'Building roads is what we have been doing for the last fifty years and is not the solution we should be seeking in 2017 and beyond,' Howe advised.[7] Plans for the road were scrapped once again; many environmental activists saw it as a big win. Friends of the Earth, for example, welcomed the decision, saying it was 'great news for Wales and the planet'.

If we are going to move away from short-termism, then it's imperative that we find ways to meaningfully integrate long-term thinking into our political and economic systems. Legally obliging politicians to think about future generations, as Wales did, is one way you can go about doing this. New Zealand's redesign of its budget is another. In May 2019, the country unveiled its first Wellbeing Budget, with all new spending required to go towards five goals: taking mental health seriously; improving child wellbeing and reducing child poverty; supporting indigenous peoples; moving to a low-carbon-emission economy; supporting a thriving nation in the digital age.

New Zealand's Treasury has also developed a set of wellbeing indicators 'to help analyse and measure intergenerational wellbeing' over time.

'Today we have laid the foundation for not just one wellbeing budget, but a different approach for government decision-making altogether,' Prime Minister Jacinda Ardern explained at the World Economic Forum. 'We're embedding that notion of making decisions that aren't just about growth for growth's sake, but how are our people faring? How is their overall wellbeing and their mental health? How is our environment doing? These are the measures that will give us a true measure of our success.'[8]

That's not just touchy-feely: there's an economic rationale behind treating government policy as long-term investments. When you invest in the most vulnerable, it pays off for everyone. Putting funds into reducing family violence, Ardern explained,[9] 'saves us costs down the line' as well as making people's lives better. Prioritizing mental-health services is another example of this sort of long-term thinking. Mental health got the biggest funding and investment boost on record, receiving NZ$1.9b. Half a billion went to the 'missing middle', anxiety and depressive disorders that don't require hospitalization but had a significant impact on people's quality of life. Improving mental health doesn't just help people, it should help the economy: every dollar spent on mental-health services will repay New Zealand with $3.50 in productivity gains and other savings, a report[10] from a Government Inquiry into Mental Health and Addiction found.

New Zealand isn't the first country to move beyond a myopic focus on GDP. There is growing recognition around the world that progress can't simply be measured in monetary terms. The Buddhist kingdom of Bhutan helped pioneer this: in the 1970s the Fourth King of Bhutan coined the phrase 'Gross National Happiness' (GNH) and developed a National Happiness Index. By 2008 GNH was in Bhutan's constitution and has been a key part of the kingdom's development ever since. In 2013, Ecuador appointed a state secretary of *buen vivir* – a world-view that describes a way of doing things that is more community-centric, and ecologically balanced and culturally sensitive. In 2016 the UAE appointed Her Excellency Ohoud Al Roumi as the country's first Minister of State for Happiness to oversee initiatives that could enhance citizen well-being. A number of countries have also started measuring the national rate of wellbeing. Still, while New Zealand isn't the first place to think about incorporating wellbeing into government policy, it's the first to place wellbeing at the centre of a major budget. Some on the left have accused it of not going far enough, while some on the right have dismissed it as airy-fairy spin. However, the entire world is watching it and there's a general consensus that it's a major sign of progress. It may not transform the country overnight, but it's a powerful statement about the importance of embedding long-term thinking into government. And not just myopic long-term thinking, but long-term thinking that takes the most vulnerable into account. Long-term thinking that takes a wider view.

And while Ardern doesn't get all the credit for the Wellbeing Budget, I'm not sure it would have gone through without a woman at the helm. Women, as I noted earlier, tend to be more empathetic and think beyond themselves. You can see this reflected in an analysis of characteristics and beliefs of male vs female leaders in the US, below. Female leaders in the US are more likely to agree with statements that demonstrate more external concern and focus. They are more family-oriented and want to improve their local and global communities. Men, on the other hand, were more likely to agree with more individualistic statements.

STATEMENT	US MALE LEADERS	US FEMALE LEADERS	FEMALE LEADERS +/-
I am interested in other cultures / countries	55%	65%	18%
I always try to recycle	53%	62%	17%
I believe all people should have equal rights	69%	76%	10%
Helping others before myself is important to me	50%	55%	10%
I like to know what is going on in the world	61%	65%	7%
Contributing to my community is important to me	48%	50%	4%
I am ambitious	47%	46%	-4%
I am career-focused	44%	42%	-5%
Being successful is important to me	66%	61%	-8%
I am adventurous	50%	45%	-10%
I am money-driven	22%	20%	-10%
I am confident	68%	59%	-13%
I make decisions quickly	43%	35%	-19%
I like to be the first to try new things	47%	37%	-21%
I take risks	41%	32%	-22%

Source: GlobalWebIndex analysis of 2.8K business leaders within the U.S. and 16.2K globally during Q3'2020 (internet users ages 18–64 only)

Around the world, female leaders seem to be leading the charge for what Katrín Jakobsdóttir, Prime Minister of Iceland, has described[11] as 'an alternative future, based on wellbeing and inclusive growth'. In early 2020 Jakobsdóttir teamed up with

Ardern and Scotland's First Minister Nicola Sturgeon to promote a 'wellbeing agenda'. New Zealand, Scotland and Iceland were the three founding members of the Wellbeing Economy Governments (WEGo) initiative, a collaborative project between national and regional governments designed to share best practices and advance wellbeing economies. At the time of writing, the only other two members of WEGo are Finland (which has a female prime minister) and Wales. So far, four out of the five members of WeGo are governments run by women. Says something, doesn't it?

Perhaps Jeff Bezos should take note of what these women are doing. The way to get people thinking far into the future isn't by spending millions of dollars building enormous clocks in limestone mountains but by integrating long-term thinking into government in meaningful ways. It is by finding ways to ensure that the perspective of a wide group of people (including the unborn) are heard in important decisions. If we want humanity to be thriving on a healthy planet when that little cuckoo pops out to mark the next millennium, we need to build a future for everyone. As we saw in the previous chapter, an influential subsection of privileged white men don't think about risk the same way the rest of us do. They have the luxury of thinking in abstract terms about the future because they know they'll always be OK. They have the luxury of building clocks in mountains to represent long-term thinking. For most of us, though, it's not an abstract concept, it's urgent and existential.

Avoid abstraction and look at problems from a wide variety of viewpoints

To show you the perils of not thinking long and wide, let me introduce you to a guy called Robert Williams, who lives in a suburb on the outskirts of Detroit, Michigan. Williams is a forty-something dad of two with a 9–5 at an automotive supplier. He was living an ordinary suburban life until, one day in January 2020, he got a weird phone call that ended up earning him an unenviable place in the history books. The call was from the Detroit Police Department; they wanted Williams to turn himself in. 'Why? What for?' he asked. He didn't have a criminal record, he was a law-abiding citizen. Nobody would tell him. Williams, who wondered whether it was some kind of prank, told the guy on the phone that he was at work and he had no intention of turning himself in. They could come to his house with a warrant if they wanted.

Which is exactly what they did. When Williams got in his car to go home, he called his wife, Melissa, and she told him the police were waiting for him. He still half-thought it was a prank at this point but, when he pulled up outside his house, Williams was arrested in front of his wife and two daughters, aged two and five; his kids, who couldn't understand what was happening, cried as they watched him being taken away. Williams was then taken to the Detroit Detention Center where he was he had his mugshot, fingerprints and DNA taken. He was questioned and held for thirty hours before being released on bail.

Williams's crime? Basically, being Black. The police had been investigating the robbery of $3,800-worth of watches from a Shinola retail store in Detroit back in 2018. There was security footage of the incident which had been run through facial recognition software: Williams came up as a match. The detectives showed Williams this footage and he pointed out that, other than being Black, he looked nothing like the guy. He'd also never been to that shop. (He was also, by the way, at work with an alibi when the theft happened, but the police never bothered to check.) 'So I guess the computer got it wrong,' one of the detectives reportedly told him in a sarcastic voice.

The computer had got it wrong. Artificial intelligence facial-recognition technology is around 90% accurate at identifying white men but is notoriously bad at identifying Black people. This is because the underlying algorithms were trained to learn how to identify faces by being fed huge datasets of faces – and the majority of those faces were white men; one research study[12] found that a widely used facial-recognition data set was estimated to be more than 75% male and more than 80% white.

Williams is the first known person[13] to have been arrested because of a facial-recognition failure. That doesn't mean that he's the first person this has happened to, however. He just had the resources to fight back: he was able to hire a defence attorney and contact the American Civil Liberties Union (ACLU), who filed a complaint with the department. The case against Roberts was dismissed but that doesn't undo the humiliation of being arrested in front of your family and neighbours. It doesn't undo the Kafkaesque nightmare of being wrongfully accused by a computer. As Robert puts it:[14] 'I never thought I'd have to explain to my daughters why daddy got arrested. How does one explain to two little girls that a computer got it wrong, but the police listened to it anyway?'

Wrongful arrests happen, of course. No system is ever perfect. But what makes this different from one-off human error is the scale of these systems. The tech bros creating the facial-recognition algorithms clearly didn't think about the broader ramifications of what they were doing. They didn't think about the bias going into the technology and they didn't think about the social consequences of the technology. They didn't take into account the fact that predominantly Black neighbourhoods are frequently over-policed and that introducing biased surveillance tools into this context would have disastrous ramifications. They didn't look at the way in which society and technology interconnect and interact. They didn't properly consider the ethical implications of what they were building.

Remember Timnit Gebru from Chapter 4 ('Embrace Imposter Syndrome')? This is what she spends her life doing: looking at the ethics of the systems that control increasingly large parts of our lives. Gebru's work starts from the understanding that technology doesn't exist in a vacuum, but is part of a larger, and very messy, social system. That may seem obvious, but it's something a lot of people in Silicon Valley don't seem to want to think about. One of the big problems with tech, Gebru tells me, is that ethics is often looked at as an abstract concept. People will ask if a model or system is 'fair', for example. But, she says in frustration. 'That question just doesn't make sense. What does "fair" mean? Fair to who? What context is it being used in?'[15]

You might have heard of the cake-cutting problem. For decades computer scientists, mathematicians, and economists have grappled with the question of how to fairly divide a resource among people with different preferences. For example: how do you divide a birthday cake with multiple different toppings among a group of people (some of whom love chocolate, some of whom hate frosting, etc.) in a way that means nobody feels cheated and nobody feels envious of someone else's slice? This problem was considered in the Book of Genesis, in relation to land. Abraham and Lot used the 'I cut, you choose' method to ensure fairness. That method works for two people. When the number of people involved gets larger, it gets a lot more difficult. In 2016 a couple of young computer scientists finally came up with an algorithm that worked. The cake-cutting problem had finally been solved! The only problem? It involved cutting the cake into an enormous number of pieces. Even with a handful of people, the number of pieces required to divvy things up fairly is greater than the number of atoms in the universe.[16] The problem may have been solved in theory, but how are you supposed to apply this to issues of fairness in real life?

A large proportion of the people who are creating the technology that affects our lives come from a very small, very privileged, very male, very white section of society. The system benefits them, so they don't really question it. Issues of fairness seem academic and abstract rather than existential and urgent. They treat ethics in AI like it's a cake-cutting problem, Gebru says. Like it's something you can sit back in your ivory tower and solve through maths and logic alone.

When it comes to AI, a lot of tech bros and white men don't seem to be too bothered about the risks related to exacerbating bias and creating unfair systems. 'It doesn't really affect them and white men don't seem to find it particularly fun to think about,' Gebru says. What they do like thinking about are risks like killer robots or an AI-instigated apocalypse. They see discrimination in a silo, not as something that pervades every aspect of life. For example, says Gebru, she was at a weird dinner a couple of years ago with a world-renowned economist. (I won't put the guy's name here but he's a big deal; he's been called one of the most influential people in the world.) A bunch of people were going around the table talking about discrimination and Famous White Guy Economist seemed to get tired of the conversation. 'He was like: "You know, of course, discrimination is bad, but why don't we talk about more important things like climate change?"' She shakes her head in disbelief. 'And I'm thinking: why don't you think those two things are related? That's what I'm talking about when I talk about white men and abstraction. They want to speak in general terms.'

When you speak in general terms like this, when fairness is an abstract concept, not a lived reality, then you get technology that exacerbates existing inequality in exponential and opaque ways. When you don't think long and wide, you get a system that only works for a narrow sliver of society. What are the implications for this? In the spirit of getting away from abstractness, let me give you a few potential scenarios that demonstrate the sort of problems this kind of thinking could cause.

1. You might get turned down for a job because the algorithm is inadvertently sexist or doesn't like your accent

Back in 2014 Amazon created a program that would look through applicants' resumés and give candidates a rating ranging from one to four stars. Yep, potential employees were basically being graded with the same rating system as Amazon's products. Congratulations, human! You might think you are a complex individual with hopes and dreams, but Amazon thinks you're about as complicated as a roll of toilet paper. Anyway, the computer models were trained on resumés that had been submitted to the company over the past ten years. As it turns out, most of the resumés were from men, leading the computer to think that any mention of the word 'women's' was a red flag. If you were on the women's chess team, for example, you got downgraded. If you went to a women's college you got downgraded. Amazon eventually discovered the problem and got rid of the tech, but it's not clear how many people were affected. Amazon has said the tool[17] 'was never used by Amazon recruiters to evaluate candidates' but hasn't denied recruiters looked at the recommendations generated by the recruiting engine. We also don't know what else the tool might have discriminated against. What if you used the word 'wheelchair' in your resumé, for example? And while Amazon may have said it fixed that program, hiring processes will continue to be automated, meaning it's unlikely this sort of problem will be unique.

Remember the research paper that Gebru co-authored? The one that got her forced out of Google? It was called *On the Dangers of Stochastic Parrots: Can Language Models Be Too Big?* and it was about AIs trained on vast amounts of text data in order to 'understand' how to read and write. The same sort of tech, broadly speaking, that Amazon used to check through potential employees' resumés. Gebru's paper warned that, because these programs are trained on enormous amounts of data, it's really hard to check them for embedded biases.

'A methodology that relies on datasets too large to document is therefore inherently risky,' the researchers conclude. It can result in programs that perpetuate 'harm without recourse'. Without people in technology companies who are thinking about these issues and are committed to preventing them before it happens, we are likely to see variations of Amazon's sexist recruiting tool over and over again. Digital interviews, for example, are becoming an increasing common part of the hiring process. Before you ever get to speak to a real-life recruiter, you've got to answer a few questions on camera. On some of the common digital hiring platforms, your facial movements get analysed, your word choice is graded, your speaking voice is assessed: all that info is combined to create an 'employability' score. The problem is, if you've got an accent that the algorithm isn't familiar with, it might not understand what you're saying and you'll find yourself with a low employability score. This might track you for life.

2. You might get arrested because a computer mistranslated your social media post

Gebru's research paper notes a famous example from 2017, where Facebook mistranslated a Palestinian man's post, which said 'good morning' in Arabic, as 'attack them' in Hebrew. The man got arrested. At no point before his arrest did anyone who spoke Arabic read the actual post. After all, computers know everything, right?

3. You might not be able to find anywhere to live because of an algorithm

You've found a great apartment to live in and have filled out the paperwork. Then you get notified that you're not allowed to live there. The management company won't tell you why exactly, it seems the tenant-screening software they used identified you as an undesirable tenant. This happened to a guy called Mikhail Arroyo[18] back in 2016. He was recovering from a fall that had resulted in a coma and his mum wanted to move him into a unit in her Connecticut apartment complex. The only problem was the computer said no. Why? It wasn't clear; the management company told Arroyo's mum to call CoreLogic, the company behind the screening software they'd used. CoreLogic is one of a number of companies providing automated tenant-screening tools – it's a booming industry. These tools scan all the available data they can find about you and assign you a score to determine how risky a tenant you are. It's like your Uber Score but you can't see it or easily appeal it.

For months Arroyo's mum called CoreLogic to try and get them to help but she couldn't get any answers; eventually she got legal help from a local non-profit. They finally found that the computer had flagged a small retail theft charge on Arroyo's record. He'd been twenty at the time, it was his first offence and involved less than $150. But that was apparently bad enough for him to be given a score that deemed him an unde-sirable tenant and effectively locked him out of housing. Should making one mistake stay with you for the rest of your life in the form of a score that marks you an undesirable tenant? What kind of impact would this have on Black and brown people who are disproportionately policed? Clearly the people design-ing these algorithms didn't think or care about that.

Maybe you've never done anything wrong in your life and your records are squeaky clean. That doesn't mean that you're safe from these algorithms. In November 2018 a naval officer called Marco Antonio Fernandez[19] came back to America after spending a year deployed in South Korea and tried to find an apartment to live in. He had top-secret security clearance; his record was as pristine as you could get. However, the tenancy-screening algorithm rejected him. It confused his name with that of an alleged Mexican drug trafficker. Fernandez had the resources to sue the company and the issue is currently going through the courts. But what if he had been someone with fewer resources? There would seemingly have been no recourse. It's very unlikely that Fernandez is the first case of mistaken identity with these sorts of algorithms; he's just currently the most high profile.

These aren't futuristic scenarios. All these things are happening now. Some of them make the news and cause a temporary outcry, others go undetected. The law is trying to play catch-up with the issues being caused by new technology, but it's a very slow process. In the meantime, how much harm is being caused?

Create teams that challenge you, instead of echoing you

No system is going to be perfect, obviously. No matter how good the intention, it's likely that there will be unintended consequences to the technology we build. However, it's very hard to argue that tech companies have good intentions or are adequately thinking about the harm they may cause. Indeed, when people like Gebru bring it up, they are pushed aside. And lest you think Gebru is just one unfortunate example, she's not. In February 2021 Google fired AI ethics lead Margaret Mitchell, who worked closely with Gebru, saying she violated the company's code of conduct by moving files outside the company. Google employee Alex Hanna said on Twitter that the company was running a 'smear campaign' against Mitchell and Gebru. Google employees have spoken out about harassment and intimidation at the company since

the firings.[20] And it's not just Google: a number of former and
current Facebook employees have spoken out about how the
company prioritizes profit over ethics. One researcher claimed[21]
they'd been told to block a medical-misinformation detection
algorithm that had reduced the reach of anti-vaccine campaigns,
for example. These companies are focused on growth, growth,
growth. They think long term, but only about themselves, not
the harm they cause.

What's the answer to this? Do we burn all the computers
and retreat to an agrarian society where we never hear the
word 'algorithm' ever again? Thankfully we don't need to be
that extreme. What's so frustrating is that there are lots of ways
to mitigate this risk and build fairer technology; there just isn't
the will to do it. One thing we need to do to avoid a *Black
Mirror* future, for example, is ensure that the people building
the technology that governs our lives are bringing in *and listening to* lots of different sorts of people with different life experiences. Big Tech likes to make a big song and dance about how
much it cares about diversity, but it's not always keen on actually listening to the 'diverse' talent it brings in. 'People often
talk about diversity like it's charity,' Gebru says with frustration.
And because they don't really believe that diversity is anything
more than an annoying PR exercise, they go about it in a really
superficial way. 'AI is a system,' Gebru stresses. 'The people
creating it are part of that system.' If they're not looked at as
being part of that system, if those people are not listened to,
then we're going to continue creating technology that harms
marginalized communities.

When she was at Google, Gebru was an outspoken advocate
for diversity. She also hired social scientists, who have been
educating people on feminist standpoint theory: essentially the

idea that knowledge is socially situated. It doesn't try to pretend that you can be entirely 'objective' because what we call objectivity is generally just what a privileged white guy thinks ('the view from nowhere'). Standpoint theory encourages you to interrogate the point of view that you're taking when you're talking about something. 'To me that means rooting things in reality,' Gebru says. 'When you start rooting things in different people's points of view and interacting with different groups of people, it becomes a little bit less abstract.'

Long and wide thinking doesn't magically happen. You need to build it into government decision-making, as Jacinda Ardern did with the Wellbeing Budget. You need to build it into corporate processes, as Gebru did. 'In order to really figure out how the technology is going to affect people, you need to go talk to the people who are impacted,' Emily Bender, a Professor of Computational Linguistics and one of the co-authors of the paper that Gebru worked on, tells me. That can't be something that is *ad hoc*. 'There need to be methodologies in place that ensure the people coming up with new technology are systematically thinking about how it is going to affect people.'[22]

In order to do all that, you need to think that other people are worth thinking about in the first place. You have to *want* to think wide. Again, women tend to do this more naturally than men because we've been socialized to think about others, not just ourselves. Impostor syndrome also plays a role: because women are more prone to self-doubt, we're more eager to listen to others. We don't think we have all the answers. Imagine what the world would look like if more men were brought up to worry about how every little thing they did might make others feel? Imagine if more men weren't so confident in their world-views. Imagine if they knew they needed a team around them who'd provide those checks and balances. That person who says 'Hold on, isn't this idea ridiculous? Why do we need to build a cuckoo clock? Why do we need a rocket?'

8

You Don't Need a Rocket

Congratulations on reaching this chapter. As a reward, I'm going to let you in on a secret; I'm going to tell you how we save the world from the climate crisis. Building very fancy cuckoo clocks in the middle of Texas is obviously one solution. But we need to go further: we need more technology! Greener technology! Sleeker, more sophisticated technology! And rockets! Rockets are super-cool, right? Let's build bigger rockets!

That's what Jeff Bezos, Elon Musk, and Richard Branson seem to think, anyway. The trio of Space Billionaires have ploughed enormous amounts of money and energy into their intergalactic ambitions. While Branson seems to be in the Billionaire Space Race largely for the fun of space tourism and the cosmic clout, Bezos and Musk have far bigger plans. Musk wants to colonize Mars and make humans a multi-planet species to avoid an extinction event. 'If there's something terrible that happens on Earth, either made by humans or natural, we want to have, like, life insurance for life as a whole,' Musk said during a virtual Mars conference in 2020. He reckons there'll be a million people on Mars by 2050. Although how much fun they'll be having on a desolate and freezing-cold planet I don't know. Perhaps more fun than their peers will be having on a ravaged Earth.

Bezos, who spends $1billion of his own Amazon stock each year financing Blue Origin, his space exploration company, also reckons that intergalactic expansion is essential for the future of mankind. 'We want to go to space to protect this planet,' he once wrote.[1] 'That's why the company is named Blue Origin – for the blue planet, which is where we're from. But we don't want to face a civilization of stasis, and that is the real issue if we just stay on this planet – that's the long-term issue.' Bezos, who stepped down from Amazon in 2021 so he could spend more time on space, believes in growth, growth, growth: to keep growing we need to plunder Near Earth objects for resources. He also hopes to set up floating space colonies. These are straight out of the *Jetsons*: climate-controlled paradises that orbit around the galaxy.

Bill Gates, the Sensible Centrist Dad of billionaires, isn't so keen on extraterrestrial exploration. 'I'm not a Mars person,' he has said.[2] When it comes to solving Earth's problems, he doesn't think 'rockets are the solution'. However, just like the rest of the billionaires, his thinking is characterized by what you could call Big Rocket Energy (BRE). It's a mindset in which the need for constant growth is a given; bigger is always better; and technology is fetishized. It's a mindset that is focused on searching for the newest biggest thing instead of asking whether you really need it. Gates, for example, thinks that sustainable growth is largely a matter of disruptive technology. In 2015 Gates started a $2 billion venture-capital fund called Breakthrough Energy that invests in tech that can 'lead the world to zero emissions' – while making some people very rich of course. A win–win! The best part of all this? If we develop the right technology, then none of us will have to change our energy-guzzling habits. Which is great news for guys like Gates who, according to one study, probably has one of the largest carbon footprints[3] in the world. Gates loves his private jet, which consumes 486 gallons of fuel each hour. He also recently invested in a private jet company. But don't be too quick to judge him! The guy uses sustainable jet fuel, which is the billionaire equivalent of recycling your takeaway containers. So it's totally fine. Gates is also the largest farmland owner in America and has drawn criticism for the environmental impact of his farms. But, again, he's investing in green technology so it's totally fine!

I'm not a Luddite, but I am wary of technological utopianism. A lot of women are. In 2019 an American thinktank called the Center for Data Innovation released a survey[4] showing that women had less favourable views of AI than men. 41% of men, compared to only 31% of women, for example, agreed with the statement: 'Technological innovations, like artificial intelligence and robotics, will make the world a better place.' And 34% of men, compared to only 21% of women, agreed with the statement: 'Self-driving cars will lead to safer roads and fewer accidents.' These results mirror other research that shows women are less impressed with technology than men. According to the 2015 Edelman Trust Barometer, which measures trust across different institutions, women are twenty points more sceptical about innovation than men. 'Women, in our study, are substantially more skeptical about innovation. Substantially,' Edelman president and CEO Richard Edelman noted.[5] 'Why? Because they are the protectors of the family. The guys are like: "Whoa, just another gadget, let's roll." No. What are the consequences to society?'

One of the risks of fetishizing new technology is that you might move too quickly and unleash a whole host of unintended problems, as we saw in the previous chapter with bias in AI. Another risk, however, is that a myopic fixation on new technology blinds you to simpler, more efficient, and more human-centric solutions. Remember when twelve young Thai soccer players got stuck in a cave back in 2018? Elon Musk decided he was going to save the day and started tweeting about he was building a kid-sized submarine to get them out: a solution rescue organizers described as 'technologically sophisticated' but impractical. In the end the boys were saved by an international team of divers working together. They were saved by a combination of existing technology, diplomacy and human ingenuity. Musk, who can't seem to stand anyone outshining him, very maturely responded to his failure by calling one of the British divers a 'pedo' in a baseless attack. The whole episode is an example of how Big Rocket Energy (or I suppose in Musk's case it was Small Submarine Energy) can stop you from appreciating solutions that are right in front of your eyes.

Instead of fetishizing the new, make the most out of now

The opinions and antics of a bunch of billionaires wouldn't really matter if it didn't have such an impact on all of our lives. Alas, it does. Gates isn't just investing in clean energy, he seems intent on turning himself into a leading voice on climate change. He may not have any actual credentials in climate science but he's obscenely rich – ergo an expert in everything. In February 2021 he came out with a book called

How to Avoid a Climate Disaster: The Solutions We Have and the Breakthroughs We Need. The general thrust of his argument was that the answer to the climate crisis lies in breakthrough new technology. It's basically a really long infomercial for his investments. Gates doesn't have much time for activists (he has been rather patronizing[6] about Greta Thunberg) or politicians. He dismisses the Green New Deal, which aims for carbon neutrality, as a fantasy. His big idea is that, if faced with the choice between (1) cutting carbon emissions now and (2) reducing the cost of net-zero green technology for the long run, we should do the latter. What does that mean from a policy point of view? It means the government (and, by extension, the taxpayer) subsidizes and supports the kind of tech companies he's invested in. It means our focus is not on some carbon neutrality now, but total carbon neutrality in the future.

Once again: Gates is not a climate expert or a scientist or an elected politician. 'I can't deny being a rich guy with an opinion,' he admits in the book. And he's absolutely entitled to his opinions. It would be unfair not to acknowledge that his opinions and his money have done a lot of good in the world. The Gates Foundation spends more on global health each year than the World Health Organization and many countries do; it's stepped in where governments have failed. However, while a lot of good can come from billionaires applying their brains and bank account to thorny issues, it's important to remember that they are not elected officials. It doesn't matter how good their intentions are, they are still imposing their world-views on us with little oversight or accountability. 'The first guiding principle of the Foundation is that it is "driven by the interests and passions of the Gates family,"' noted an editorial in *The Lancet*.[7] 'Is this kind of governance really good enough?' The Gates Foundation has also been criticized for aggressively pursuing an agenda and stifling dissenting opinion. In 2007, for example, the head of WHO's malaria research, Arata Kochi, sent a memo complaining that the foundation 'was stifling debate on the best ways to treat and combat malaria, prioritizing only those methods that relied on new technology or developing new drugs'. Again, it doesn't matter how good Gates's intentions are or how smart he is, the fact a single person has so much power should give us all pause for thought.

I don't think it can be stressed enough that the likes of Gates, Musk and Bezos are not just rich guys with opinions. They're guys with the resources and influence to turn their opinions into policies and shape our future. Thomas Carlyle famously said that 'The history of the world is but the biography of great men.' The future of the world may well be the tech investments of a few rich men.

Would that really be so bad? An awful lot of people don't seem to think so. Musk has a cult following so devoted that they would probably sacrifice their first-born child if it would help Daddy Musk get to Mars. Meanwhile, despite the fact he's not a climate expert, despite the fact he only decided to divest from oil and gas in 2019, the media is giving Gates's climate views an enormous amount of airtime and rapidly turning him into a leading voice in the field. It's not hard to understand why so much of the media is so enamoured with Gates: the vision that he is peddling is very comforting. It's certainly a lot more comforting than Greta Thunberg's vision. I know I don't want to give up flying or modern comforts. I don't really want to change my behaviour. I'd love to invest in some futuristic gadgets and make a ton of money while simultaneously helping to save the world. Who wouldn't?

The problem with this kind of silver-bullet thinking is that it's just another form of procrastination. It's an excuse for not doing anything now. And the fact is, there's a lot that we can be doing now to radically change the course of the climate crisis.

Like what? Well, as a number of actual climate experts pointed out in response to Gates's books, we actually have a lot of the technology that we need to avoid a climate catastrophe. Talking to the *Guardian,* for example, Michael E. Mann, one of the world's most eminent climate scientists, criticizes Gates's view as overly technocratic, ignoring the importance of political solutions, and 'premised on an underestimate of the role that renewable energy can play in decarbonizing our civilization'. Gates doesn't think the wind and solar energy we've got at the moment are anywhere near close to making a significant difference. However, the price of solar has plummeted. Writing about Gates's book in the *New York Times,*[8] the climate activist Bill McKibben noted that 'the price drop is 50 to 100 years ahead of what the International Energy Agency was forecasting in 2010, mostly because we're getting better at building and installing solar panels. Every time we double the number of panels installed, the price drops another 30 to 40 per cent, and there's plenty of runway left.' Building new sun- and wind-power facilities is close to being cheaper than operating existing coal-fired power. 'Most people, Gates included, have not caught on yet to just how fast this engineering miracle is happening,' McKibben says. We should still be investing in the sort of new technology that makes Gates so excited, but we can do what needs to be done with sun and wind. Instead of putting all our energy into building something new, we should be scaling up and improving what we've got now. And instead of just focusing on technology alone, we need to be looking at how we match that with political solutions.

So what does the opposite of Big Rocket Energy look like? It looks a little like Dr Ayana Elizabeth Johnson. Dr Johnson is a marine biologist and policy expert. She's also a rising star in the environmental movement; she has written a book about solutions to the climate crisis and co-hosts a podcast on the issue. Cheesy popcorn kicked off her career: when she was five years old, she was on a family vacation in Florida and, thanks to a severe milk allergy, broke out in hives after feeding cheese popcorn to fish at a coral reef. (Feeding fish snacks is probably strictly prohibited now but this happened back in the mid-1980s.) Johnson's mum took her into a cabin on the boat they were in to wash the cheese dust off; the cabin had a glass-bottom and Johnson found herself with a private view of the ocean. She was hooked. And, no, I will not apologize for that pun!

Twenty years or so after that popcorn incident, Johnson found herself on a boat in the Caribbean, doing fieldwork for a PhD in sustainable coral-reef management. One of the problems she was looking at was bycatch, the baby fish and inedible fish that get caught up in traps and have to be thrown away. Bycatch is a major issue. It makes fishing unsustainable and it can throw the equilibrium of delicate reef systems out of whack.

I'd bet a million dollars (which I don't actually have) that if you tasked Elon Musk with reducing bycatch, he'd design some kind of AI-powered submarine that herded the right fish into traps. Or perhaps he'd design fish-based facial-recognition systems to identify the targets and suck them into high-tech underwater tunnels where they'd be transported via fish-sized Teslas to their final destination. Whatever he designed, anyway, it would be flashy and expensive. Johnson's solution was neither. After doing hundreds of scuba dives and observing how fish were getting caught in traps, she just made a tweak to the fish traps. Her improved fish trap had a narrow vertical hole in the corner through which 80% of the bycatch would escape. It was cheap, easy and useful. It made fishing more sustainable without hurting fishermen's income. It made the most of what was at hand at the moment rather than focusing on building something completely new.

Designing that fish trap was something of an 'aha' moment for Johnson. 'It showed me that it's not about fancy technology,' she explained on a podcast.[9] 'There are these really valuable, low tech solutions. And if you design your research to fill a need that is expressed by the local government and you work with fishermen that you can actually be useful.'

Johnson also realized that she didn't want to spend her career writing 'papers that no one was gonna read and wouldn't ever result in any action'. She felt that the best way she could make a difference to the health of the ocean wasn't by focusing on fish, but focusing on humans. More specifically, thinking about ocean policy from the perspective of the people most affected by it. 'What I realized is that I really needed to just be talking to fishermen,' Johnson said on the same podcast. 'I needed to talk to the people who had for generations been on the water, under the water, seeing what's changed and whose livelihoods depended on getting management right.'

So that's what she did; Johnson spent hundreds of hours interviewing over 400 fishermen in the small Caribbean island of Barbuda. One of the most important questions she asked them was what kind of rules would they put in place to manage fishing in the ocean? A lot of people were surprised to be asked. People didn't normally ask them about policy or care about their opinion. Johnson got valuable ideas and insights from these interviews and the end result was an initiative that helped the citizens of Barbuda craft their own marine regulation. 'With these new policies, the small island of Barbuda has become a Caribbean ocean conservation leader and global role model,' *National Geographic* wrote in 2014.[10]

Talking to the people most affected by an issue and getting their input on the policies that govern their lives – it's not exactly rocket science, is it? However, as we saw in the previous chapter, doing this sort of community consultation properly takes time and is a lot of hard work. And that work is often unacknowledged and underappreciated; it's not as sexy or as attention-grabbing as building cool technology and it doesn't get the same sort of media attention and adulation. Indeed, thanks to our cult of individual genius, there's almost a disdain for listening to ordinary people's opinions. We all know the quote attributed to Henry Ford: 'If I had asked people what they wanted they would have said faster horses.'[11] Steve Jobs similarly said that customers don't know what they want until you show it to them. There's obviously truth to that. However, as with pretty much everything in life, what's needed is balance. At the moment we're too obsessed with *new*. Let's balance that with building on what we have now.

Constructive innovation can be more important than disruptive innovation

We also need to strike a balance between constructive innovation and disruptive innovation. You've probably heard the phrase 'disruption' or 'disruptive innovation' at least a million times over the past decade; there may be no buzzword that better sums up the modern era. The phrase was popularized by a 1995 *Harvard Business Review* article by Clayton Christensen describing how start-ups or industry outsiders could change the rules of an existing market or create a whole new market segment via the discovery of new types of customers. Fittingly, Christensen's idea of 'disruption' was rapidly disrupted. The concept morphed into a sort of license for tech bros to wreak havoc that's probably best epitomized by Facebook's former internal motto: 'Move Fast and Break Things'. There were posters with that slogan plastered all over Facebook's offices and it was on the company's IPO paperwork. 'Unless you are breaking stuff, you are not moving fast enough,' Mark Zuckerberg explained.[12] What mattered was speed above all else. Getting new things into the market even if they were riddled with mistakes. In 2014, after some embarrassing data breaches, Facebook changed its slogan to the very catchy: 'Move Fast With Stable Infra'. As you might have inferred, 'infra' means infrastructure: the idea is that you move fast while continuing to mess up the world, you just don't advertise it so much!

If Silicon Valley epitomizes disruptive innovation, then Ayana Elizabeth Johnson's approach to the climate might be described as 'constructive innovation'. While tech bros are focused on a sort of scorched-earth approach – do whatever you want, never mind who gets hurt in the process, and then disingenuously ask for forgiveness later – Johnson is focused on cooperation rather than competition. It's not about one group 'winning', it's about creating value, and providing climate justice, for everyone. And you can't do that if the climate movement is dominated by white guys. Johnson's book on the climate crisis opens with an essay by eighteen-year-old Mexican–Chilean climate activist Xiye Bastide called 'Calling In', that sums that up. 'A vibrant fair and regenerative future is possible, not when thousands of people do climate justice activism perfectly, but when millions of people do the best they can.'

Remember Taiwan's digital minister, Audrey Tang, from earlier in the book? Her entire approach to technology is another example of constructive innovation: it's about listening to people, building consensus and creating tools that work for everyone. Instead of obsessing over new technology, Tang is resourceful about finding new ways to leverage what's already at her disposal. Take misinformation, for example. During the pandemic Taiwan deployed what Tang described as a 2–2–2 'humour over rumour' system for fighting misinformation. Tang hired comedians to help craft viral responses to fake news and a response to misinformation was provided within twenty minutes, in 200 words or fewer, with two fun images. In the early stages of the pandemic, for example, rumours were spreading that face masks were made from the same material used to make toilet paper, which was going to lead to a shortage of toilet paper. People immediately ran out and bought as much bog roll as they could. The government's official response? A meme showing Taiwanese premier Su Tseng-chang wiggling his bum with a caption saying: 'We only have one pair of buttocks.' It sounds ridiculous but it was effective; humour can cut through in ways straight fact-checking can't. It was certainly a lot more effective than using AI to add warnings to possible misinformation, which is what Facebook does. Not everything has a purely technological solution. You have to think of the human element as well.

Fei-Fei Li is on something of a mission to do just that. Unless you pay attention to tech, then you may not have heard of Li. The Stanford professor is not a household name the way Musk is. But she's done far more to change the world than he has – indeed, were it not for Li's work then we might not be as close to self-driving cars as we are now. Li created this thing ImageNet, which is, to be incredibly simplistic, an enormous database of images. That doesn't sound very exciting on the surface, but it's thanks to ImageNet that AI has become so sophisticated. When Li came up with the idea of ImageNet, one of the big issues in AI, which was then a very niche and nascent area, was that computers were rubbish at object recognition. The machine-learning models at the time were not making much progress at getting AI to see a picture of a cat and recognize that it was a cat. Li, who studied neuroscience and physics at Princeton, thought there was a lesson to be found in emulating the way children learn. Childhood development, in many ways, is exposure to enormous amounts of data that you slowly learn to organize. To make computers smarter, Li decided, you needed to massively increase the amount of data they were fed. That seems sort of obvious now, but this was in the early days of the internet, way before everyone was obsessed with the idea of data. At that time Li's idea of collecting 15 million images and organizing them into 22,000 labels was regarded as a little bit out there by some. However, ImageNet eventually led to a breakthrough in object recognition. *Wired*[13] notes that Li is 'one of a tiny group of scientists – a group perhaps small enough to fit around a kitchen table – who are responsible for AI's recent remarkable advances'.

Since creating ImageNet, Li has started to worry that she's created a monster. Like Gebru, she's sick of hearing influential male tech leaders warn about killer robots when the far more urgent issue with AI is the ways it is exacerbating inequality. Li knows a thing or two about inequality. She was born in China and emigrated to New Jersey with her parents when she was sixteen; at the time she didn't speak any English. She worked lots of odd jobs in restaurants and dry-cleaning shops when she was a kid to help support the family. And she also looked after her chronically ill mother.

That experience, she tells me from her office in Stanford, showed her the importance of humility. 'Seeing human vulnerability, seeing all the hope in the hospital, seeing the clinicians helping my mom, it made a profound difference.' It grounded her and made her realize that 'no matter what technology we're making, that human element, that human impact is so important'.[14] A lot of tech types pay lip service to that, but Li is trying to operationalize through an approach she calls 'human-centred AI'. In 2019 she became the co-director of the Stanford Institute for Human-Centered Artificial Intelligence, a new institute which advocates for AI that improves human lives and focuses on an interdisciplinary approach to the field. While a lot of tech types seem to think they know better than anyone else ('I think more like an engineer than a political scientist,' Bill Gates says proudly in his book on climate change), Li is adamant that AI shouldn't be in the hands of technologists alone. You need to involve philosophers and ethicists and experts across every industry. You need a 'collective mindset', Li says.

Is Li optimistic about the future now? Does she think AI is going to save the world? 'What drives me is a sense of responsibility,' she tells me.

I don't know if that means optimism or pessimism, but what wakes me up every day is this intense sense of responsibility. When I first entered the field of AI twenty years ago it was just a personal intellectual passion, right? Nobody cared about this field at that time, but I just loved it. I would never have dreamed what a seismic impact and profound change it's leading in our society. And that realization has instilled a tremendous sense of responsibility.

I'm not saying Li is perfect by any means. But talking to her is incredibly refreshing. She – like Gebru – is the complete opposite to a guy like Elon Musk. She doesn't think she knows it all. She's humble. And when she talks about feeling a sense of responsibility, you believe her.

Again, the lesson from all this isn't that new technology is bad and we should be elevating more analogue solutions. Rather, it's that we shouldn't fetishize technology or soundbite solutions. Instead of worshipping egomaniacs who think their latest rocket is going to save the world, we need to be injecting more humility and humanity into technology. And we need to realize that technology alone isn't going to move us forward, we need to couple it with low-tech solutions. Sometimes those solutions look like a bigger hole in a fish trap, sometimes they look like optimism.

Optimism and realism are a powerful package: propel people forwards with an optimism grounded in reality

It can be hard to find much optimism when it comes to the climate – as Christiana Figueres, a Costa Rican diplomat who was head of the UN Climate Change Conference when the Paris Agreement was achieved in 2015, knows only too well. Figueres was appointed to lead the UN Framework Convention on Climate Change six months after the disaster that was the 2009 Copenhagen Conference. There had been high hopes that COP15 (which had been branded 'Hopenhagen')[15] would result in a new global climate-change treaty and set the world on a unified path towards improving the environment. Instead of progress and unity, however, there was division, discord – and blood. During the last night of negotiations, Claudia Salerno, Venezuela's chief climate negotiator, repeatedly banged her hand violently on the table in an attempt to be heard by her Danish hosts. Suddenly realizing she was injured, Salerno raised her bloody palm in the air. 'Do you think a sovereign country has to actually cut its hand and draw blood?' she demanded. 'This hand, which is bleeding now, wants to speak, and it has the same right of any of those which you call a representative group of leaders.'

Salerno's bloody hand came to symbolize the fiasco that was Copenhagen. The only thing to show for days of non-stop negotiations was a simple statement recognizing the scientific case for keeping temperature rises to no more than 2°C above pre-industrial levels. There was no roadmap for getting to that point; just a lot of resentment, particularly from vulnerable countries. The path ahead looked bleak.

Over a decade later, speaking to me from quarantine in Costa

Rica, Figueres still seems a tiny bit traumatized by Copenhagen. The experience had been so disheartening, she says, she simply couldn't see a way forward. 'I had succumbed to the self-defeating, grieving, angry feelings that all of us who were "Copenhagen survivors" had walked away with. Even as I accepted the responsibility to take on the helm of the climate negotiations, I didn't really think that there was anything we could do in the short-term that was dramatically different to Copenhagen.' She remembers a journalist asking if a global agreement on climate change could be reached and replying: 'No, not in my lifetime.'

As soon as she said that, Figueres felt guilty. 'When I said those words, they were like a dagger into my own heart because, as I expressed them, I realized that if what I was saying was true, then I was condemning my daughter's generation and all generations after that to utter misery. I was condemning nature to ecosystem failures that we had never witnessed.'[16]

Figueres decided that she wasn't willing to participate in that. She realized that, actually, the situation wasn't hopeless. 'If we were in this situation thirty years ago, or even ten years ago, it would have been very different. We didn't have the technology, the policies, the capital, to change things. But right now we do.'

But technology, policies, capital – none of that's good enough if people are divided and disillusioned. To avoid a repeat of Copenhagen, Figueres knew she had to bring her colleagues out of the 'fog of doom and gloom they were in' and inject them with a sense of purpose and responsibility. But to motivate everyone else, she had to motivate herself. She had to change her own attitude. So she started practising mindfulness. Personally, I hate the word 'mindfulness' as it has been completely corporatized and overused. But true mindfulness isn't an app you can download or a product you buy. All it is, Figueres explains, is 'becoming much more aware on a daily level of everything that we have in front of us that we can be deeply grateful for'. It's easy to just focus on the negative, on the things we didn't do, the things we didn't achieve.

> If you put on your negative glasses, then every day can look very negative and very dark. But if you intentionally seek out the positive you will be surprised how many wonderful things happen to us during the day, and how many things we can be grateful for. Starting from little things like the miracle of a tiny leaf growing on your balcony.

If you're a grump like me and find it a tad difficult to be grateful for a weed on your balcony, all hope is not lost. You don't just become mega-optimistic overnight, Figueres tells me, it's a path. It starts by choosing to be grateful for small things.

> Optimism for me is a deliberate choice that we have to make every day, almost at every moment of the day. It's a deliberate choice to focus on the positive and harvest our internal conviction, that there is enough potential within us and collectively to make the changes that we want for a much better world.

Women, it seems, tend to naturally be more grateful than men. A 2012 survey of 2,000 Americans, commissioned by the John Templeton Foundation, suggests there might be a gratitude gender gap: 'Women are more likely than men to express gratitude on a regular basis (52% women/44% men), feel that they have much in life to be thankful [for] (64% women/50% of men), and express gratitude to a wider variety of people.'

Numerous other studies have found that women report feeling more grateful than men in their everyday lives.[17]

Analysis of the Twitter conversation of business executives provides similar results. Female leaders are more likely to share positivity on social media, whereas male leaders are more likely to share neutral sentiment:

Female leaders are more likely to share
positivity on social media

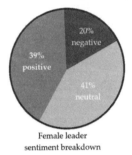

Female leader
sentiment breakdown

Male leader
sentiment breakdown

	FEMALE LEADERS	MALE LEADERS
Positive Conversation Drivers	• Optimistic views for each day • Gratitude regarding their experiences and accomplishments • Congratulations to others on their achievements	• Sharing positive news • Praise for political, business, and sports figures • Highlighting industry and personal progress
Negative Conversation Drivers	• Criticism of political figures and systems • Anger and frustration regarding racism	• Negative judgment for how quarantine and COVID-19 has been handled • Annoyance at the actions of those with opposing viewpoints

So women are good at feeling grateful: what next? Figueres views change as a series of concentric circles. You're at the very centre of those circles: change has to come from the self. You have to be the change you want to see in the world. The next circle is the group that works most closely with you: in Figueres's case it was her team in the United Nations Secretariat. The next circles consisted of corporations, youth activists, scientists, etc. The point is that you start with yourself and work outwards. 'Once you've got everyone working together, on the same page and behind the same message, you create a sort of "surround sound system".' Everyone is unified behind the same messaging and inspired by the same vision. What does that mean? It means that 'no matter what direction governments turned, they would hear the same message'. While governments may have been her primary audience in her role at the UN, Figueres knew she couldn't start by trying to convince them of her vision. She needed to create this sort of surround system so they would have the confidence to be courageous in Paris. They needed to know that if they took ambitious action, 'they would not be hung out to dry by the rest of society'. 'It can't be a top-down process. There has to be the fertilization of so many other enabling forces that are bottom-up.'[18]

In December 2015, 195 nations adopted the Paris Agreement unanimously; it was widely recognized as a historic achievement. While many factors contributed to success in Paris, Figueres credits a collective sense of optimism. Not the sort of pie-in-the-sky optimism that characterizes populists like Boris Johnson and Donald Trump (*we're going to make everything really great again . . . you just wait and see*) but an optimism grounded in a shared vision and the creation of real value. Figueres describes this as 'stubborn optimism': an optimism that empowers you and propels you forward. Stubborn optimism is grounded in action. That's different from 'hope', which can be passive and vague.

What about Greta Thunberg, though? Nobody could really say that she's a beacon of optimism. One doesn't imagine Thunberg goes around waxing lyrical about tiny plants on her balcony; she's probably more likely to explain that the only reason they're growing now is because the climate is messed up and we're all going to die a painful death. I could do some mental gymnastics and tell you that Thunberg practises her own form of stubborn optimism, but I'm really not sure that's true. If one word sums up Thunberg, it's 'angry'. Does Figueres think that's counter-productive? Ever the diplomat, Figueres notes that for some people Thunberg's approach is effective; it shakes them out of complacency. But while fear alone might get you to sit up, it's optimism that keeps you going.

'We need hundreds of Elon Musks and that's how we'll get this done,' Gates said in an interview on CBS,[19] in reference to climate change. No doubt Musk agrees with this thesis. Indeed I wouldn't be surprised if he's funding some secretive cloning start-up that is trying to achieve just that. (Speaking of which, let's all take a minute to remember how Jeffrey Epstein had ambitions of impregnating twenty women at a time and seeding the human race with his DNA as a first step in creating technologically modified super-humans. So much ego in that man, no wonder there wasn't any room for a moral compass.) Sorry for the disgusting Epstein imagery. Point is: we don't need hundreds of Musks. There simply isn't enough space on the planet for all that ego. What we desperately need is a lot less Big Rocket Energy and a lot more humility. It's possible to think big while keeping your feet rooted firmly on the ground.

9

Get Real

BOOM. BOOM. BOOM.

Alexandria Ocasio-Cortez was crouched in her office bathroom, afraid for her life. It was 6 January 2021 and thousands of pro-Trump rioters were outside the US Capitol, protesting the fact that Joe Biden had won the election. It was starting to look like they might force their way into the building and a staffer had hurried into Ocasio-Cortez's office and told her she should hide. Now someone was banging loudly at the door.

AOC had good reason to fear for her safety. As an outspoken young woman of colour with unapologetically progressive views, she was a symbol of everything many on the right hated. From the moment she'd shot to fame by unseating ten-term incumbent congressman Jo Crawley in New York she'd had a target on her back. Donald Trump and his followers were obsessed with her and the rest of the progressive women of colour who make up the group of congresswoman known as the 'Squad'. In 2019, for example, a gun shop in North Carolina put up a massive advertising billboard with photos Ocasio-Cortez, Ilhan Omar of Minnesota, Rashida Tlaib of Michigan and Ayanna Pressley of Massachusetts. 'The 4 Horsemen are idiots' the sign read above the word CHEROKEE

GUNS. The Squad were also the target of constant online harassment and regularly received death threats online.

It wasn't just angry Trump supporters who hated the Squad; many of their Republican colleagues were not shy about expressing their disdain for them either. The summer before, Republican congressman Ted Yoho had confronted AOC on the steps of the Capitol and called her 'disgusting' for talking about how poverty can drive crime. He was then overheard calling her a 'fucking bitch'. Meanwhile, Marjorie Taylor Greene, a QAnon supporter and new congresswoman from Georgia, had made her hatred for the Squad a central pillar of her campaign. Shortly before getting elected, she'd posted a picture on Facebook of her holding an assault rifle alongside Ocasio-Cortez, Omar and Tlaib. 'We need strong conservative Christians to go on the offense against these socialists who want to rip our country apart,' her post's caption read.[1] So, yeah, Ocasio-Cortez had good reason to believe that the banging on the door was not going to end well.

BANG. BANG. BANG.

'Where is she? Where is she?'

BOOM. BOOM. BOOM.

The thumping at the door was now accompanied by a man's angry yells. Ocasio-Cortez's heart was racing. She peeked through the door hinges and saw a glimpse of a white guy in a black beanie demanding to know where she was. Terrified, she held breath trying not to make a sound.

'Hey! It's OK! Hey, come out,' one of her staffers yelled. Hesitant, AOC crept slowly out.

It transpired that the guy banging on the bathroom door was a Capitol police officer who was trying to move AOC to a more secure location. But he hadn't yelled 'Capitol Police' when he came in or announced himself. There was no partner with him. Things just weren't adding up. 'It didn't feel right because he was looking at me with a tremendous amount of anger and hostility,' Ocasio-Cortez said later.[2] 'Just the very uncertainty that you don't know if that person is trying to protect you or not is deeply unsettling.' There were, after all, lots of police officers among the rioters that day.

The officer gave AOC and her staffer directions to a different building where they could take shelter. But his directions were vague and the pair were so rattled that it was only when AOC and the staffer got to the other building that they realized he didn't give them a specific place to go and they had no idea where was safe. So they just stood there frozen for a minute, next to a deserted Dunkin' Donuts in an empty basement, the sound of rioters trying to break in reverberating through the halls, with absolutely no clue what to do next. Then, then they started running again, sprinting up a spiral staircase and running frantically between various offices trying to find somewhere safe to shelter.

Eventually, Occasio-Cortez saw congresswoman Katie Porter, a friendly face, who ushered her in. Ocasio-Cortez was in panic mode at that point. She was fully expecting a rioter with a gun to run through the corridor at any moment and shoot her. Porter wasn't fully up to speed on what was happening – she hadn't heard the intelligence reports and you couldn't hear the rioters where she was yet – and so was a little calmer. 'Don't worry, I'm a mom,' Porter said breezily. 'I've got everything here we need to live for, like, a month in this office.' Those included a pair of sneakers for AOC, who was wearing high heels, in case she needed to run for her life. They pushed furniture against the door so they were barricaded in. And then, along with a number of staffers, they sat and waited. As the sun started to set – which was very early in the afternoon since it was January in Washington DC – they turned off all the lights because they were afraid that if rioters saw lights in a window they'd target that office. And then they sat and waited in the dark.

As they sheltered, new intelligence reports came in. Bombs had been found a couple of blocks away from the building. AOC's anxiety escalated. What would they do if the building exploded, she thought? As the minutes crept by, she kept expecting someone to burst in to the office or for the whole thing to just go up in flames. Still, she thought, at least this wasn't her first term in office! If she died at least she'd be dying in her second term! After a while the situation calmed down but AOC still didn't feel safe leaving. She went to Ayanna Pressley's office, ate dinner with her, and stayed in the building until about four in the morning.

6 January 2021 was one of the darkest days in modern American history. It was the first time that the US Capitol building had been breached since the early 1800s, when it was burned during a war with the British. Trump supporters, some of whom were carrying swastikas[3] or wearing shirts that said things like 'Camp Auschwitz',[4] were rampaging through lawmakers' offices, smashing windows and stealing things. One police officer was bludgeoned to death with a fire hydrant; another was crushed against a door. A thirty-four-year-old woman participating in the riot was trampled to death by her fellow mob. 'She's dying!' her friend yelled. But rioters kept stampeding over her.

Had the people storming the Capitol been Muslims scream-ing *Allahu Akbar*, Fox News would have never shut up about the incident; they'd have demanded a stricter Muslim ban. Had the people storming the Capitol been African-Americans chanting 'Black Lives Matter', they'd have been shot *en masse*. The incident would have been talked about like another 9/11. People would never forget. But because the majority of the rioters were white Trump-supporters the insurrection was quickly glossed over by conservative media outlets and Republican politicians. *Let's move on,* the message was. *Let's forget about that little bit of nastiness. You're over-reacting, it wasn't that bad.*

Ocasio-Cortez did not want to just move on. One of the men arrested for allegedly storming the Capitol had previously tweeted 'Assassinate AOC'. If the rioters had found her, they were not just going to sit her down and have a polite chat over tea and biscuits. They would have quite literally torn her apart. And yet people kept telling her that she was over-reacting.

AOC wasn't having that. She wasn't going to be gaslit. So, on a Monday evening on 1 February 2021, almost a month after the insurrection, AOC went on Instagram Live to share her story. 'My story is one of many stories of what happened in the Capitol,' she stressed at the beginning of a ninety-minute livestream that was watched by over 140,000 people. 'There were food-service workers there that were afraid for their lives. There were custodial workers that had to clean up after the wreckage of white supremacists, and many of those workers were Black and brown and immigrants.' Her story wasn't the most important part of that day, but she wanted to share it because many of the people who helped facilitate the attack were now denying all responsibility. They were telling every-one to move on while dodging all accountability. And she was not having that.

Ocasio-Cortez's voice started shaking at that point and she apologized in advance to loved ones who were going to learn something about her they hadn't known before. 'The reason I'm getting emotional in this moment is because these folks who tell us to move on, that it's not a big deal, that we should forget what's happened, these are the same tactics of abusers,' Ocasio-Cortez said. 'I'm a survivor of sexual assault. And I haven't told many people that in my life. But when we go through trauma, trauma compounds on each other.'

When you go through trauma, AOC continued, people are constantly trying to tell you that you didn't experience what you experienced. 'If you are a survivor of abuse or neglect or verbal abuse or sexual assault, you know there's the trauma of going through what you went through and then there's the trauma afterwards of people not believing you or trying to publicly humiliate you or trying to embarrass you.' And so you internalize all that shame because a lot of times you don't want to believe that happened to you either. But, AOC said, admitting that you've been through trauma is a really important first step towards healing. She'd really struggled with telling her story, she said, she'd thought about all the things people would say: oh, she's making it about her; oh, it wasn't a big deal. But she'd decided she had to tell it. She had to take control of her own narrative. She wouldn't let the abusers win.

Another well-known tactic of abusers is turning themselves into the victim and acting like you're the abusive one. Which, AOC noted, is exactly what the Republicans were doing. Just that week, fourteen Republicans had written a self-righteous letter to house speaker Nancy Pelosi[5] demanding that AOC apologize for accusing Republican Ted Cruz, who had challenged the election results, thus helping incite the crowds, of attempted murder. AOC had been tweeting about stock-market manipulation and Cruz tweeted that he agreed with her. 'You almost had me murdered three weeks ago so you can sit this one out,' she retorted. This was beyond the pale for Republicans: in their universe, inciting actual violence is no big deal – but calling that violence out is just not on.

These are the tactics that abusers use, AOC repeated. 'I'm not gonna let it happen to me again. I'm not gonna let it happen to the other people who've been victimized by this situation again.' Speaking out about this wasn't easy, she said. As a survivor of sexual assault, she struggled with the fact that she might not be believed. Particularly since Republicans were constantly calling her untruthful or saying she exaggerated. But, she said, she was telling everyone this story because it is supremely important to hold people accountable. If you don't hold people accountable for the wrongs they've done, then they will just go ahead and do it again. Ted Cruz and other politicians who challenged the election results, like Senator Josh Hawley, had had almost a month to apologize for their role in inciting violence that day. But they'd just brushed it off. So what did that tell her? It told her those people would do it all again and that they remained a danger to their colleagues.

That's why we need accountability. Accountability is not about revenge or getting back at people. It's about creating safety. And we are not safe when people who hold positions of power are willing to endanger the lives of others if they think it will score them a political point.

Everything Ocasio-Cortez said she was afraid was going to happen if she shared her story happened. She was called a liar and a hysterical narcissist by her detractors. Fox's Kim Klacik suggested AOC had just made it all up for money. One of AOC's colleagues, Nancy Mace, similarly said the congresswoman had made the whole thing up. (Numerous fact checks showed she hadn't.) 'This is a masterclass in emotional manipulation – a genuine political/rhetorical skill. Gotta hand it to her,' wrote journalist and Twitter personality Michael Tracey.

You do 'gotta hand it to her'. That ninety-minute livestream was a masterclass not in manipulation, but in the power of intimacy. What do I mean by intimacy? Not hugs and kisses, obviously, but rather a more human, more vulnerable style of leadership. Intimacy means not being afraid to let people see the real you. It means not being afraid to appear imperfect or reveal your vulnerabilities. It means not shedding your humanity at the office door. Intimacy isn't a word that you usually associate with the traditional authoritarian leadership model; leaders are supposed to be strong and not reveal their vulnerabilities. Particularly if you're a woman, of course. In the past, female leaders have often had to overcompensate so as not to seem like the 'weaker' sex. See 'Iron Lady' Margaret Thatcher for the most obvious example.

Thankfully, however, things are beginning to change. AOC exemplifies a powerful new style of intimate and authentic leadership both men and women are beginning to lean in to. Instead of loftily standing on top of a pedestal, she forges a more one-to-one connection with the people she represents. Instead of seeing vulnerability as a weakness, she recognizes it can be a strength. Instead of trying to act like society's vision of a leader, she gets real.

Have the courage to be vulnerable

A few days after her livestream, AOC organized a special event where lawmakers could share their own experience of the attack on the Capitol. Rashida Tlaib hadn't been there on 6 January, but in a speech on the House floor, she explained how scared she'd been to watch things unfold from afar. She also shared what it was like to live in constant fear of her life because there were people who couldn't stand the fact she is a Muslim.

'On my very first day of orientation, I got my first death threat,' she said. 'It was a serious one. They took me aside, the FBI. I didn't even get sworn in yet and someone wanted me dead for just existing. More came later. Uglier, more violent.' The congresswoman from Michigan shared how some threats had mentioned her son by name and how one celebrated the mosque massacre in New Zealand where fifty-one people were killed by a white supremacist.

'Each one paralysed me,' Tlaib said. 'So what happened on January 6th, all I could do was thank Allah that I wasn't here.'

Getting more emotional, she said: 'The trauma for just being here and existing as a Muslim is so hard.' And not just because she was worried about her own safety but because she was worried about the safety of her diverse group of staff. As she said this, Tlaib began to cry.

There was a time when crying on the job might have been the end of your career or irreversibly damaged your image. In 1972, for example, Maine senator Edmund Muskie was the frontrunner for the Democratic presidential nomination. His presidential chances were dashed, however, when he shed tears at a press conference where he accused a newspaper of writing nasty things about his wife (the newspaper said she liked drinking and telling jokes, which was apparently very scandalous). Muskie went to his grave insisting that he hadn't been crying, it was just snowflakes melting on his face, but the 'watershed incident', as it was called, seemed to seal his political fate.

Former Colorado congresswoman Pat Schroeder, meanwhile, is famous for breaking down in tears in 1987 when she announced that she wouldn't be seeking the Democratic nomination for president. 'Women across the country reacted with embarrassment, sympathy and disgust,' the *Chicago Tribune* wrote a week later. In 2007 Schroeder told *USA Today* that women are still writing to her to criticize her for it. 'I want to say, "Wait a minute, we are talking about twenty years ago." It's like I ruined their lives, twenty years ago, with three seconds of catching my breath.'

Crying hasn't always been seen as a sign of weakness. According to Tom Lutz, the author of *Crying: The Natural and Cultural History of Tears*, eighteenth-century upper-class men frequently cried, and were 'viewed as brutes if they didn't'. Norms change, and crying has made a comeback. Obama cried at least five times in office. David Cameron cried while being praised by William Hague and when he resigned after the Brexit vote. Even Vladimir Putin has cried. Crying (under the correct circumstances) is now an established piece of the PR toolkit: leaders see it as a handy way to help humanize themselves. Unless you're Donald Trump, that is. 'When I see a man cry I view it as a weakness,' Trump has said. 'The last time I cried was when I was a baby,' he told *People* magazine in 2015.[6]

The pandemic has made getting in touch with your feelings

even more acceptable. In April 2020 CNN host Brian Stelter tweeted[7] that he had 'crawled in bed and cried for our pre-pandemic lives. Tears that had been waiting a month to escape. I wanted to share because it feels freeing to do so. Now is not a time for faux-invincibility.' He later said: 'I think I'd be worried about anyone who *hasn't* teared up in the last month.' And, with the exception of Trump, a lot of politicians did. Mark Meadows, Trump's chief of staff, repeatedly cried in front of staffers. Charlie Baker, the Republican governor of Massachusetts, broke down multiple times while discussing the pandemic. Then again, he is famous for crying. His daughter has said he's the 'guy that cries over *Extreme Makeover: Home Edition*.'[8] Over in the UK, health secretary Matt Hancock looked like he was trying to shed a tear on *Good Morning Britain* as he watched an eighty-one-year-old named William Shakespeare become the first man in the world to get a coronavirus vaccine. Hancock was widely suspected of faking the waterworks, which shows you just how mainstream crying has become.

The fact that it has become more acceptable for leaders to cry is a positive thing. However, it doesn't need to be said that cynically shedding a tear in the hope of good PR isn't the same as demonstrating vulnerability. Vulnerability means speaking from the heart and not being afraid to show your authentic self – which is what Tlaib did that. Leaders who are able to do that can create deeper and more meaningful connections; they don't need PR stunts to humanize them.

Jacinda Ardern is a case in point. You remember Jacinda Ardern's reaction after mass shootings at two mosques in Christchurch left fifty dead and forty injured in 2018, don't you? There's an iconic image of her wearing a headscarf to visit a mosque; genuine grief is etched all over her face and her hands are clasped tightly together. Her reaction to the massacre won her praise worldwide. Here was a leader who was not afraid to quickly label the attacks 'terrorism'. Here was a leader who was not afraid to call an Australian politician's disgusting suggestion of a link between Muslim immigration and violence 'a disgrace'. Here was a leader who respectfully donned a hijab and gave heartfelt hugs to members of New Zealand's Muslim population. Here was a leader who was not afraid to speak from her heart. Here was a leader who said to New Zealand's Muslims: 'you are us!' Most importantly, here was a leader who actually meant it. And here was a leader who matched her grief with action: who promised to introduce new gun measures in Parliament immediately.

We're used to hearing stirring speeches from our leaders. We're used to hearing them say all the right words and promise to do all the right things. We're used to seeing a little tear now and again. But we're not used to seeing them actually *feel*. You're not used to seeing grief like that written all over their face. The response to Ardern's handling of the Christchurch massacre isn't just a testament to her leadership, it demonstrates how hungry we all are to see that kind of empathetic leadership. How hungry we all are to see a world leader act like a real human with real feelings. While empathy and vulnerability are not synonyms, you need the latter to have the former.

It should be said, of course, that there's such a thing as being too vulnerable. It's called the 'pratfall effect': if people already think you're a bit of an idiot and then you make yourself vulnerable, they will think less of you. Vulnerability only humanizes you when people already have a high opinion of you or when you've already established your credentials. Had AOC only been a congresswoman for a week when she made that that ninety-minute livestream, for example, it probably wouldn't have had quite the same effect. Had Tlaib been a new congresswoman when she cried, people might not have viewed it as quite so powerful. And had Ardern cried over the mosque attack but not matched her emotion with action, she could have been accused of crocodile tears.

Tlaib's tears following the Capitol riots and Ardern's grief after the Christchurch massacre are both examples of vulnerability following extreme events; they're examples of leaders who have the courage to respond to tragedy with humanity rather than with machismo. Vulnerability can be a lot more banal, however. It can simply be a matter of sharing personal stories and experiences with people in order to connect with them on a more individual level. An analysis of the Twitter conversations of business leaders suggests women seem to do this more naturally than men. The analysis found female leaders share their personal stories and journey at a 26% higher rate than male leaders, and are substantially more likely to post using first person singular qualifiers like 'I' or 'me'. When using first person plural qualifiers like 'we' or 'our', men are also more likely to be referring to society as a whole whereas women are using it to share anecdotes and announcements about the companies they lead.

use of first person pronouns

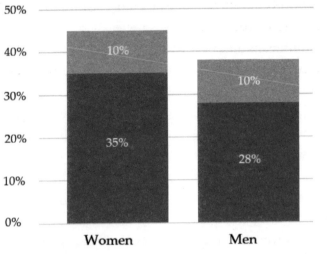

■ first person singular (I, me, etc.)   ■ first person plural (we, our, etc.)

Don't mistake informality for intimacy

We've all been there. You get home after a long day and rifle through the fridge looking for sustenance. Weirdly a magic food fairy hasn't loaded your shelves with gourmet meals; there's just a sad bowl of week-old leftovers that smells like it might give you listeria.

AOC found herself in that situation shortly after becoming a new congresswoman. After getting back home to the Bronx after Congress's new-member orientation in 2018, she opened her fridge to find some old mac and cheese. Should she eat it, she quizzed her then 800,000 Instagram followers (as of March 2021 she's got 8.9 million)? Or should she throw it away? Don't risk it, her followers advised, so she ate some noodles instead.

We've all become familiar with how Ocasio-Cortez uses social media to chat directly with her followers but, at the time, it was novel enough to make headlines. Congressmembers just didn't do that sort of thing – or at least they didn't do it very well. Politicians and new media tended to be an awkward combination or feel forced and unnatural, but AOC excels at using the internet to demystify her life as a congresswoman. Her use of new media platforms to connect directly with people has been compared to President Franklin D. Roosevelt's famous fireside chats in the 1930s and 40s; she has a way of making you feel like you're sitting opposite her, having a chat with a friend you've known for ever. One Sunday night over 4,000 people watched AOC make Instant Pot black bean soup on Instagram Live; she chopped chipotle peppers and chatted politics and policy, answering questions about things like the federal jobs guarantee. When she arrived in Washington DC for her first week in Congress, she took her followers along for the ride, showing them the 'secret underground tunnels' that connect congressional buildings and chatting with them on Instagram Live while she did laundry in a coin-operated machine.[9] 'Congressional life getting off to a glamorous start,' she joked, before adding that nobody tells you that being in politics means 'your clothes are stinky' because you're always running around.

So what's the lesson here? Poll people on your mouldy leftovers and do your laundry on Instagram? Not exactly. It's important not to confuse informality with intimacy. Donald Trump, for example, used social media like no other head of state has ever done. He used Twitter to speak directly to people in his own idiosyncratic voice; it was completely unfiltered and very informal. But it was never intimate. He spoke (OR

RATHER YELLED) at you, using Twitter as a megaphone rather than a telephone. Trump's use of social media felt like being in a bar with an angry, albeit charismatic drunk. AOC's use of social media is like sitting in your living room chatting to a friend who is telling you about her exciting new job.

A lot of politicians have tried (and mostly failed) to replicate the way AOC uses social media. Remember Beto O'Rourke, for example? The guy who was a Democratic darling for a while and ran for the Democratic 2020 primaries? In 2019, in the midst of the primaries, he decided it would be a really great idea to livestream his trip to the dentist. (I mean, seriously, dude?) Viewers were treated to extreme close-ups of his mouth interspersed with questions he asks his dental hygienist, Diana, about her experiences growing up in El Paso near the US–Mexico border. A quick sample of the coverage that followed this weird stunt? 'Beto O'Rourke Instagrams his trip to the dentist, and people hate it,' the *San Francisco Chronicle*'s headline read.[10] 'Beto O'Rourke's Instagram of dentist visit prompts oversharing concerns,' MarketWatch wrote. The general consensus was that this was taking things way too far.

The difference between AOC polling people on her leftovers and O'Rourke's dentist visit is that the former feels like you're getting an exclusive invite into the unglamorous bits of a glamorous person's life and the latter feels like you're watching a stunt. I won't just pick on men here. Elizabeth Warren is also an example of a politician who has stumbled on social media. Shortly after announcing she was running for president in the 2020 Democratic primary, Warren did an Instagram livestream from her family kitchen on New Year's Eve. 'Hold on a sec, I'm gonna get me a beer,' she said midstream. The moment was widely panned as awkward and inauthentic. Some of the brouhaha over Warren's beer may have been down to sexism – pretty much everything she did was deemed 'unlikeable'. Nevertheless, the moment felt forced. It felt a little too much like she was leaning into the male-centric playbook that a president ought to be someone you'd like to have a beer with, rather than really being herself. Instagram Live also probably doesn't come naturally to Warren in the same way that it does to AOC. I think there's an idea now that you have to use social media to connect with people, but intimacy can be cultivated in far more analogue, and far more formal, ways.

Madeleine Albright is a case in point. (Some trivia I can't resist: Albright's first 'serious job' was when she was thirty-nine and worked for then-Senator Ed Muskie as his chief legislative assistant. He's the guy who pretended he wasn't crying, he just had snow on his face.) Anyway, Instagram wasn't around when Albright served as the first female US Secretary of State from 1997 to 2001 under President Bill Clinton. Instead, she was famous for communicating through a very different sort of visual platform: jewellery. Throughout her diplomatic career, Albright used pins (brooches) to indicate her mood and opinions – when people asked her what she was thinking, she'd say 'read my pins'.

I'm not able to read Albright's pin when I call her up for an interview, as we're using old-fashioned phone technology rather than video-conferencing; however, she helpfully describes this one for me. Today she's wearing a pin shaped in the letter V. Alas, this is not in my honour but because she's doing a talk later and the 'V' stands for victory over the coronavirus. There's a long history behind that V, she tells me. Her family spent World War II in London; her dad, the diplomat Josef Korbel, was a Czechoslovakian diplomat working for the government in exile. During the Blitz, they'd go down to the cellar of the Notting Hill house they were staying in, which backed on to Portobello Road – all of them crowded in the cellar except her dad, who was busy writing broadcasts for the BBC. They'd listen to those broadcasts – 'I used to think my father was in the radio' – and every one began with the opening motif of Beethoven's Fifth played on drums. That iconic opening was an important symbol for Allied forces. The short–short–short–long (da-da-da-DUM) rhythm of Beethoven's Fifth corresponded in Morse code to the letter V for victory. It was a symbol of solidarity and hope. Winston Churchill famously also used to make the 'V' hand gesture as a sign of resistance and victory – although sometimes he did it with his palms facing inwards, which means something a lot ruder. He was informed of this but continued to do it anyway.

Albright didn't deliberately set out to start wearing symbols on her chest. 'The pins were an accident, frankly,' she says.

What happened was that I was sent to the United Nations in 1993. And it was the end of the Gulf War, and the cease-fire had been translated into a series of sanctions resolutions. I was the ambassador and so I said terrible things about Saddam Hussein constantly. There was a poem in the papers in Baghdad comparing me to many things, but among them an unparalleled serpent. And, by chance, I had a snake pin and I started wearing the snake pin when we talked about Iraq and then the journalist asked about it.

'This is fun,' she thought, why not do more of it? She was living in New York at the time and went out to buy a bunch of costume jewelry to depict what she was doing as Secretary of State.

> So on good days, I wore flowers and butterflies and balloons, and on bad days, I wore carnivorous animals and spiders. And the ambassadors noticed. And they'd say: What are we gonna do today? And I would say: Read my pins. And that's how the whole thing started. I had a lot of fun with that.'[11]

Because it's associated with women, jewellery is often thought of as something frivolous. But instead of trying to hide that aspect of herself, Albright used it to talk about foreign policy in a more intimate way. 'I love being a woman,' she says. 'I love getting my hair done and wearing my pins and at the same time delivering some pretty tough messages.' Intimacy doesn't have to be touchy-feely. It's about creating a closeness. In Albright's case this was in the form of a visual language you were invited to decode. It was a way of bringing you into a process that normally felt shut off and difficult to understand.

Humour is another way of doing this. However, again, there's a big difference between informality and intimacy when it comes to humour. Elon Musk, for example, is famous for his use of memes on social media and for having the sense of humour of a twelve-year-old boy. The naming conventions for Tesla's cars, for example, are a sex joke. First came the Model S, then the Model X, then the Model 3 (Ford threatened to sue Musk over a Model E so it became a Model 3). Musk finds this hilarious and has made the same sex joke multiple times. His humour has helped him create a loyal fanbase of dudes who think he is hilarious, but I wouldn't classify this as creating intimacy. Instead of using humour to bring people in, Musk uses it to shut people out. It's him and his band of fanboys against everyone else.

By contrast, it's worth looking at how Mary Robinson has been trying to use humour to fight the climate crisis. Robinson co-hosts a podcast on the climate crisis, Mothers of Invention, with Maeve Higgins, a young Irish comedian and writer. The show shines a spotlight on women of colour and indigenous women around the world who are implementing solutions in their own communities; it's not a comedy show but it injects levity into a serious issue. One of Robinson's big regrets, she tells me, is that she didn't use the power of comedy earlier in her career. 'I've always had a good sense of humour. But I didn't use humour all that much, especially as President, because I was too overawed by the responsibility.' She looks back now at her big speeches to the Houses of Parliament and cringes. 'The tone is so preachy. And there's no self-depreca-tion, no humour whatsoever. I'd never do that now.'[12]

When Robinson is asked for advice now she always says, 'Learn the power of humour.' Well, she clarifies: if it's a very young person, you know a thirteen- or fifteen-year-old, I'd say, "Don't be afraid to interrupt: it may be the only way to get your voice heard." But for the older woman who's already successful, I say: "Learn to use humour, it can be very power-ful." And it shows how relaxed you are about being in the posi-tion you're in.' Creating intimacy with humour doesn't mean making infantile sex jokes, it means breaking down barriers and bringing people in.

10

Pass the Mic

The worst boss I ever had, back when I was a trainee solicitor at a corporate law firm, was a woman. She (I'll call her Evil Boss) would give me little pep talks about how I shouldn't wear make-up to work if I wanted people to take me seriously. She advised me, in the interest of 'female solidarity', to never leave the office at 7 p.m., even if I had nothing to do, and just sit alone in the office and read case law all night. She'd often tell me that maybe I'd be better suited to marketing instead of law – and she made very clear this was an insult. I tried, somewhat unsuccessfully, not to take all of this personally. She was clearly scarred at the sexism she'd encountered rising up the ranks in a male-dominated industry and at times it felt to me like she was determined that everyone else should suffer like she had. Partly because of that experience, I ended up depressed, doubting myself, and leaving law. I went into . . . marketing.

You probably know Evil Boss pretty well. Not personally, I mean, but you know her type. The female boss who hates other women is a well-known stereotype. The stereotype is so ingrained that study after study shows both men and women prefer male bosses. Indeed, women are more likely to say that they prefer a male boss than men are. In a 2011 study on the issue that analysed responses from 60,000 people, participants characterized female bosses as 'emotional', 'catty', or 'bitchy'.

Of course, there are some female bosses who act in toxic ways to other women. But do you know where these types of women tend to be clustered? Male-dominated places like the old law firm I worked at. (And, for the record, most of the senior women I worked with at that law firm were very pleasant to work with.) A researcher called Robin Ely, who is now a business professor at Harvard, has done extensive research[1] into why some women are so bad to work for. She found that women in overwhelmingly male companies tended not to support each other. When it feels like there is only room for one woman to succeed, you lean into the patriarchy and turn on your competition. And it's not just women who do this, studies have shown minorities can do this too.

While there are certainly some women who aren't great to work for, there are also plenty of men who aren't brilliant bosses. The stereotype that women don't help each other and are terrible to work for is incredibly unfair. Much of it is down to sexism and the higher standards we hold women to. Research shows that people are three times more likely to associate giving praise[2] with female managers and twice as likely to associate critical comments with male managers. We expect women to be nice all the time and so, when they are assertive or critical, we punish them for it. Criticism by a woman leads to larger drop in job satisfaction than criticism from a man. Perhaps I was guilty of that myself to some degree when it came to Evil Boss. Internalized misogyny, eh? It's a real bitch.

The worst boss I've ever had may have been a woman, but the best boss I've ever had has also been a woman. She went out of her way to mentor me and find me opportunities. She ensured I always got credit for my work, made me feel valued, and gave me a lot of confidence. She also realized that staying in the office all night doesn't make you a better employee and taking time off was important. Even after I left that job, she continued to support my career. Most of the women I've worked with have been a lot more like my brilliant boss than they have my evil boss.

We need to push back against the stereotype of the catty female boss. While there are certainly toxic female leaders out there, plenty of data shows that women are better at developing talent[3] and motivating others than men are. And that matters, because working to develop and promote other people may be the most important and underrated leadership skill there is. Effective leaders demonstrate all the qualities we've looked at so far: they build trust, they avoid ego, they collaborate. But above all else the most effective leaders don't create followers, they create other leaders. They don't need to always hog the spotlight; they let other people shine. That point has been somewhat lost in our authoritarian model of leadership, which fetishizes individual achievement. It's also been minimized in a lot of the discussion around female leadership, which has focused on self-empowerment and told women that success means raising your voice and taking up space. However, real leadership isn't about being the loudest voice in the room, it's about being secure enough in yourself to pass the mic to others. Real leadership isn't about taking up space, it's about knowing when to yield it.

Knock down the barriers to power

There's an anecdote from the Obama era that you see in a lot of books and articles about women and leadership. You may be familiar with it, but if you're not, it goes like this. When Obama took office, two-thirds of his top aides were men. The women in his circle had a hard time getting a word in edge-ways during meetings because men constantly talked over them and took credit for their ideas. So they came up with a strategy they called 'amplification': when one woman said something important, other women in the room would repeat that point and give credit to that woman. It meant that women's voices were heard more and they were acknowledged for their contributions. Obama reportedly noticed and started calling on women more and, during Obama's second term, there were just as many women as men in the president's inner circle.

It's a great example of how women can strategically lift each other up, I don't deny that. However, I want to be clear that passing the mic doesn't just mean elevating people in your inner circle. Corporate feminism has created a bunch of alter-natives to the old boy's network: powerful women can gather together in fancy women-only member clubs so they can crack the glass ceiling together. There's nothing wrong with that *per se*. However, when it comes to female leadership there's been far more focus on women building their own private elite spaces rather than knocking down exclusionary barriers to make power more inclusive. The Squad, however, have been very deliberate at doing the latter rather than the former. They've made clear that they're not a clique intent only on advancing each other's careers, they're working to bring more outsiders into insider-only places. And, again, that goes beyond superficial 'diversity.' It's not about peppering the halls with diverse faces, but amplifying diverse voices. Not because it's the politically correct thing to do, but because it raises the bar when it comes to leadership. It's often said that talent is equally distributed, but opportunity is not. Great leaders recognize that and get rid of the barriers that stop the best talent from rising to the top.

While the people at the top love to think we live in a meritocracy, our systems are currently set up so that it isn't actually the best rising to the top, often it's people who are funnelled through established pipelines to power. In American politics, that pipeline tends to involve an Ivy League education; when Joe Biden was inaugurated in 2021, he became the first US president without an Ivy League education to hold office since Ronald Reagan's election in November 1980. Joe Biden and Kamala Harris were also the first presidential ticket without an Ivy League education in forty-four years. While an Ivy League education ups your chance of getting into politics, being born into a political family is your best route to power. You are 8,500 times more likely to become a senator if your dad is one.

In Britain, the pipelines to power have long been Eton and Oxbridge. Twenty of the UK's heads of government went to Eton. Boris Johnson is the fifth Eton-educated PM since 1945 and one third of the UK's fifteen prime ministers since 1945 are Old Etonians. Twenty-eight British Prime Ministers went to Oxford (thirteen were educated at Christ Church). Fourteen British Prime Ministers went to Cambridge (six went to Trinity College). Not everyone surrounding the Prime Minister might have gone to Eton, but there is a very good chance they went to private school. While only 7% of people in Britain went to private schools, two-thirds of Boris Johnson's cabinet were privately educated;[4] ministers in Johnson's cabinet are nine times more likely to have attended a fee-paying school for all or part of their secondary education than the general population. Of the thirty-three ministers making up

Johnson's cabinet in 2019, 45% were Oxbridge-educated; a further 24% attended Russell Group universities. In the House of Commons, 24% of MPs attended Oxford or Cambridge. If you think that sounds bad, it's not as bad as it was. 91% of Margaret Thatcher's 1979 cabinet had been to a fee-paying school.

The system isn't just designed so that the same sort of people get into power, it's also designed to keep the same people in power. One US example of this is the massive advantage that you have if you are an incumbent. Sitting members of Congress are almost always re-elected, thanks to visibility, experience campaigning and a campaign bank account. That means the party behind them doesn't have much interest in encouraging fresh blood. In March 2018 the Democratic Congressional Campaign Committee (DCCC), the campaign and fundraising arm of the Democratic Party, essentially formalized this policy with a 'blacklist'. It announced that it wouldn't work with political vendors – e.g. ad agencies, political consultancies, direct mail companies – that work with candidates challenging incumbent Democrats. Their rationale for this was that they wanted to keep control of Congress and they thought the best way to do this was to protect incumbents. This – excuse me while I use some political jargon – completely screwed over some of the new people running. Marie Newman, a progressive who was challenging Dan Lipinksi,[5] an eight-term Illinois congressman who took his dad's old seat in Congress, said that the new rule was preventing her from running her campaign properly. She had a bunch of pollsters, consultants and mail firms leave because they didn't want to get backlisted. Newman being sidelined was a big deal; Lipinski may have been a Democrat but he was what is known in

America as a 'moderate Democrat', which is what is known in most Western countries as an anti-abortion right-winger. Newman had also only narrowly lost against him when running in 2018 with pretty much zero name recognition. There was a real chance to change things with Lipinski, but instead of supporting her the DCCC seemed more interested in keeping a guy who was basically a Republican in power.

The Squad very quickly spoke out about this blacklist policy. Which, let's be clear, wasn't in their best interest. Since they all had jobs already protecting incumbents, the new policy protected them. However, AOC and Ayanna Pressley, who had both unseated incumbents, made it very clear that they didn't want to pull the ladder up behind them. AOC told her millions of followers to 'pause' donations to the DCCC and 'give directly to swing candidates instead'. Congressmembers are also expected to raise money and pay at least $15,000 a year in 'dues' to the DCCC to help it fund campaigns; AOC refused to do this. 'DCCC made clear that they will blacklist any org that helps progressive candidates like me,' Ocasio-Cortez tweeted. 'I can choose not to fund that kind of exclusion.' Instead, Ocasio-Cortez said that she would raise money for candidates herself and that she had raised over $300,000 for other candidates. She later formed a political action committee to help fundraise for progressive primary candidates.

Ayanna Pressley also spoke out on Twitter. 'The fact that I challenged an incumbent meant a lot of folks were told not to come anywhere near my campaign,' she explained. Without people who were willing to take a risk and go against the status quo, there was a big chance she would never have got into Congress.[6] 'If the DCCC enacts this policy to blacklist vendors who work with challengers, we risk undermining an entire universe of potential candidates and vendors – especially women and people of color – whose ideas, energy, and innovation need a place in our party.' Pressley explained that she wouldn't be airing all this on Twitter if people in the DCCC had been listening to their concerns, but they weren't. 'When a candidate takes the risk to run, Democrats should not be in the practice of creating litmus tests or roadblocks that have a chilling effect on new candidates or those who would invest their sweat equity in support,' she said.[7]

You know what's really funny about the DCCC blacklist policy? It was part of a document they were going to tout as a brilliant diversity initiative. The DCCC had created a new form for political vendors that set out a few ground rules and policies. One was that you couldn't work with primary challengers. Another was that the DCCC would prioritize businesses with non-white, women or LGBTQ owners. The document is a perfect representation of how superficial most 'diversity' initiatives are. We'll pass you the mic, it says, if you promise to parrot exactly what we want to hear. We want a few token women and brown people in the room so we don't look racist, but we don't want to do anything meaningful to actually disrupt the status quo and increase access to our elite little club.

You know what happens when you push for meaningful diversity and inclusion? You get accused of being disruptive. A number of AOC's Democratic colleagues criticized her fundraising. Rep. Gregory W. Meeks, a congressman from New York, told Fox News that 'DCCC dues are about supporting others because you want to be part of the team.' It's such a disingenuous attitude. The message is: *be grateful you're part of the cool kids' club now and do as you're told.*

Instead of settling comfortably into the Establishment, the Squad have continued to ruffle feathers and advocate for change. In July 2020 the Squad launched The Squad Victory Fund, a joint committee to raise money to support each other and help other progressive candidates. 'We find ourselves in unprecedented times that call for unprecedented organizing, unprecedented mobilizing, and unprecedented legislating,' Pressley said in a written statement. 'Together, we'll continue to do the work of ensuring that those closest to the pain are closest to the power.' This isn't skin-deep diversity. This isn't the Squad focusing on electing other women of colour. The Squad promised to use their prominence to advance a core set of values, no matter what sort of body that came in. That's what real diversity looks like. Not more brown women who act the same as the white men who came before them, but people who lean into a very different sort of leadership and amplify the sort of voices that haven't traditionally been heard. That starts with looking around and realizing who isn't in the room and who isn't being represented.

Ask whose voices aren't being heard

'Why is she here?'

Amina Mohammed used to hear that question a lot. In the early stages of her career, she worked at an architectural design office in Nigeria; the men would look at her quizzically and make disparaging comments, wondering what a woman was doing in the office. They thought she couldn't understand the native languages, but she could.

Mohammed is a long way from that office now. She's the Deputy Secretary-General of the United Nations and, when we chat, she's sitting on the thirty-eighth floor of the UN building in New York. Talking to her, you don't get the impression she much cared if people asked why she was there: she just got on with it and showed them why she was there. When she was young, she had her heart set on studying hotel catering management in Italy and found the perfect place to do it. Her dad, however, wasn't convinced. No, he told her, you're going to university here in Nigeria. No, she replied, I'm going to Italy. Fine, he said, but you're not getting any money from me. Fine, she replied, I'll raise the money myself.

But how, exactly, was she going to raise the money? This was the 1970s. You couldn't just put a GoFundMe online. After giving it some thought, Amina decided she'd bet people that she could walk across Nigeria. "I felt that was better than asking people to give me money for my studies,' Mohammed tells me over Zoom. 'It was a challenge. "I bet you I can do this!", "No you can't!" "Put your money down!"'

People put their money down and the teenager enlisted a friend for the challenge. The pair woke up at 4 a.m. and set off to walk the 76 km from Kaduna to Zaria in Northern Nigeria. They hadn't done any training for their trip, nor had they considered exactly how safe their route was. There were, Mohammed recalls, some very dodgy stretches. About halfway on their trek her friend gave up, but she kept on going. At the end of it she got £4,000. 'And so off I went to Italy.'[8]

Mohammed has kept on going ever since. She worked with three Nigerian presidents on implementing the Millennium Development Goals; she was the Nigerian Minister of Environment; she advised former UN Secretary-General Ban Ki-moon on poverty and climate change; she led successful negotiations on the UN's Sustainable Development Goals, which aim to eradicate poverty by 2030; she is now one of the most powerful and respected diplomats in the world.

Nothing Mohammed has achieved was handed to her – she fought for it. And, along the way, she'd hear people ask 'Why is she here?' Now when the Deputy Secretary-General enters a room, she makes a point of looking around and asking a very different question: 'Who isn't here? Who aren't we listening to?' She also makes a point of regularly asking others in the room to take her spot at the head of the table and lead a discussion. I'll say: 'Can you come and take the chair? I'm not giving you my job, but I'm giving you the opportunity to see what it's like to head the table.' The people in her department have adopted the same practice, operating a rotating system so it's not always the team leader who is running a meeting. This isn't just a symbolic gesture, Mohammed stresses, it's done with purpose. 'Yielding space must be meaningful, you don't just do it for the sake of it. And sometimes people don't know what to do with the space you have given them. So you have to build their confidence and help them until they are comfortable.'

When you're in a hierarchical institution with established protocols, you also have to be OK with making others feel uncomfortable at times. Mohammed recalls an important UN event where she decided, at the last moment, to bring up a young person from the audience to share the stage with her. Spontaneity isn't really a feature of the United Nations, and Mohammed second-guessed herself for a moment. The Queen of Sweden was in the audience, she noted, and she remembers thinking: 'The Queen's going to go bonkers. Everybody's going to have a fit. All those things went through my mind in sixty seconds.' It would have been easier to just stick to protocol and deliver her speech as planned, but she brought the girl up on stage to speak anyway. 'Leadership demands that you should be able to share that space,' she stresses.

Making space for more voices isn't just the right thing to do; it makes you a better leader. 'Of course you're going to benefit from what comes from voices you haven't heard,' Mohammed says. 'If you're smart, you'll know that you don't have a monopoly of knowledge. And so therefore the more voices you have, the more powerful you will be in helping to lead on the issues. We need to lean forward and share in leadership; not see it as something that, once you get it, you hang on to for dear life.'

Listening to more voices also helps keep you grounded, stops you becoming out of touch. It stops you becoming the sort of leader you disdained when you were at the bottom of the pecking order. 'I've been in the audience, I've been in the crowd for a very long time,' Mohammed says. 'And when you get to the pulpit, you had better remember what was said in the crowd.'

Passing the mic isn't just about sharing space, it's about learning to listen. Which is something women in general, not just Mohammed, tend to be pretty good at. Women, broadly speaking, excel at 'active listening': they don't just passively *hear* what someone is saying, they're also analysing their body language and facial expressions, they're figuring out what they're not saying. Active listening means you're not just dashing off a draft of your reply as the other person talks, you're really thinking about what the other person is saying. Much of the conversation around women in leadership has focused on telling women to speak up; really we should be telling men to listen.

One reason women might be better at listening is because we tend to have a lot of practice at it. We're not really used to holding court uninterrupted, so we're more eager to listen to others. A study conducted in the 1990s found that when women head legislative committees, they're likely to call more witnesses, allow more debate and permit more committee discussions than men heading similar committees. Like Mohammed, they're more likely to ask who isn't in the room and bring in other voices.

Finally . . . for the love of god (who's a woman, obvs) let's stop talking about 'empowerment'

During the occasional fit of procrastination (to which I am prone), I consider Googling my Evil Boss. I've managed to resist the temptation, but I like to think she's talking about female empowerment and has changed and is in fact very nice now. However, I do have a theory that the more people bang on about 'empowerment', the less interested they are in actually changing the face of power.

What exactly does empowerment mean anyway? To some extent, corporate feminism and self-help culture have turned empowerment into a commodity. *Buy this shampoo, it'll empower you! Buy this car, it'll empower you! Buy this self-help book, it'll empower you!* Society's vision of an Empowered Woman™ is basically an upper-middle-class white woman who ticks all the conventional metrics of success. She's well-groomed, has a lot of money, a high-powered job, a perfect family, and she makes time for mindfulness and green juice. The Empowered Woman buys herself expensive things *because she's worth it.* Of course, the Empowered Woman is not selfish; she also donates money to those poor unempowered women in developing countries.

Empowerment culture isn't just a sneaky way of getting women to buy more scented candles, though. It's a lot more insidious than that: it's often a way of reinforcing current power structures. The thing about the word 'empowerment' is that it means someone *giving* you power or enabling you; it suggests that you are somehow incapable of helping yourself. The conversation around women in leadership, Amina Mohammed tells me forcefully, is incredibly patronizing.

> The condescending nature with which we are welcomed into that arena of leadership is a narrative we have to change. People need to understand that women in leadership is an asset. There's still this sort of idea that it's something that is graciously bestowed upon us. But you know what? Power is never given, it's taken.

Want a perfect example of the condescending attitudes towards women in leadership? In early 2021, Japan's ruling Liberal Democratic party (LDP) benevolently decided to allow a few women into its meetings. Japan had just suffered a bout of embarrassing PR after the head of Tokyo's Olympic organizing committee had claimed meetings with too many women tended to 'drag on' because they talked too much. The LDP's secretary general decided that the perfect damage-control move[9] would be too announce that it would invite small groups of women to its meetings – on the condition that they didn't say anything. Men expecting applause for inviting women to sit silently in a room with them pretty much sums up what 'empowerment' really is. While the LDP's empowerment tactics made international news, this sort of attitude is so widespread it's rarely even remarked upon. I give talks about diversity to companies sometimes; at one of these talks, to a big tech company in San Jose, this guy stood up at the end to announce to the room (which was 98% male) that he'd just hired a woman. I honestly think he wanted me to applaud him for it. What benevolence: a guy like him giving a feeble woman a chance.

The reason there's this patronizing approach to female leadership is that a lot of people still think that women simply don't have the qualities required for leadership. Corporate feminism doesn't think women have the qualities required for leadership. It has told women that *empowerment* means leading like a man. It has told women 'feminine' qualities are weaknesses rather than strengths; empowerment means doing power poses, speaking loudly, competing rather than collaborating; it means never saying sorry. Corporate feminism will pass you the mic (and it will be a very expensive pink mic) but tell you to speak from the script that a man wrote; it's the only way to guard your power and you earned this, queen!

A new generation of female leaders are roundly rejecting this. They're not sitting around waiting to be *empowered*, they're redefining what power looks like. 'We never need to ask for permission or wait for an invitation to lead,' Ilhan Omar of Minnesota responded in a 2019 panel[10] when she was asked what she would say to women of colour who are frustrated by comments that seek to minimize their impact. 'There's a constant struggle oftentimes with people who have power about sharing that power. We are not really in the business of asking for the share of that power; we're in the business of trying to grab that power and return it to the people.' That desire to share power rather than to hoard it? That's what real leadership looks like.

Conclusion

Woman Up – why this decade is crucial

Remember the sperm from the prologue? Well, nature and science eventually did its thing and my partner and I will have a little girl by the time you're reading this. I've never been a natural optimist (I don't just see the glass half-empty, I moan about how I really don't like the glass and I wish I'd been given another one), but when you spend so much time and money trying to procreate you are forced into optimism. You stay up all night wondering if you're doing the right thing and thinking about the kind of world you're bringing your hypothetical child into. If you don't find a way to conclude that the world isn't in such dire straits after all then you'd have to conclude that your decision to procreate makes you a monster. And nobody wants to think they're a monster.

So, cognitive dissonance aside, why am I optimistic? Because I think we're seeing a fundamental – and fundamentally important – shift in how we think about leadership. First, we're seeing the global rise of decentralized protest movements demanding systemic change. From Chile to Lebanon to France to the United States, we've seen the rise of massive movements that don't have a single charismatic figurehead, but are truly people-powered. These are sometimes described as 'leaderless'. In 2019, for example, the Center for Strategic and International Studies, an influential think-tank, published a piece declaring that we were in an 'Age of Leaderless Revolution.'[1] In 2020 the *New York Times* published a piece with the headline 'Today's Activism: Spontaneous, Leaderless, but Not Without Aim'.[2] But these movements aren't leaderless. They are, as the three women who kickstarted Black Lives Matter – Patrisse Cullors, Alicia Garza and Opal Tometi – have repeatedly said, 'leader-full'. There isn't one single charismatic leader at the helm dictating the direction of the movement and bossing people around, there are lots of leaders working together. These people aren't motivated by getting their names on the front page or etching out a place in history, they're interested in creating a more equitable future.

We're also starting to see more high-profile politicians come from the worlds of community organizing, activism and 'feminine' professions such as teaching. Cori Bush was a community leader and Black Lives Matter activist before she won a seat in Congress representing Missouri. Nadia Whittome came into politics through activism rather than through the traditional route of interning with an MP. Jamaal Bowman, a (male) member of the Squad, was a headteacher who became a leading advocate against standardized testing before he defeated sixteen-term incumbent Eliot Engel and became a New York congressman. These people aren't abandoning their backgrounds as soon as they enter the halls of power, they're redefining what leadership looks like.

Another big shift that happened in 2019/20 was the rejection of the #Girlboss. Elizabeth Holmes was far from the only #Girlboss who had a fall from grace; a number of millennial women who had leaned into the masculine model of leadership blazed out ingloriously or were caught up in controversy. Steph Korey, the CEO of fancy millennial luggage brand Away, for example, was mired in scandal during 2019 over her allegedly toxic[3] management style. (Korey issued a lengthy apology at the time and stepped down as CEO; a few weeks later she disputed the reporting[4] about her management style and took her job back.) Audrey Gelman, CEO of the Wing, a fancy women's co-working space, was forced to resign in 2020 after her employees went on a virtual strike protesting her leadership and the Wing's treatment of Black and brown employees. Ivanka Trump, the #Girlboss who wrote a pseudo-feminist book about working women, had her #Girlboss credentials summarily removed. 'The End of the Girlboss Is Here,'[5] the journalist Leigh Stein declared in an influential essay published a few months after the pandemic started. 'The girlboss didn't change the system; she thrived within it. Now that system is cracking, and so is this icon of millennial hustle.'

It's easy to fake it until you make it when everything is going well, but when the system starts cracking, the traits that define a good leader are thrown into sharp relief. The pandemic prompted a widespread reassessment of the sort of characteristics leaders should display. Much of the world looked to the likes of Jacinda Ardern and sobbed, *Why can't we have someone like her in charge?* There was a growing realization that 'feminine' qualities aren't a weakness, they're a strength.

And they're not just a strength, they're essential for managing the complex problems the world faces. 'We live during the hinge of history,' the philosopher Derek Parfit wrote in 2011. 'Given the scientific and technological discoveries of the last two centuries, the world has never changed as fast. We shall soon have even greater powers to transform, not only our surroundings, but ourselves and our successors.' The world has only got more hingey since Parfit wrote those words. The decade following the pandemic may be the most consequential in human history. As Christiana Figueres has noted,[6] when it comes to climate change, 'This is the decade in which, contrary to everything humanity has experienced before, we have everything in our power. We have the capital, the technology, the policies. And we have the scientific knowledge to understand that we have to halve our emissions by 2030.'

It's not just the climate where we must act now. The next few years, as AI leaders have warned, is also when we need to rethink and reboot AI; if we don't do it soon, we will lose controls of the systems we have set in motion. I'm not talking killer robots (although that's certainly a possibility, seeing how the world is currently going), I'm talking about coding inequality deeper into our system. As Tabitha Goldstaub, one AI expert, has warned: 'We could get transported back to the dark ages,[7] pre-women's lib, if we don't get this right.'

If there's one point I hope you take away from this book, it's that the challenges the world faces can't be overcome by a few brilliant individuals acting alone. They can't be overcome by authoritarian leaders who think they know best, don't listen to others and are afraid of other people overshadowing them. They can't be overcome by a group of leaders who all look, sound and act the same. We are at a moment in time where we have the resources and capabilities to either destroy the world or to save it. Which of those paths we end up taking very much depends on the leaders we have and the way they lead.

It has never been so obvious that our male-coded model of leadership isn't working. If we want a better world, then we need more men who act like Jacinda Ardern, not more women who act like Donald Trump. If we want a better world, then it's time to woman up.

Notes

Prologue

1 Joanna Taylor, 'Men sharing why they don't have female role models has sparked a debate about masculinity', *Independent*, Indy100, 19 August 2020, https://www.indy100.com/offbeat/women-role-models-men-twitter-debate-9677686

2 Jamie Grierson, 'Doctor Who casting: Time Lords clash over "loss of role model for boys"', *Guardian* 21 July 2017, https://www.theguardian.com/tv-and-radio/2017/jul/21/doctor-who-casting-peter-davison-laments-loss-of-role-model-for-boys

3 Govenor Phil Murphy, @GovMurphy, Twitter, https://twitter.com/GovMurphy/status/1307119237954232325?s=20

4 Margaret King quote on Margaret Thatcher wearing suits in a man's world

5 Sheryl Sandberg, *Lean In* (WH Allen, 2013)

6 John Sutherland, 'The face of power: do all world leaders look the same?', *Guardian*, 7 August 2015, https://www.theguardian.com/artanddesign/2015/aug/07/the-face-of-power-do-all-world-leaders-look-the-same

7 Shankar Vedantam, 'Women Held to Higher Ethical Standard than Men, Study shows' NPR, 2 June 2016, https://www.npr.org/2016/06/02/480487259/women-held-to-higher-ethical-standard-than-men-study-shows?t=1618784186462

8 Valentina Zarya, 'The CEO is to Blame for a Company in Crisis – But Only if She's a Woman', *Fortune*, 26 October 2016, https://fortune.com/2016/10/26/ceo-blame-woman-crisis/

9 Helena Vieira, 'Gender quotas and the crisis of the mediocre man', LSE, 13 March 2017, https://blogs.lse.ac.uk/businessreview/2017/03/13/gender-quotas-and-the-crisis-of-the-mediocre-man/

10 Timothy Besley, Olle Folke, Torsten Persson and Johanna Rickne, 'Gender Quotas and the Crisis of the Mediocre Man: Theory and Evidence from Sweden', *American Economic Review 2017*, 107(8): 2204–2242 https://doi.org/10.1257/aer.20160080 , https://pubs.aeaweb.org/doi/pdfplus/10.1257/aer.20160080

11 'Female-led countries' COVID-19 outcomes "systematically and significantly better"', University of Liverpool, 18 August 2020, https://news.liverpool.ac.uk/2020/08/18/covid-19-outcomes-systematically-and-significantly-better-in-female-led-countries/

12 Jack Zenger and Joseph Folkman, 'Research: Women are Better Leaders during a Crisis', *Harvard Business Review*, 30 December 2020, https://hbr.org/2020/12/research-women-are-better-leaders-during-a-crisis

13 'Think 2020's disasters are wild? Experts say the worst is yet to come', *NBC News*, 10 September 2020, https://www.nbcnews.com/science/environment/think-2020s-disasters-are-wild-experts-say-worst-yet-come-rcna114

14 Future of the human climate niche, Chi Xu, Timothy A. Kohler, Timothy M. Lenton, Jens-Christian Svenning, Marten Scheffer, Proceedings of the National Academy of Sciences May 2020, 117 (21) 11350-11355; DOI: 10.1073/pnas.1910114117 https://www.pnas.org/content/117/21/11350

15 John Podesta, 'The climate crisis, migration, and refugees', one of eight briefs commissioned for the 16th annual Brookings Blum Roundtable, '2020 and beyond: Maintaining the bipartisan narrative on US global development', Brookings, 25 July 2019, https://www.brookings.edu/research/the-climate-crisis-migration-and-refugees/

16 Paul Lewis, Sean Clarke, Caelainn Barr, Josh Holder and Niko Kommenda, 'Revealed: one in four Europeans vote populist', *Guardian,* 20 November 2018, https://www.theguardian.com/world/ng-interactive/2018/nov/20/revealed-one-in-four-europeans-vote-populist

17 Saira Asher, 'Barack Obama: Women are better leaders than men', *BBC News*, 16 December 2019, https://www.bbc.co.uk/news/world-asia-50805822

18 Arianne Cohen, 'What is a "Peter problem"? Jaw-dropping study of UK CEOs reveals more named Peter than women', *Fast Company,* 29 July 2020, https://www.fastcompany.com/90534066/what-is-a-peter-problem-jaw-dropping-study-of-u-k-ceos-reveals-more-named-peter-than-women

19 Sarah A. Soule, Davina Drabkin and Lori Nishiura Mackenzie, 'The Stereotypes in MBA Case Studies', *Harvard Business Review*, 24 June 2019, https://hbr.org/2019/06/the-stereotypes-in-mba-case-studies?registration=success

Chapter 1: Lean Out

1 Sarah Hedgecock, 'Elizabeth Holmes on Using Buusiness to Change the World', *Forbes*, 5 October 2015, https://www.forbes.com/sites/sarah-hedgecock/2015/10/05/elizabeth-holmes-on-using-business-to-change-the-world/#c908ef765dd7

2 Nick Bilton, 'She never looks back: Inside Elizabeth Holmes's chilling final months at Theranos, *Vanity Fair*, 20 February 2019, https://www.vanityfair.com/news/2019/02/inside-elizabeth-holmess-final-months-at-theranos

3 John Carreyrou, 'Blood-Testing Firm Theranos to Dissolve', 5 September 2015, *Wall Street Journal, https://www.wsj.com/articles/blood-testing-firm-theranos-to-dissolve-1536115130*

4 John Carreyrou, *Bad Blood* (Penguin Random House, 2018)

5 Taylor Dunn, Victoria Thompson and Rebecca Jarvis, 'Ex-Theranos employees describe culture of secrecy at Elizabeth Holmes' startup: "The Dropout" podcast ep. 1', *ABC News*, 12 March 2019, https://abcnews.go.com/Business/theranos-employees-describe-culture-secrecy-elizabeth-holmes-startup/story?id=60544673

6 Deborah Petersen, 'Elizabeth Holmes: "I Wasn't Weighted by Influences That I Couldn't Do It"', Stanford Business 'Insights', https://www.gsb.stanford.edu/insights/elizabeth-holmes-i-wasnt-weighted-influences-i-couldnt-do-it

7 *Ibid.*

8 Nicolas Kayser-Bril, 'Female historians and male nurses do not exist, Google Translate teels its European users', Algorithm Watch, 17 September 2020, https://algorithmwatch.org/en/google-translate-gender-bias/

9 Mark Johanson, 'Is your voice holding you back?', BBC Worklife, 4 March 2015, https://www.bbc.com/worklife/article/20150302-when-your-voice-is-a-turnoff

10 David Robson, 'The reasons why women's voices are deeper today', BBC Worklife, 13 June 2018, https://www.bbc.com/worklife/article/20180612-the-reasons-why-womens-voices-are-deeper-today

11 Michelle Obama in conversation with Elizabeth Alexander at the Barclay Center as part of the book tour for *Becoming*, 2 December 2018, quoted in *The Guardian:* https://www.theguardian.com/us-news/2018/dec/03/michelle-obama-lean-in-sheryl-sandberg

12 David R. Feinberg, Lisa M. DeBruine, Benedict C. Jones, David I. Perrett, 'The Role of Femininity and Averageness of Voice Pitch in Aesthetic

Judgments of Women's Voices', *Sage Journals*, 1 January 2008, https://journals.sagepub.com/doi/abs/10.1068/p5514

13 Arwa Mahdawi, 'All it takes for a woman to be reduced to an object is too much eyeliner', *Guardian,* 1 February 2020, https://www.theguardian.com/world/2020/feb/01/study-too-much-makeup-women-misogyny

14 Nadia Whittome, @NadiaThittomeMP, Twitter, 13 December 2019, https://twitter.com/NadiaWhittomeMP/status/1205340043046506496?s=20

15 Speech by Kate Green to Labour's National Women's Conference, 26 September 2015, https://press-archive.labour.org.uk/post/129922098464/speech-by-kate-green-to-labours-national-womens

16 Christopher Watson, 'House of Commons treds: The age of MPs', House of Commons Library, 3 November 2020, https://commonslibrary.parliament.uk/house-of-commons-trends-the-age-of-mps/

17 Nadia Whittome interview with the author, 8 January 2021.

18 Mona Eltahaway quote (via Nadia Whittome)

19 Jessica Moulite, 'Exclusive: Rep. Ayanna Pressley Reveals Beautiful Bald Head and Discusses Alopecia for the First Time'. The Root, 16 January 2020,   https://theglowup.theroot.com/exclusive-rep-ayanna-pressley-reveals-beautiful-bald-1841039847

20 Clyde Habermann, 'NYC; At Yale, A Discourse On Hair', *New York Times*, 26 May 2001, https://www.nytimes.com/2001/05/26/nyregion/nyc-at-yale-a-discourse-on-hair.html

21 Rebecca Klar, 'Pressley: Democrats don't need "any more black faces that don't want to be a black voice"', The Hill, 14 July 2019, https://thehill.com/homenews/house/453007-pressley-democrats-need-any-more-black-voices-that-dont-want-to-be-a-black

22 Maureen Dowd, 'It's Nancy Pelosi's parade', *New York Times,* 6 July 2019, , https://www.nytimes.com/2019/07/06/opinion/sunday/nancy-pelosi-pride-parade.html

Chapter 2: Build Trust (by banishing bullshit)

1 Priyanka Pulla, 'Nipah virus: Anatomy of an outbreak', *The Hindu*, 2 June 2018, updated 21 January 2020, https://www.thehindu.com/news/national/kerala/anatomy-of-an-outbreak-how-kerala-handled-the-nipah-virus-outbreak/article24060538.ece

2 Amrita Dutta, '"Couldn't afford to show fear": Kerala's health minister KK

Shailaja on dealing with Nipah', *Indian Express*, 21 July 2019, https://indianexpress.com/article/express-sunday-eye/extraordinary-measures-kk-shailaja-kerala-nipah-virus-5835834/

3 Sneha Mary Koshy, 'Kerala Nurse Died After Treating Nipah Patient, Left Heartbreaking Note', NDTV, 23 May 2018, https://www.ndtv.com/kerala-news/nurse-lini-who-treated-kerala-nipah-victim-left-heartbreaking-note-for-husband-1855625

4 Amrita Dutta, ' "Couldn't afford to show fear": Kerala's health minister KK Shailaja on dealing with Nipah', *Indian Express,* 21 July 2019, https://indianexpress.com/article/express-sunday-eye/extraordinary-measures-kk-shailaja-kerala-nipah-virus-5835834/

5 *Ibid.*

6 'Shailaja teacher was like family, Mullappally didn't even dall: Nipah hero Lini's husband'. *New Indian Express*, 20 June 2020, https://www.newindianexpress.com/states/kerala/2020/jun/20/shailaja-teacher-was-like-family-mullappally-didnt-even-call-nipah-hero-linis-husband-2159216.html

7 Anna M. M. Veticad, 'Virus: A lesson from Mollywood on how to tackle coronavirus', *Al-Jazeera*, 1 May 2020, https://www.aljazeera.com/opinions/2020/5/1/virus-a-lesson-from-mollywood-on-how-to-tackle-coronavirus

8 Hannah Ellis-Peterssen, '"Namaste Trump": India welcomes US president at Modi rally', *Guardian*, 24 February 2020, https://www.theguardian.com/world/2020/feb/24/namaste-donald-trump-india-welcomes-us-president-narendra-modi-rally

9 'Congress blames "Namaste Trump" event for COVID-19 spread in Gujarat', *New Indian Express*, 6 May 2020, https://www.newindianexpress.com/nation/2020/may/06/congress-blames-namaste-trump-event-for-covid-19-spread-in-gujarat-2139949.html

10 Asif Bukhari, 'India Could Be on the Brink of a Coronavirus Catastophe – and Modi Will Be to Blame', *Jacobin*, 4 July 2020, https://jacobinmag.com/2020/04/india-modi-political-prisoners-coronavirus-crisis

11 Sonia Faleiro, 'What the world can learn from Kerala about how to fight covid-19', *MIT Technology Review*, 13 April 2020, https://www.technologyreview.com/2020/04/13/999313/kerala-fight-covid-19-india-coronavirus/

12 Jaideep C. Menon, P. S. Rakesh, Denny John, Rajesh Thachathodiyi, Amitava Banerhee, 'What was right about Kerala's response to the COVID-19 pandemic?', BMJ Global Health, July 2020, https://gh.bmj.com/content/5/7/e003212

13 Kavumpurathu Raman Thankappan, 'Combating corona virus disease 2019 and comorbidities: the Kerala experience for the first 100 days', *International Journal of Noncommunicable Diseases*, vol. 5, issue 2, pp. 26–42, 29 June 2020, https://www.ijncd.org/article.asp?issn=2468-8827;year=2020;volume=5;issue=2;spage=36;epage=42;aulast=Thankappan

14 Edelman Trust Barometer 2021, https://www.edelman.com/trust/2021-trust-barometer

15 George Orwell, 'Politics and the English Language',.

16 Compiled by Stacy Cowley, 'Voices from Wells Fargo: "I Thought I Was Having a Heart Attack"', *New York Times,* 21 October 2016, https://www.nytimes.com/2016/10/21/business/dealbook/voices-from-wells-fargo-i-thought-i-was-having-a-heart-attack.html?_r=0

17 Renae Merle, 'Wells Fargo CEO faces bipartisan scolding, defends bank's reputation', *Washington Post*, 12 March 2019 https://www.washington-post.com/business/2019/03/12/wells-fargo-ceo-faces-bipartisan-scolding-defends-banks-reputation/

18 Transcript of House Hearing, 116th Congress — HOLDING MEGABANKS ACCOUNTABLE: AN EXAMINATION OF WELLS FARGO'S PATTERN OF CONSUMER ABUSES, 12 March 2019 https://www.congress.gov/event/116th-congress/house-event/LC64177/text?s=1&r=1

19 Ben Eisen, 'Wells Fargo clawed back $15 million pay from former CEO Tim Sloan', *Marketwatch/ Wall Street* Journal, 16 March 2020, https://www.marketwatch.com/story/wells-fargo-clawed-back-15-million-in-pay-from-former-ceo-tim-sloan-2020-03-16

20 Marina Pitofsky, 'Porter brings back whiteboard to grill former pharma CEO on cancer drug price hike', 1 October 2020, https://thehill.com/homenews/house/519255-katie-porter-brings-back-viral-whiteboard-to-grill-pharma-exec-on-cancer-drug

21 Amanda Arnold, 'How Representative Katie Porter Will Get It Done', *New York* magazine*, The Cut,* 17 December 2020, https://www.thecut.com/2020/12/katie-porter-on-child-care-hearings-and-her-priorities.html

22 Source: Brandwatch | 53M mentions | 12/1/19–11/30/2020 | Twitter | Executives are defined as people that have C-Suite titles in their bio (e.g., CEO, CFO, etc.) and share relevant business content that validates that they are in fact a leader in a business organization. Within this analysis, we listened to a list of 179K Executives.

23 P. D. Joshi, C. J. Wakslak, G. Appel and L. Huang, 'Gender differences in communicative abstraction', *Journal of Personality and Social Psychology*, 118

(3), pp. 417–35, APA PsychNet, https://psycnet.apa.org/doiLanding?doi
=10.1037%2Fpspa0000177

24 Mark Travers, 'Men and Women (Sort of) Speak Two Different Languages',
Psychology Today, 31 October 2019, https://www.psychologytoday.com/
us/blog/social-instincts/201910/men-and-women-sort-speak-two-
different-languages

25 Chris Woolston, 'Male authors boost research impact through self-hyping
studies', *Nature*, 31 January 2020, https://www.nature.com/articles/
d41586-020-00266-3

26 Chris Buckley and Steven Lee Myers, 'Where's Xi: China's Leader
Commands Coronavirus Fight From Safe Heights', *New York Times,* 8
February 2020, https://www.nytimes.com/2020/02/08/world/asia/xi-
coronavirus-china.html

27 Caitlin Oprysko and Susannah Luthi, 'Trump labels himself "a wartime
president" combating coronavirus', *Politico*, 18 March 2020, https://www.
politico.com/news/2020/03/18/trump-administration-self-swab-corona-
virus-tests-135590

28 James Griffiths, Jenni Marsh, Tara John, Fernando Alfonso II and Amir
Vera, 'April 26 coronavirus news', CNN, 26 April 2020, https://edition.
cnn.com/world/live-news/coronavirus-pandemic-04-26-20-intl/h_
031e1d192acb92fdd2191ca04f6e6f9e

29 Sara Dada, Henry Charles Ashworth, Marlene Joannie Newa, Roopa Dhatt,
'Words matter: political and gender analysis of speeches made by heads of
government during the COVID-19 pandemic', *BMJ Global Health*, vol. 6,
issue 1, January 2021, https://gh.bmj.com/content/6/1/e003910

30 Tsai Ing-wen official remarks on 19 March 2020, https://english.presi-
dent.gov.tw/News/5985

31 'Germany: Angela Merkel's coronavirus address horored as "Speech of the
Year"', DW, https://www.dw.com/en/germany-angela-merkels-corona-
virus-address-honored-as-speech-of-the-year/a-55984728

32 Angela Merkel speech, 18 March 2020, official translation on German
government website https://www.bundesregierung.de/breg-en/issues/
statement-chancellor-1732296

33 Emmanuel Macron speech, 16 March 2020, official website of the French
president https://www.elysee.fr/emmanuel-macron/2020/03/16/adresse-
aux-francais-covid19)

34 Shannon Schumacher and Moira Fagan, 'Confidence in Merkel is at all-
time high in several countries during her last full year in office', Pew
Rearch Center, 2 October 2020, https://www.pewresearch.org/fact-tank

/2020/10/02/confidence-in-merkel-is-at-all-time-high-in-several-countries-during-her-last-full-year-in-office/

35 Ta-Nehisi Coates, 'Mark Penn revealed', 10 August 2008, https://www.theatlantic.com/entertainment/archive/2008/08/mark-penn-revealed/5622/

36 Dylan Scott, 'Single-payer's big test: can Medicare-for-all win in competitive House distrcits?', Vox, 1 June 2018, https://www.vox.com/policy-and-politics/2018/6/1/17378840/california-democratic-primary-2018-medicare-for-all

Chapter 3: Don't be a Hypocrite

1 Melissa Quinn, 'Trump offered Barrett Supreme Court nomination three days after Ginsburg's death', CBS News, 30 September 2020, https://www.cbsnews.com/news/amy-coney-barrett-supreme-court-nomination-trump-ruth-bader-ginsburg-death/

2 CBS News, 'What Amy Coney Barret said about filling a Supreme Court seat in an election year.' https://www.cbsnews.com/video/amy-coney-barrett-on-replacing-supreme-court-justices-election-year-2016/

3 Matthew S. Schwartz, '"Use my words against me": Lindsey Graham's shifting position on court vacancies', NPR, 19 September 2020, https://www.npr.org/sections/death-of-ruth-bader-ginsburg/2020/09/19/914774433/use-my-words-against-me-lindsey-graham-s-shifting-position-on-court-vacancies.

4 Yahoo News, @YahooNews, Twitter, 3 October 2018, https://twitter.com/YahooNews/status/1047509950778335232?s=20

5 Matthew S. Schwartz, '"Use my words against me": Lindsey Graham's shifting position on court vacancies,' NPR, 19 September 2020 https://www.npr.org/sections/death-of-ruth-bader-ginsburg/2020/09/19/914774433/use-my-words-against-me-lindsey-graham-s-shifting-position-on-court-vacancies

6 Jay van Bavel interview with the author, 17 January 2021.

7 University of Zurich, 'The female brain reacts more strongly to prosocial behavior than the male brain, study finds', Science Daily, 9 October 2017, https://www.sciencedaily.com/releases/2017/10/171009123213.htm

8 Jonathan Weisman and Jennifer Steinhauer, 'Senate Women Lead in Effort to Find Accord', New York Times, 14 October 3013, https://www.nytimes.com/2013/10/15/us/senate-women-lead-in-effort-to-find-accord.html

9   'Working Together and Across the Aisle, Female Senators Pass More Legislation Than Male Colleagues', Quorum, February 2015, https://www.quorum.us/data-driven-insights/working-together-and-across-the-aisle-female-senators-pass-more-legislation-than-male-colleagues/

10 Mary Robinson interview with author, 28 October 2020.

11 Mary Robinson interview with author, 28 October 2020.

12 Mary Robinson interview with author, 28 October 2020.

13 Nadia Whittome interview with the author, 8 January 2021.

14 Gender Shades project, gendershades.org/overview.html

15 Josh Horwitz, 'If you're a darker-skinned woman, this is how often facial -recognition sofrware decides you're a man', Quartz, 13 February 2018, https://qz.com/1205604/if-youre-a-darker-skinned-woman-the-best-facial-recognition-software-frequently-thinks-youre-a-man/

16 Nicolas Rivero, 'The influential project that sparked the end of IBM's facial recognition program', Quartz, 10 June 2020, https://qz.com/1866848/why-ibm-abandoned-its-facial-recognition-program/

17 Khari Johnson, 'AI Weekly: A deep learning pioneer's teachable moment on AI bias', Venturebeat, 26 June 2020, https://venturebeat.com/2020/06/26/ai-weekly-a-deep-learning-pioneers-teachable-moment-on-ai-bias/

18 Timnit Gebru, interview with the author, 20 November 2020.

19 Casey Newton, 'The withering email that got an ethical AI researcher fired at Google', Platformer, 3 December 2020, https://www.platformer.news/p/the-withering-email-that-got-an-ethical

20 Karen Hao, 'We read the paper that forced Timnit Gebru our of Google. Here's what it said', MIT Technology Review, 4 December 2020, https://www.technologyreview.com/2020/12/04/1013294/google-ai-ethics-research-paper-forced-out-timnit-gebru/

21 'Standing with Dr. Timnit Gebru – #ISupportTimnit #BelieveBlackWomen', Google Walkout for Real Change, 4 December 2020, https://googlewalkout.medium.com/standing-with-dr-timnit-gebru-isupporttimnit-believeblackwomen-6dadc300d382

22 Khari Johnson, 'Researchers are starting to refuse to review Google AI papers', Venturebeat, 7 December 2020, https://venturebeat.com/2020/12/07/researchers-are-starting-to-refuse-to-review-google-ai-papers/

23 Yvette D, Clarke, @RepYvetteClarke, Twitter, https://twitter.com/RepYvetteClarke/status/1339297358815834113?ref_src=twsrc%5Etfw%7Ctwcamp%5Etweetembed%7Ctwterm%5E1339297358815834113%7Ctwgr%5E%7Ctwcon%5Es1_&ref_url=https%3A%2F%2Fwww.

technologyreview.com%2F2020%2F12%2F17%2F1014994%2Fcongress-wants-answers-from-google-about-timnit-gebrus-firing%2F

24 'Google Workers, Demanding Change at Work, Are Launching a Union With the Communications Workers of America', Alphabet Workers Union, 4 January 2021, https://alphabetworkersunion.org/press/releases/2021-01-04-code-cwa-google-union/

25 Jay Van Bavel interview with the author, January 18 2021

26 Margaret Thatcher Conservative Party Conference speech, 10 October 1980, Brighton https://www.margaretthatcher.org/document/104431

27 Russell Berman, 'The Story Elizabeth Warren Isn't Telling', *The Atlantic*, 10 January 2020, https://www.theatlantic.com/politics/archive/2020/01/elizabeth-warren-republican-electability/603178/

28 Elizabeth Warren interview with Harry Kreisler, Conversations with History series, March 7, 2007 https://conversations.berkeley.edu/warren_2007

29 Helaine Olen, Elizabeth Warren was once a Republican. She shouldn't hide it., *Washington Post,* 16 April 2019 *https://www.washingtonpost.com/opinions/2019/04/16/elizabeth-warren-was-once-republican-she-shouldnt-hide-it/*

30 Eleanor Ainge Roy, 'Jacinda Ardern and ministers take pay cut in solidarity with those hit by Covid-19', *Guardian*, 15 April 2020, https://www.theguardian.com/world/2020/apr/15/acinda-ardern-and-ministers-take-20-pay-cut-in-solidarity-with-those-hit-by-covid-19

31 Jack Peat, 'MPs given an extra £10,000 to work from home', *London Economic*, 9 April 2020, https://www.thelondoneconomic.com/politics/mps-given-an-extra-10000-to-work-from-home-183913/

32 Camille Baker, 'From the Mediterranean to Mexico, Capt. Pia Klemp Believes Rescuing Refugees is Worth Facing Prison Time', *The Intercept*, 10 July 2019, https://theintercept.com/2019/07/10/mediterranean-migrant-rescue-pia-klemp/

33 '*Sea Watch* vs the Libyan Coastguard', https://forensic-architecture.org/investigation/seawatch-vs-the-libyan-coastguard

34 Elisabeth Schumacher, 'German boat captain Pia Klemp faces prison in Italy for migrant rescues', DW, 8 June 2019, https://www.dw.com/en/german-boat-captain-pia-klemp-faces-prison-in-italy-for-migrant-rescues/a-49112348

35 Daniel Trilling, 'How rescuing drowning migrants became a crime', *Guardian*, 22 September 2020, https://www.theguardian.com/news/2020/sep/22/how-rescuing-drowning-migrants-became-a-crime-iuventa-salvini-italy

36 Crispian Balmer, 'Italian magistrates set to level charges against sea rescuers, NGOs', *Reuters*, 3 March 2021, https://www.reuters.com/article/uk

-europe-migrants-italy/italian-magistrates-set-to-level-charges-against-sea-rescuers-ngos-idUKKCN2AV2J0

37 Pia Klemp, Facebook post, August 20 2019.

38 Lorenzo Tondo and Maurice Stierl, 'Banksy funds refugee rescue boat operating in Mediterranean', *Guardian,* 27 August 2020, https://www.theguardian.com/world/2020/aug/27/banksy-funds-refugee-rescue-boat-operating-in-mediterranean

39 Banksy, Instagram (@Banksy), 29 August 2020, https://www.instagram.com/p/CEeHxqgF7gU/?utm_source=ig_embed..

40 Michael A. Fuoco, 'Trial and error: They had larceny in their hearts, but little in their heads', Pittsburgh Post-Gazette, 21 March 1996, https://news.google.com/newspapers?id=ZNlRAAAAIBAJ&sjid=DXADAAAAIBAJ&pg=6777%2C3720310

Chapter 4: Embrace Imposter Syndrome

1 Sebastian Ocklenburg, 'Do Men Rate Their Own Intelligence Highter Than Women Do?', *Psychology Today*, 27 February 2020, https://www.psychologytoday.com/us/blog/the-asymmetric-brain/202002/do-men-rate-their-own-intelligence-higher-women-do

2 'Cameron is "jolly" but has no fixed ideology, says Mandelson', ConservativeHome, 10 July 2020, https://www.conservativehome.com/leftwatch/2010/07/cameron-is-jolly-but-has-no-fixed-ideology-says-mandelson.html

3 Boris Johnson, Brexit means Brexit and we are going to make a Titanic success of it, 2 November 2016 https://www.spectator.co.uk/article/brexit-means-brexit-and-we-are-going-to-make-a-titanic-success-of-it

4 *Ibid.*

5 Johnson to the Treasury Committee, Wednesday 23 March 2016, https://parliamentlive.tv/event/index/66ab01e2-3d9b-4eb9-9186-2a669355c082?in=10:09:15

6 Nina Feldman, Max Marin, Alan Yu, 'In Philadelphia, A Scandal Erupts Over Vaccination Startup Led By 22-Year-Old', NPR, 29 January 2021, https://www.npr.org/sections/health-shots/2021/01/29/962143659/in-philadelphia-a-scandal-erupts-over-vaccination-start-up-led-by-22-year-old

7 'Hd Live! Interview with Andrei Doroshin: Vaccine Rollout in Philadelphia', YouTube, HealthDay, 19 January 2021, https://www.youtube.com/watch?v=OJOLWSC3u4c

8 Max Marin, Nina Feldman, Alan Yu, 'Philly Fighting COVID kicked out of city vaccine program after sudden switch to for-profit', Whyy, 25 January 2021, https://whyy.org/articles/philly-fighting-covid-kicked-out -of-city-vaccine-program-after-sudden-switch-to-for-profit/

9 Max Marin, Nina Feldman, Alan Yu, 'Group entrusted with Philly vaccine clinic abandoned testing, stranding communities', Whyy, 20 January 2021, https://whyy.org/articles/group-entrusted-with-philly-vaccine-clinic-abandoned-testing-stranding-communities/

10 Stephanie M. Rizio, Ahmed Skali, 'How often do dictators have positive economic effects? Global evidence, 1858–2010', *The Leadership Quarterly*, vol. 31, issue 3, June 2020, Elsevier, ScienceDirect, https://www.sciencedirect.com/science/article/pii/S1048984317308093?via%3Dihub#

11 Andrew Cuomo interview on All Things Considered, NPR, 14 October 2020, https://www.npr.org/2020/10/14/923736968/new-york-governor-on-his-new-book-american-crisis

12 'Cuomo Faces Inquiry Over Use of State Resources for Pandemic Book', *New York Times* 19 April 2021, https://www.nytimes.com/2021/04/19/nyregion/andrew-cuomo-book-investigation.html

13 Marina Villeneuve, Cuomo set to earn $5M from book on COVID-19 crisis, 17 May 2021, https://apnews.com/article/andrew-cuomo-pandemic-book-deal-08136b1149764bd2a630a08ab50b6703

14 Andy Newman, 'Harlem Deer Caught in City-State Tussle Has Died', *New York Times*, 16 December 2016, https://www.nytimes.com/2016/12/16/nyregion/harlem-deer.html

15 'No. 202.5: Continuing Temporary Suspension and Modification of Laws Relating to the Disaster Emergency', Executive Order, New York State, Governor Andrew M. Cuomo,18 March 2020, https://www.governor.ny.gov/news/no-2025-continuing-temporary-suspension-and-modification-laws-relating-disaster-emergency

16 Jimmy Vielkind, Joe Palazzolo and Jacob Gershman, 'In Worst-Hit Covid State, New York's Cuomo Called All the Shots', *Wall Street Journal*, 11 September 2020, https://www.wsj.com/articles/cuomo-covid-new-york -coronavirus-de-blasio-shutdown-timing-11599836994

17 Hannah Kuchler and Andrew Edgecliffe-Johnson, 'How New York's missteps let Covid-19 overwhelm the US', *Financial* Times, 22 October 2020, https://www.ft.com/content/a52198f6-0d20-4607-b12a-05110bc48723

18 *Ibid.*

19 Jimmy Vielkind, Joe Palazzolo & Jacob Gershman, 'In Worst-Hit Covid

State, New York's Cuomo Called All the Shots', *Wall Street Journal*, 11 September 2020, https://www.wsj.com/articles/cuomo-covid-new-york -coronavirus-de-blasio-shutdown-timing-11599836994

20 J. David Goodman and Danny Hakim, 'Cuomo Aides Rewrote Nursing Home Report to Hide Higher Death Toll', *New York Times*, 4 March 2021 https://www.nytimes.com/2021/03/04/nyregion/cuomo-nursing-home-deaths.html

21 Mike Baker, 'Seattle's Virus Success Shows What Could Have Been', *New York Times,* 11 March 2021, https://www.nytimes.com/2021/03/11/us/ coronavirus-seattle-success.html?smid=tw-share

22 *Ibid.*

23 'Michelle Obama: "I still have impostor syndrome"', BBC News, online, 4 December 2018, https://www.nytimes.com/2021/03/11/us/coronavi-rus-seattle-success.html?smid=tw-share

24 Sanna Marin interviewed by Sirin Kale, *Vogue*, 16 October 2020, https:// www.vogue.co.uk/arts-and-lifestyle/article/sanna-marin-finland-prime-minister-interview

25 'Open Minded, Ep. 5m Rt Hon Jacinda Ardern', Mentemia, YouTube, 20 December 2020, https://www.youtube.com/watch?v=MGKwczxm0pQ

26 Jack Zenger and Joseph Folkma, 'Research: Women Score Higher Than Men in Most Leadership Skills', *Harvard Business Review*, 25 June 2019, https://hbr. org/2019/06/research-women-score-higher-than-men-in-most-leadership -skills

27 Tomas Chamorro-Premuzic, 'Why Do So Many Incompetent Men Become Leaders?', *Harvard Business Review*, 22 August 2013, https://hbr. org/2013/08/why-do-so-many-incompetent-men

28 Amanda Klabzuba & Michael Mumford, 'When Confidence Is Detrimental: Influence of Overconfidence on Leadership Effectiveness', *The Leadership Quarterly*, August 2011 https://www.researchgate.net/ publication/251637910_When_Confidence_Is_Detrimental_Influence_ of_Overconfidence_on_Leadership_Effectiveness

29 Mary Robinson interview with the author, 27 October 2020

30 University of California–Berkeley, 'What we think we know – but might not – pushes us to learn more', *ScienceDaily*, 23 May 2019, https://www. sciencedaily.com/releases/2019/05/190523161150.htm

31 Mary Robinson interview with the author, 27 October 2020

32 Stefan Kornelius, 'Angela Merkel, The Chancellor and Her World, the authorized biography', translated by Anthea Bell and Christopher Moncrieff, Alma Books, 2013.

33 Angela Merkel, press conference following a visit to a refugee camp near Dresden, 31 August 2015.

34 Philip Oltermann, 'How Angela Merkel's great migrant gamble paid off', *Guardian*, 30 August 2020, https://www.theguardian.com/world/2020/aug/30/angela-merkel-great-migrant-gamble-paid-off

35 'Germany: Half of refugees find jobs within five years', DW, https://www.dw.com/en/germany-half-of-refugees-find-jobs-within-five-years/a-52251414

36 Ludovica Gambaro, Daniel Kemptner, Lisa Pagel, Laura Schmitz and C. Katharina Spiess, 'Integration of Refugee Children and Adolescents In and Out of School: Evidence of Success but Still Room for Improvement', DIW Weekly Report, German Institute for Economic Research, 19 August 2020 https://www.diw.de/documents/publikationen/73/diw_01.c.797310.de/dwr-20-34.pdf

Chapter 5: Collaborate Ruthlessly

1 'Fork the Government', NPR, 23 December 2020, https://www.npr.org/transcripts/949764249

2 'Name-based rationing system for purchases of masks to be launched on February 6; public to buy masks with their (NHI) cards', Taiwan Centers for Disease Control, 4 February 2020, https://www.cdc.gov.tw/En/Bulletin/Detail/ZlJrIunqRjM49LIBn8p6eA?typeid=158

3 Audrey Tang interview with author over Skype, April 6 2021

4 TurboVax, @turbovax, Twitter, 14 February 2020, https://twitter.com/turbovax/status/1360970495038996482?s=20

5 Adam Grant and Sheryl Sandberg, 'Madam C.E.O., Get Me a Coffee', *New York Times*, 6 February 2015, https://www.nytimes.com/2015/02/08/opinion/sunday/sheryl-sandberg-and-adam-grant-on-women-doing-office-housework.html

6 'Audrey Tang, Double Ten Day and the Transcultural Republic of Citizens', *China Heritage*, 10 October 2020, http://chinaheritage.net/journal/audrey-tang-double-ten-day-the-transcultural-republic-of-citizens/

7 *Ibid.*

8 'President Tsai talks COVID-19, leadership with Cornell Law Forum' *Taiwan Today*, 16 December 2020, https://taiwantoday.tw/news.php?unit=2&post=190937

9 Transparency and Open Government, memorandum for the heads of executive departments and agencies, 21 January, 2009 https://obamawhitehouse.archives.gov/the-press-office/transparency-and-open-government

10 https://www.pewresearch.org/internet/2016/12/28/white-house-responses-and-policy-impact-of-petitions/#fn-17830-8

11 Dan Froomkin, After Two Years, White House Finally Responds to Snowden Pardon Petition—With a "No", *The Intercept,* 28 July 2015 https://theintercept.com/2015/07/28/2-years-white-house-finally-responds-snowden-pardon-petition/

12 White House's 'We The People' Petitions Find Mixed Success, NPR, https://www.npr.org/2013/01/03/168564135/white-houses-we-the-people-petitions-find-mixed-success

13 Asawin Suebsawen, "My God, What Have We Done?": White House Staffers React to Insane Online Petitions, Mother Jones, 18 January 2013 https://www.motherjones.com/politics/2013/01/we-the-people-white-house-petitions-obama-administration/

14 Polis, https://pol.is/home&sa=D&ust=1552459295447000

15 Chris Horton, 'The simple but ingenious system Taiwan used to crowd-source its laws' *MIT Technology Review,* 21 August 2018, https://www.technologyreview.com/2018/08/21/240284/the-simple-but-ingenious-system-taiwan-uses-to-crowdsource-its-laws/

16 Sally Jewell, interview with the author, 9 December 2020.

17 2019 survey, reported on by CNBC https://www.cnbc.com/2019/09/17/elon-musk-named-the-most-inspirational-leader-in-tech.html

18 'He can set unrealistic goals', Mark Matousek, 'Former Tesla employees reveal what it's like to work with Elon Musk', *Insider,* 1 October 2019, https://www.businessinsider.com/ex-tesla-employees-reveal-what-its-like-work-elon-musk-2019-9?r=US&IR=T#he-has-very-high-standards-6

19 Michael J. Coren, 'Former Tesla executive: "Everyone is Tesla isin an abusive relationship with Elon"', *Quartz,* 13 Decmber 2018, https://qz.com/1495131/former-tesla-executive-says-employees-in-abusive-relationship-with-elon-musk/

20 Elon Musk, @elonmusk, Twitter, 16 March 2020, https://twitter.com/elonmusk/status/1239650597906898947

Chapter 6: Rethink Risk

1 Tom Sykes, 'Iceland's Incest Prevention App Gets People to Bump their Phones Before Bumping in Bed', *Daily Beast,* 23 April 2013, updated 11 July 2017, https://www.thedailybeast.com/icelands-incest-prevention-app-gets-people-to-bump-their-phones-before-bumping-in-bed

2 Jenna Gottlieb and Jill Lawless, 'New app helps Icelanders avoid accidental incest', *Associated Press*, 18 April 2013 https://apnews.com/article/6845e5 f1d9a04abf9d9eecc097b617ef.

3 'Icelandic Names', Nordic Names, https://www.nordicnames.de/w/index.php?title=Icelandic_Names

4 Jon Henley, 'Icelandic girls can't be called Harriet, government tells family' *Guardian,* 26 June 2014, https://www.theguardian.com/world/2014/jun/26/iceland-strict-naming-convention-cardew-family

5 Michael Lewis, 'Wall Street on the Tundra, *Vanity Fair*, 3 March 2009, https://www.vanityfair.com/culture/2009/04/iceland200904?printable=true

6 Halla Tómasdóttir interview with the author, 8 December 2020

7 Neil Reynolds, 'Iceland's tax reduction lesson for Canada', *Globe and Mail*, 15 August 2007, https://www.theglobeandmail.com/report-on-business/icelands-tax-reduction-lesson-for-canada/article20400309/

8 Robert H. Wade, Silla Sigurgeirsdottir, 'Iceland's meltdown: the rise and fall of international banking in the North Atlantic', *Brazilian Journal of Political Economy*, Rev. Econ. Polit. Vol. 31, no. 5, 2011, http://www.scielo.br/scielo.php?script=sci_arttext&pid=S0101-31572011000500001

9 Arthur Laffer, 'Overheating is not dangerous', Morgunblaðið, Reykjavik, 17 November 2007.

10 Halla Tómasdóttir interview with the author, 8 December 2020.

11 University of Exeter, 'Women can be just as daring and risk-taking as men', 5 October 2017, https://www.sciencedaily.com/releases/2017/10/171005102626.htm

12 Rowena Mason, 'Boris Johnson boasted of shaking hands on day Sage warned not to', *Guardian*, 5 May 2020, https://www.theguardian.com/politics/2020/may/05/boris-johnson-boasted-of-shaking-hands-on-day-sage-warned-not-to

13 Bruce Y. Lee, 'Trump Back at White House, Says "Don't be Afraid" Of Covid-19 Coronavirus, Is That Reasonable?', *Forbes*, 6 October 2020, https://www.forbes.com/sites/brucelee/2020/10/06/trump-back-at-white-house-says-dont-be-afraid-of-covid-19-coronavirus-here-are-the-problems/?sh=6c32a13b5447

14 Michael Safi, 'Bangladesh election: Sheikh Hasina heads for tainted victory', *Guardian*, 27 December 2018, https://www.theguardian.com/world/2018/dec/28/bangladesh-election-sheikh-hasina-heads-for-tainted-victory

15 Patrick Wintour, 'Ana Brnabic: "I do not want to be handed Serbia's gay

PM"', *Guardian*, 28 July 2017, https://www.theguardian.com/world/2017/jul/28/ana-brnabic-serbia-prime-minister-interview

16 Garikipati, Supriya and Kambhampati, Uma, Leading the Fight Against the Pandemic: Does Gender 'Really' Matter? (June 3, 2020). Available at SSRN: https://ssrn.com/abstract=3617953

17 Matthew A. Winkler, "Cathie Wood, the Best Investor You've Never Heard Of', *Bloomberg Opinion*, 18 February 2020, https://www.bloombergquint.com/gadfly/cathie-wood-s-tesla-bet-puts-ark-invest-in-spotlight

18 Ark Invest website https://ark-invest.com/

19 Jennifer Rogers, 'ARK Invest's Cathie Wood: "Be on the right side of change"', Yahoo News, 5 February 2021, https://news.yahoo.com/ark-invests-cathie-wood-side-224355767.html.

20 Vicky Ge Huang, '"My friends thought I was going to fail": Cathie Wood on launching Ark', *CityWire*, 4 April 2019, https://citywireusa.com/professional-buyer/news/my-friends-thought-i-was-going-to-fail-cathie-wood-on-launching-ark/a1210917

21 Renato Capelj, '3 Reasons Why Tesla Will Hit $6,000, According to Ark Invest's Catherine Wood', Interview with Benzinga at Forbes 30 Under 30 Summit in Detroit 2019 https://www.benzinga.com/fintech/19/11/14746784/3-reasons-why-tesla-will-hit-6-000-according-to-ark-invests-catherine-wood

22 Jeff Wilser, 'Cathie Wood: Ahead of the Curve', Coindesk, 8 December 2020, https://www.coindesk.com/cathie-wood-most-influential-2020

23 Ranato Capelj, '3 Reasons Why Tesla Will Hit $6,000, According To Ark Invest's Catherine Wood', Interview with Benzinga at Forbes 30 Under 30 Summit in Detroit 2019, https://www.benzinga.com/fintech/19/11/14746784/3-reasons-why-tesla-will-hit-6-000-according-to-ark-invests-catherine-wood

24 *Ibid.*

25 James Altucher, 'NYC is dead forever. Here's why', LinkedIn, 13 August 2020, https://www.linkedin.com/pulse/nyc-dead-forever-heres-why-james-altucher/

26 Jane Wells, 'Miami's commercial real estate boom picks up steam as pandemic pushes companies to seek new digs', CNBC, 23 December 2020, https://www.cnbc.com/2020/12/22/miamis-commercial-real-estate-boom-picks-up-steam-amid-covid-pandemic.html

27 Daniel Cusick, 'Miami Is the "Most Vulnerable" Coastal City Worldwide', *Scientific American*, 4 February 2020, https://www.scientificamerican.com/article/miami-is-the-most-vulnerable-coastal-city-worldwide/

28 *Ibid.*

29 Sarah Miller, 'Heaven or High Water' Popula, 2 April 2019, https://popula.com/2019/04/02/heaven-or-high-water/

30 Graphs adapted from Flynn, J., Slovic, P. and Mertz C.K. (1994) Gender, Race, and Perception of Environmental Health Risk, *Risk Analysis,* 13, pp. 1101-1108

31 Aaron M. McCright, Riley E. Dunlap, 'Cool Dudes: The Denial of Climate Change Among Conservative White Males in the United States', ResearchGate, October 2011, https://www.researchgate.net/publication/244062439_Cool_Dudes_The_Denial_of_Climate_Change_Among_Conservative_White_Males_in_the_United_States

32 Julia Pyper, 'Why Conservative White Males Are More Likely to Be Climate Skeptics', *New York Times,* 5 October 2011, https://archive.nytimes.com/www.nytimes.com/cwire/2011/10/05/05climatewire-why-conservative-white-males-are-more-likely-11613.html?pagewanted=all

33 GlobalWebIndex analysis of 100K people in the US during Q3'2020 (internet users ages 16 – 64 only)

34 Dan Kahan, 'What Fearless White Men Are Afraid of', Balkin,com, 22 August 2005, https://balkin.blogspot.com/2005/08/what-fearless-white-men-are-afraid-of.html

35 Dan Kahan, 'Checking in on the "white male effect" for risk perception', Cultural Cognition Project at Yale Law School, 7 October 2012, http://www.culturalcognition.net/blog/2012/10/7/checking-in-on-the-white-male-effect-for-risk-perception.html

36 Andrew Bolt, 'The Disturbing Secret to the Cult of Greta Thunberg', *Herald Sun,* 1 August 2019, https://www.heraldsun.com.au/blogs/andrew-bolt/the-disturbing-secret-to-the-cult-of-greta-thunberg/news-story/55822063e3589e02707fbb5a9a75d4cc

37 'The UN is "taking advantage of hysterical teen" Greta Thunberg', YouTube, 24 September 2019, https://www.youtube.com/watch?v=UDXKTXuM2TY

38 Meg Vertigan and Camilla Nelson, 'Why angry middle-aged men are so threatened by Greta Thunberg', *Quartz,* 2 October 2019, https://qz.com/1719873/greta-thunberg-comes-under-attack-from-misogynistic-men/

39 John Carlin, 'A Nordic revolution: The heroines of Reykjavik', *Independent,* 20 April 2012, https://www.independent.co.uk/news/world/europe/nordic-revolution-heroines-reykjavik-7658212.html

40 Matt Phillips, 'Risky Borrowing is Making a Comeback, but Banks Are on the Sideline', *New York Times,* 11 June 2019, https://www.nytimes.com/2019/06/11/business/risky-borrowing-shadow-banking.html

Chapter 7: Think Long and Wide

1 The Long Now Foundation, https://longnow.org/about/

2 Carl Benedikt Frey and Michael A. Osborne, 'The Future of Employment: How Susceptible Are Jobs to Computerisation?', 17 September 2013, https://www.oxfordmartin.ox.ac.uk/downloads/academic/The_Future_of_Employment.pdf

3 James B. Stewart, 'Amazon Says Long Term and Means It', *New York Times*, 17 December 2011, https://www.nytimes.com/2011/12/17/business/at-amazon-jeff-bezos-talks-long-term-and-means-it.html

4 'Gifted Men and Women Definte Success Differently, 40-Year Study Shows', Association for Psychological Science, 19 November 2014, https://www.psychologicalscience.org/news/release.s/gifted-men-and-women-define-success-differently-40-year-study-shows.html

5 'Well-being of Future Generations (Wales) Act 2015', https://www.legislation.gov.uk/anaw/2015/2/contents/enacted

6 'Promoting Wales to the World: Our International Work', https://www.futuregenerations.wales/making-it-happen/international/

7 'M4 Relief road: Well-being commissioner opposes plans', *BBC News*, 22 February 2017, https://www.bbc.co.uk/news/uk-wales-politics-39052153

8 Jacinda Ardern speech on wellbeing budget, May 2019.

9 'Ardern's "wellbeing" budget spreads good vibes in New Zealand', *France 24*, 30 May 2019, https://www.france24.com/en/20190530-arderns-wellbeing-budget-spreads-good-vibes-new-zealand

10 Government Inquiry into Mental Health and Addiction', https://www.mentalhealth.inquiry.govt.nz/inquiry-report/he-ara-oranga/

11 Megan Whitby, 'Icelandic Prime Minister calls for "alternative future" based on wellbeing"', Spa Opportunities, 5 February 2020, https://www.spaopportunities.com/index.cfm?pagetype=news&codeID=344502

12 Steve Lohr, 'Facial Recognition is Accurate, if you're a White Guy', *New York Times*, 9 February 2018, https://www.nytimes.com/2018/02/09/technology/facial-recognition-race-artificial-intelligence.html

13 Nancy Kaffer, 'He was arrested because of a computer error. Now he wants to fix the system', *Detroit Free Press*, https://eu.freep.com/story/opinion/columnists/nancy-kaffer/2020/06/24/robert-williams-detroit-police-facial-recognition/3247171001/

14 Robert Williams, 'I was wrongfully arrested because of facial recognition. Why are police allowed to use it?', *Washington Post*, https://www.

washingtonpost.com/gdpr-consent/?next_url=https%3a%2f%2fwww.
washingtonpost.com%2fopinions%2f2020%2f06%2f24%2fi-was-wrong-
fully-arrested-because-facial-recognition-why-are-police-allowed-use-
this-technology%2f

15 Timnit Gebru, interview with author, 20 November 2020.

16 Erica Klarreich, 'Computer scientists have come up with an algorithm that
can fairly divide a cake among any number of people', *Scientific American*,
13 October 2016, https://www.scientificamerican.com/article/the-math-
ematics-of-cake-cutting/

17 Jeffrey Dastin, 'Amazon scraps secret AI recruiting tool that showed bias
against women', *Reuters*, https://www.reuters.com/article/us-amazon-
com-jobs-automation-insight/amazon-scraps-secret-ai-recruiting-tool-
that-showed-bias-against-women-idUSKCN1MK08G

18 Colin Lecher, 'Automated background checks are deciding who's fit for
a home', *The Verge*, 1 February 2019, https://www.theverge.com/2019
/2/1/18205174/automation-background-check-criminal-records
-corelogic

19 Cyrus Farivar, 'Tenant screening software faces national reckoning', *NBC
News*, 14 March 2021, https://www.nbcnews.com/tech/tech-news/
tenant-screening-software-faces-national-reckoning-n1260975

20 Khari Johnson, 'AI Weekly: Facebook, Google, and the tension between
profits and fairness', *VentureBeat*, 12 March 2021, https://venturebeat.com
/2021/03/12/ai-weekly-facebook-google-and-the-tension-between-
profits-and-fairness/

21 *Ibid.*

22 Emily Bender interview with author, 21 December 2020.

Chapter 8: You Don't Need a Rocket

1 'Jeff Bezos: Blue Origin 'is the most important work I'm doing', *Fast
Company*, 4 February 2021, https://www.fastcompany.com/90601154/
jeff-bezos-blue-origin-space#:~:text=We%20want%20to%20go%20
to,that's%20the%20long%2Dterm%20issue

2 Tim Levin, 'Bill Gates say he's not "a Mars person" like Elon Musk and
would rather spend his money on faccines than a trip to space', *Business
Insider*, 16 February 2021, https://www.businessinsider.com/bill-gates-
elon-musk-mars-climate-electric-vehicles-2021-2?r=US&IR=T

3 Sarah Young, 'Bill Gates, Jennifer Lopez and Paris Hilton among

Celebrities with "Harmful" Carbon Footprints, Study Finds', *Independent*, 24 October 2019, https://www.independent.co.uk/life-style/celebrity-super-emitters-bill-gates-jennifer-lopez-study-flights-carbon-footprint-a9169136.html

4 Daniel Castro, 'Many Women Aren't Sold On AI. That's a Problem', Center for Data Innovation, 12 March 2019, https://datainnovation.org/2019/03/many-women-arent-sold-on-ai-thats-a-problem/

5 John Cook, 'Study: Women are way more skeptical of tech advances than men', 12 March 2015, https://www.geekwire.com/2015/study-women-are-way-more-skeptical-of-tech-advances-than-men/

6 Emma Brockes, 'Bill Gates: "Carbon neutrality in a decade is a fairytale. Why peddle fantasies?"', *Guardian*, 15 February 2021, https://www.theguardian.com/technology/2021/feb/15/bill-gates-carbon-neutrality-in-a-decade-is-a-fairytale-why-peddle-fantasies

7 'What has the Gates Foundation done for global health?', *The Lancet*, 9 May 2009, https://www.thelancet.com/journals/lancet/article/PIIS0140673609608850/fulltext?rss=yes

8 'How Does Bill Gates Plan to Solve the Climate Crisis?', *New York Times*, 15 February 2021, https://www.nytimes.com/2021/02/15/books/review/bill-gates-how-to-avoid-a-climate-disaster.html

9 The Outside Podcast, August 20, 2020 https://www.outsideonline.com/2416316/ayana-elizabeth-johnson-alex-blumberg-how-to-save-planet-podcast

10 'Small Caribbean Island Shows Bold Ocean Leadership: Barbuda Overhauls Reef and Fisheries Management for Sustainability', *National Geographic*, 13 August 2014, https://blog.nationalgeographic.org/2014/08/13/small-caribbean-island-shows-bold-ocean-leadership-barbuda-overhauls-reef-and-fisheries-management-for-sustainability/

11 Henry Ford famous horses quote

12 'Mark Zuckerberg, Moving Fast And Breaking Things', *Business Insider*, 14 October 2010, https://www.businessinsider.com/mark-zuckerberg-2010-10?r=US&IR=T

13 Jessi Hempel, 'Fei-Fei's Quest to Make AI Better for Humanity', *Wired*, 13 November 2018, https://www.wired.com/story/fei-fei-li-artificial-intelligence-humanity/

14 Fei-Fei Li interview with author, 4 February 2021.

15 Mark Sweney, 'Copenhagen climate change treaty backed by "Hopenhagen" campaign', *Guardian*, 23 June 2009, https://www.theguardian.com/media/2009/jun/23/hopenhagen-climate-change-campaign

16 Christiana Figueres interview with the author, 24 November 2020.

17 Summer Allen, 'Do Men Have a Gratitude Problem?', *Greater Good Magazine*, 15 August 2018, https://greatergood.berkeley.edu/article/item/do_men_have_a_gratitude_problem

18 Source: Brandwatch | 53M mentions | 12/1/19–11/30/2020 | Twitter | Executives are defined as people that have C-suite titles in their bio (e.g., CEO, CFO, etc.) and share relevant business content that validates that they are in fact a leader in a business organization. Within this analysis, we listened to a list of 179K Executives.

19 Christiana Figueres interview with the author, 24 November 2020.

20 Bill Gates on CBS 16 February 2021 https://www.cbsnews.com/news/bill-gates-elon-musk-climate-change/

Chapter 9: Create Intimacy

1 Veronica Stracqualursi, 'Marjorie Taylor Greene posts image of herself with gun alongside "Squad" congresswomen, encourages, going on the "offense against these socialists"', *CNN*, 4 September 2029, https://edition.cnn.com/2020/09/04/politics/marjorie-taylor-greene-gun-post-squad/index.html

2 Jarrell Dillard, 'Ocasio-Cortez Reveals Past Sexual Assault, Faults GOP Over Riot', *Bloomberg*, 2 February 2021, https://www.bloomberg.com/news/articles/2021-02-02/ocasio-cortez-accuses-gop-critics-of-dimin-ishing-riot-trauma

3 Elly Belle, 'Nazis Stormed The Capitol. Why Are People Afraid to Call Them That?', *Refinery29*, 8 January 2021, https://refinery29.com/en-us/2021/01/10254568/nazi-shirts-swastika-flags-capitol-riot-trump-supporters

4 Curt Devine and Scott Bronstein, 'Man in "Camp Auschwitz" sweatshirt during Capitol riot identified', *CNN*, 11 January 2021, https://edition.cnn.com/2021/01/10/politics/man-camp-auschwitz-sweatshirt-capitol-riot-identified/index.html

5 Letter to Nancy Pelosi, Congress of the United States, 1 February 2021, https://roy.house.gov/sites/roy.house.gov/files/Joint%20Letter%20to%20Speaker%20Pelosi%20re%20Rep%20AOCs%20Cruz%20Tweet.pdf

6 Trump *People* 2015 quote on crying

7 Brian Stelter, @brianstelter, Twitter, 18 April 2020, https://twitter.com/brianstelter/status/1251532625942130689?s=20

8 Eric Levenson, 'The Tracks of His Tears: When and Why Charlie Baker Cries', Boston.com, 29 October 2014, https://www.boston.com/news/local-news/2014/10/29/the-tracks-of-his-tears-when-and-why-charlie-baker-cries

9 Marie Solis, 'Why Everyone's Obsessed with Alexandria Ocasio-Cortez's Instagram Stories', *Vice*, 16 November 2018, https://www.vice.com/en/article/vbadpy/alexandria-ocasio-cortez-instagram-stories-congress

10 Filippa Ioannou, 'Beto O'Rourke Instagrams his trip to the dentist, and people hate it', *SFGate*, 10 January 2019, https://www.sfgate.com/politics/article/Beto-2020-candidates-dentist-instagram-o-rourke-13524139.php

11 Madeleine Albright interview with the author, 27 October 2020.

12 Mary Robinson interview with author, 28 October 2020.

Chapter 10: Pass the Mic

1 lga Khazan, 'Why Do Women Bully Each Other at Work?', *The Atlantic*, September 2017, https://www.theatlantic.com/magazine/archive/2017/09/the-queen-bee-in-the-corner-office/534213/

2 Martin Abel, 'Why female bosses get different reactions than men when they criticize employees', *The Conversation*, 10 September 2020, https://theconversation.com/why-female-bosses-get-different-reactions-than-men-when-they-criticize-employees-145970

3 Jack Zenger and Joseph Folkman, 'Are Women Better Leaders than Men?', *Harvard Business Review*, 15 March 2012, https://hbr.org/2012/03/a-study-in-leadership-women-do

4 Amy Walker, 'Two-thirds of Boris Johnson's cabinet went to private schools', *Guardian*, 25 July 2019, https://www.theguardian.com/education/2019/jul/25/two-thirds-of-boris-johnsons-cabinet-went-to-private-schools

5 Gabby Birenbaum, 'In a victory for progressives, the DCCC ends its consultant blacklist', *Vox*, 10 March 2021, https://www.vox.com/2021/3/10/22323348/dccc-consultant-blacklist-maloney-aoc

6 Ayanna Pressley, @AyannaPressley, Twitter, 30 March 2019, https://twitter.com/AyannaPressley/status/1112050770814349313?s=20

7 Ayanna Pressley, @AyannaPressley, Twitter, 30 March 2019, https://twitter.com/AyannaPressley/status/1112050774283030529?s=20

8 Amina Mohammed interview with the author, 3 November 2020.

9 Justin McCurry, 'Japan's ruling party invites women to meetings – but won't let them speak', *Guardian*, 18 February 2021, https://www.theguardian.com/world/2021/feb/18/japans-ruling-party-invites-women-to-meetings-but-wont-let-them-speak

10 *Associated Press*, Philadelphia, 'House Democrats who tangled with leader not backing down', 13 July 2019, https://spectrumlocalnews.com/ap-online/2019/07/14/house-democrats-who-tangled-with-leader-not-backing-down

Conclusion: Woman Up – why this decade is crucial

1 Samuel Brannen, 'The Age of Leaderless Revolution' Center for Strategic and International Studies', 1 November 2019, https://www.csis.org/analysis/age-leaderless-revolution

2 John Eligon and Kimiko de Freytas-Tamura, 'Today's Activism: Spontaneous, Leaderless, but Not Without Aim', *New York Times*, 3 June 2020, https://www.nytimes.com/2020/06/03/us/leaders-activists-george-floyd-protests.html

3 Zoe Schiffer, 'Emotional Baggage', *The Verge*, 5 December 2019, https://www.theverge.com/2019/12/5/20995453/away-luggage-ceo-steph-korey-toxic-work-environment-travel-inclusion

4 Away C.E.O. Is Back, Just Weeks After Stepping Down, *New York Times*, Jan 13 2020 https://www.nytimes.com/2020/01/13/business/steph-korey-away.html

5 Leigh Stein, 'The End of the Girlboss is Here', *Gen*, 22 June 2020, https://gen.medium.com/the-end-of-the-girlboss-is-nigh-4591dec34ed8

6 Christiana Figueres, Damian Carrington, 'Christiana Figueres on the climate emergency: "This is the decade and we are the generation"', *Observer*, 15 February 2020, https://www.theguardian.com/environment/2020/feb/15/christiana-figueres-climate-emergency-this-is-the-decade-the-future-we-choose

7 Nicole Kobie, 'Artificial Intelligence Isn't Good for Women, But We Can Fix It', *Teen Vogue*, 4 April 2018, https://www.teenvogue.com/story/artificial-intelligence-isnt-good-for-women-but-we-can-fix-it

Acknowledgements

My Twitter DMs are usually a frightening place: 90% troll accounts with names like @trumpmagalovexxx calling me a communist and something that rhymes with Jeremy Hunt. So, the first person I'd like to thank is my wonderful editor Harriet Poland for messaging me out of the blue one day and making my Twitter DM inbox a much brighter place. Harriet had an idea for a book about female leadership and after some back and forth this book was born! Thanks also to Izzy Everington and the rest of the brilliant team at Hodder for being so brilliant to work with. A big thank you also to Devon Zdatny and Jennifer Bridgeman at First & First Consulting for helping me source data for the book – and to my great friend and fellow dog mum, Kate Mills, for helping me wrangle with Excel.

I probably would not have written this book had I not stumbled into a career in journalism. And I wouldn't have stumbled into journalism had it not been for Jessica Reed at the *Guardian*. Jessica answered a cold pitch I sent one day over a decade ago and gave me a chance to write an op-ed. Every single one of my pitches before that had gone unanswered and the confidence boost this gave me was, as the management consultants say, game-changing. Jessica is the very best sort of editor: she's not afraid of trying out new voices and she goes above and beyond when it comes to nurturing new talent. Thank you also to Amana Fontanella-Khan at the *Guardian*, another brilliant editor who has been incredibly kind and encouraging. All my editors at the *Guardian* have brilliant, so thanks to them all. And a massive thank you to my very first editor, Robert Holloway, who gave me an internship at AFP and got me interested in journalism to begin with. Small words of encouragement can change the course of someone's life so I'd also like to shout out all the teachers and mentors who have helped my writing and encouraged my work over the years: Robert Young, Bernard O'Donoghue, Mrs Ballantyne, Mr Macmillan, Karen Dwyer.

A massive thank you also to all the wonderful people I interviewed for this book. I feel so privileged to have had a chance to chat to so many inspirational people.

Now for the personal stuff. I feel hashtag blessed to have such a wonderful family who have always supported me. My mum and dad were brilliant role models and my sister is one of the most inspirational people I know. My wife is an actual saint and, to top it all off, she came with a brilliant family who have all been so supportive throughout the book-writing process. Obviously I have to thank my new daughter too. She wasn't much help with the book while in utero TBH, but it was extremely helpful that she was born on time, after I handed in the book. She's only a month old but if her lung-power is anything to go by I can already tell she's going to be a force in the world!

Finally, thank you to all the readers. I appreciate you picking this up and taking the time to read it. And if you pre-ordered this book then please allow me to tell you just how wonderful you are!